EQUITY & TRUSTS

EQUITY & TRUSTS

Katharine Davies and Sue Farran

SECOND EDITION

Hall and Stott Publishing Ltd
27 Witney Close
Saltford
BS31 3DX

British Library Cataloguing in Publication Data

ISBN 978 0 995653 08 5

Typeset by Style Photosetting Ltd, Mayfield, East Sussex

PREFACE

There are many excellent textbooks on equity and trusts and it might be asked 'why another'? For students undertaking conversion courses, or trying to juggle studies with family responsibilities, part-time jobs or other commitments, there are only so many hours in the day, so our aim was to produce a text that was more than a 'nutshell' but less daunting than a 'magnus opus'. At the same time we wanted students to appreciate that the law is full of imperfections and inconsistencies and that equity in particular can be a fickle thing. So we have gone beyond mere description and have engaged in some discussion and pointed to further reading, most of which is available online, so that the enquiring student can research more widely. We were also mindful that many law students want to know how the law works in practice regardless of whether or not the reader aspires to a legal career. In this respect we are very grateful to Gill Steel for her valuable contribution from the practitioner perspective.

We are grateful to Hall and Stott Publishing for the opportunity to be in the vanguard of their publications and to Northumbria University for the resource support which underpins a work of this nature.

We hope that this book will prove to be a welcome companion to all those seeking to understand and apply the principles and practices of the fascinating but not always straightforward laws of equity and trusts.

Katharine Davies and Sue Farran
Newcastle upon Tyne
April 2019

CONTENTS

TABLE OF CASES

C

D

E

L

M

X

Y

Z

TABLE OF LEGISLATION

chapter 1

Introduction to Equity and the Trust

After reading this chapter, you will be able to:

- understand what is meant by equity and the role it plays in the English legal system
- appreciate the historical development of the courts of equity and the merger of two systems of courts into one
- learn about the 'equitable maxims' and their application
- understand the origins of the trust and its use to achieve particular objectives
- realise the flexibility and continuing relevance of the trust in the 21st century.

1.1 Introduction

The main focus of this book is the equitable institution of the trust, but the scope and influence of equity is much broader than this. This chapter introduces you to the historical and philosophical origins of equity and gives you some idea of the pervasiveness of equity in the law as we know it today. We will then look at the origins of what today is referred to as the 'trust', drawing attention to the purpose and effect of this particular legal device and its contemporary uses and relevance.

1.2 What is equity?

Equity is a branch of the law with a history dating back to around the 13th century. Its principles and remedies developed over the following centuries and are now found interwoven throughout most of the areas of law in operation today. The law of equity is largely based upon case precedent and as such, but also due its inherent nature, it has the flexibility to evolve as society changes.

This inherent flexibility has at times attracted criticism on the grounds that the outcomes in equity are uncertain and unpredictable. Over the centuries equity has become less flexible and more grounded in precedent and rules, but from time to time equity shows that it is not 'past the age of child-bearing' (a remark once made by Justice Bagnall in the case of *Cowcher v Cowcher* [1972] 1 WLR 425). As you read through this book you will learn the doctrines that have developed within equity and how these have changed and been applied both historically and in the modern context.

However, equity is not just a body of rules and doctrines. It is also a legal philosophy based on ideas of morality and rightness. Equity recognises that the law is not always fair or just, either because of the way it works or the way in which it is administered. When we claim that something is 'inequitable', we are recognising this unjustness. This moral dimension to equity can be understood by appreciating the origins of equity and the relationship between equity and the other major body of law – the common law.

1.3 Historical development

The standardisation of law was integral to the unification of Britain under William the Conqueror from 1066 onwards. Within 20 years of the Norman Conquest, local courts (County courts presided over by a sheriff and Hundred courts dealing with very local matters and presided over by local dignitaries in the feudal system) had been established which reflected the provincial government system and which administered local laws. By 1250 a common law had emerged in order to establish a set of laws which were recognised by everyone, rather than local laws which varied across the country. In order to establish a body of common law, a conscious effort was made to find out what laws were being practised by the common people. The King (Henry I – 1068-1135, then Henry II – 1154-1189) also made sure that the judges of his court (the *Curia Regis*) moved around the country in order to administer the same law to all localities. In the period 1150–1700, in order to standardise procedures and the types of claims that were being brought before the King's courts of common law, a system of 'forms of action' or standardised 'writs' emerged. These were legal templates or protocols which the facts of any claim brought by writ before the court had to fit. If they did not fit there was no recourse to the court. As life became more complicated and different types of legal claims arose – for example in contract and tort – these forms of action proved to be straitjackets on legal development, leaving many potential litigants dissatisfied. Even if a case did fit within an existing form of writ, only damages were awarded by the courts of common law and sometimes this was not appropriate. If the common law failed to provide justice, it became possible to petition the King in Council directly – as the 'fountain of justice' – and ask him to settle the dispute. Over time, and with the growth of the administrative machinery of the court, the King began to refer these petitions to his Chancellor (a member of the King's administrative office which included the Exchequer and Chancery), and by the late 15th century the Chancellor was issuing decrees or judgments in his own name and expanding the role of his office – Chancery. During this early period of equity, the system operated in a discretionary fashion in accordance with the opinion of the Chancellor at that time. Indeed Sir George Jessel stated in the case of *Re Hallett's Estate* (1880) 13 Ch D 696 at 710:

> ... it must not be forgotten that the rules of Courts of Equity are not, like the rules of Common Law, supposed to have been established from time

> immemorial. It is perfectly well known that they have been established from time to time – altered, improved and refined from time to time. In many cases we know the names of the Chancellors who invented them. No doubt they were invented for the purpose of securing the better administration of justice, but still they were invented.

These early Chancellors were ecclesiastics and filled the royal duty of being keepers of the King's conscience at a time when religion played a key part in people's lives, and spirituality and temporality were closely linked. These Chancellors would not have seen themselves as developing a new system of law but rather as interpreting the existing (common) law in light of their own moral views and providing a remedy where it was just and equitable to do so. To begin with, the Chancellors expanded the existing common law system of writs by using legal fictions or analogies. The Chancellor or his staff would question petitioners directly in the search for the truth, and any orders made would be against the person complained of. These orders went beyond just the award of damages and could extend to ordering a person to carry out an obligation or desist from causing a harm. They were intended to act on the offender's conscience and included remedies found today such as injunctions, rectification of agreements and orders of specific performance. Moreover the Chancellor was free to recognise rights which were not recognised in the common law courts and was not bound by the existing system of writs or forms of action as were the common law courts. Nevertheless, over time, a body of principles emerged from the office of the Chancellor, and by the late 17th century, equity, much like the common law, had become established as a body of principles, based upon precedent. This coincided with the appointment of lawyers as Chancellor rather than ecclesiastics, Lord Nottingham being the first in 1673. Around this period the administration of decisions began to develop into a formal court system known as the Court of Chancery. There were therefore two parallel systems of law: that of equity administered in the Court of Chancery and that of the common law administered in the King's courts. This led ultimately to conflict, not least because the Court of Chancery could send someone to jail for trying to enforce a common law judgment, culminating in what became known as the *Earl of Oxford's Case* (1615) 21 ER 485. The upshot of this rather complicated land case was that the King, James I, decreed that if there was a conflict between the common law and equity, equity would prevail.

Lawyers and litigants soon became wise to the merits of 'forum shopping' and cases would move between the two systems of courts, either by choice in order to seek a better outcome, or because the matter raised issues of law and equity, in which case the plaintiff was required to bring two separate claims – one at the King's/Queen's Bench for the common law aspect and another at Chancery in relation to the equitable matters. This was clearly unsatisfactory and to say the least confusing, time consuming and costly. Moreover, just as the common law courts had stagnated under a restricted range of writs, so too did the courts of Chancery stagnate due to becoming overloaded with cases, inordinate delays which meant cases could go on for years, corruption and under-staffing – there were only two judges in Chancery until 1813: the Lord Chancellor and the Master of the Rolls.

Some reforms were introduced; for example in 1854 the Common Law Procedure Act permitted common law courts to grant equitable remedies, and in 1858 the Chancery Procedure Amendment Act gave the Court of Chancery the power to grant damages alongside or alternatively to equitable remedies. It was not, however, until 1873 and 1875, following the enactment of the Judicature Acts, that the courts were able (regardless of the division) to recognise and give effect to both legal and equitable rights, defences and remedies at the same time. Under the Judicature Acts the previously separate courts of Queen's Bench, Exchequer, Common Please, Chancery, Probate, Divorce and Admiralty were abolished and a Supreme Court of Judicature was created. Each division of the new High Court (Queen's Bench; Chancery; Probate, Divorce and Admiralty) exercised legal and equitable jurisdiction. This merger or fusion of the administration of justice in one set of courts did not remove the possibility of conflict between equity and common law, nor did it change the substantive rules of each body of law. Indeed in s 25(1) of the 1873 Judicature Act we find the following provision:

> Generally, in all matters not hereinbefore mentioned in which there is any conflict or variance between the rules of equity and the rules of common law with reference to the same matter, *the rules of equity shall prevail*. (emphasis added)

The Judicature Acts were replaced by the Supreme Court of Judicature Act 1925, and then the Supreme Court Act 1981 (later renamed the Senior Courts Act), the stated purpose of which was to consolidate 'the Supreme Court of Judicature (Consolidation) Act 1925 and other enactments relating to the Supreme Court in England and Wales and the administration of justice therein'.

So it remains today that administratively the rules of the common law and equity may be dealt with via one claim in one court. Whether the reforms of the late 19th century did more than fuse the administration of justice remains a moot point. It would appear that over a century later the concepts of the common law and equitable principles remain separate at the theoretical level, and that in many cases the application of equity will lead to a result that is different from that which would have been achieved were only the common law to be applied.

A fairly recent example of the use of an equitable remedy, which has been used increasingly in the later part of the 20th century and into this century, is in the development of the remedy of proprietary estoppel – a situation where a promise made, and on which the recipient has acted, is not delivered, to the detriment of the recipient. This remedy has been used to ensure, for example, that a person working on a farm for low or no remuneration but who instead was promised the farm on the death of the promisor actually received it when the promisor failed to make the gift in his will. This remedy achieved the delivery of the farm – ie the perfecting of the promise – whereas making a claim under the Inheritance

(Provision for Family and Dependants) Act 1975 would only have resulted in an award of a sum of money in lieu of reasonable maintenance and not the farm nor its equivalent in monetary value – *Thorner v Major* [2009] UKHL 18; *Suggitt v Suggitt* [2011] EWHC 903.

1.4 Maxims

During the development of equity as a branch of the law, certain guiding principles were established to underpin the objective of providing a fair and just solution to the complainant. These principles are known as the maxims of equity and there are said to be at least 12 agreed maxims, although the precise list will differ depending on the author.

The courts frequently refer to these maxims when considering an equitable claim or deciding whether to grant an equitable remedy. However, it should be noted that some are merely overarching principles rather than, for example, grounds for a claim, and others are default principles that the court will apply where necessary or appropriate. The maxims are useful guiding principles but they are not rules, and you will discover that in some cases the maxims appear to be departed from or applied in an inconsistent manner. Some of these maxims are the following:

Equity will not suffer a wrong to be without a remedy

This maxim is fairly self-explanatory and clearly stems from the earliest manifestations of equity in the medieval times (see above and for an illustration, see **1.5** 'What is a trust?' below). It does not mean that every moral wrong will be remedied by the court, but where the common law has failed to provide a solution, equity will step in and fill the gap where appropriate.

He who comes to equity must come with clean hands

The person bringing an equitable claim or seeking an equitable remedy must demonstrate that his or her past record of dealings is clean and fair. This is particularly relevant in the context of requests for the court to exercise its discretion to grant an injunction or an order of specific performance of a contract.

A relatively recent and interesting example, and one that has now run to nine cases, is the case of *Douglas and Others v Hello! Ltd* (No 1) [2001] QB 967, involving unauthorised photographs of the wedding ceremony of celebrities Catherine Zeta-Jones and Michael Douglas. The litigation involved two glossy magazines specialising in stories and photos of celebrities. The Court of Appeal lifted an interim injunction preventing Hello! magazine from publishing the rogue pictures on the basis that one of the claimants, OK magazine, had pulled a similar stunt at a previous wedding, that of Gloria Hunniford – another celebrity of the time. The maxim applied because OK magazine had not come to court with clean hands and this resulted in the overturning of the injunction.

It should be noted, however, that equity does not demand that a claimant shall have led a saintly lifestyle prior to the trial, and it will only take into account behaviour that has a strong relevance to the equitable matter being considered.

He who seeks equity must do equity

Where someone is seeking equitable relief from the court, that individual must be willing to act fairly and be prepared to carry out his or her own obligations at the same time as obtaining the remedy.

This maxim, therefore, relates to current or future conduct of the claimant as opposed to previous conduct.

In *O'Sullivan v Management Agency and Music Ltd* [1985] QB 428, the singer/songwriter, Gilbert O'Sullivan, sought redress for excessive profits paid to his agent during the course of their professional relationship. He was successful in arguing that the agent was in breach of his fiduciary duty and as such liable to pay the excess profits to O'Sullivan. However, the court required O'Sullivan to also 'do equity' by acknowledging that the agent was entitled to a fair payment for the work done, and so the award to O'Sullivan was reduced to reflect the reasonable remuneration deserved by the agent.

Equity regards as done that which ought to be done

Most frequently applied in the context of the remedy of specific performance in contract law, this maxim is also relevant to the finding of a constructive trust (see **Chapter 4**).

An interesting example is the Privy Council case, *AG for Hong Kong v Reid* [1994] 1 AC 324. The public prosecutor in Hong Kong took bribes of approximately HK$12m to obstruct prosecutions in breach of his duty to the Crown. The Court held that a constructive trust in favour of the Crown arose as soon as the bribe monies were received by Reid. So, at that moment, equity considered done that which ought to be done, ie Reid, as holder of the legal title to the money, held it on constructive trust for the Crown.

Equity is equality

A common sense, default provision, 'equity is equality' can be applied to situations where the court is dividing up property between individuals in the absence of another suitable basis for the division.

During the course of a divorce in *Jones v Maynard* [1951] Ch 572, the court applied this maxim when splitting the money in a bank account between the couple. Rather than attempting to dissect every transaction in the account, it was considered more appropriate to simply divide the money between the two of them.

Good reasons to depart from this maxim *might* be, for example:

- Where the parties have not contributed equally to the purchase of an asset, in which case it may be that the shares are proportionate to their contribution (see **Chapter 4**).
- Where the parties have expressly declared that the shares in an asset should be unequal, for example when executing a deed of transfer of land.

Delay defeats equity

This principle is equity's equivalent of a limitation period, although in true equitable fashion there is no set time limit for the bringing of an action.

The old case of *Sayers v Collyer* (1884) 28 Ch D 103 provides an amusing illustration where a house was being used as a beer shop in breach of a covenant on the title deeds. The plaintiff, who had a right to enforce the covenant, was not granted the injunction he desired because he had delayed in bringing an action for three years. This delay was exacerbated by the fact that during the three-year period he had been drinking in the said beer house.

The question of delay or, as it is sometimes referred to, 'the equitable doctrine of laches' may be particularly relevant where an equitable remedy is being sought. So, for example, in the case of *Ong v Ping* [2015] EWHC 1742 (Ch), rectification of a contract relating to the sale of land was being sought. The defendant tried (unsuccessfully) to raise the equitable doctrine of laches, or delay, to defeat the rectification. Similarly, in the case of *Salt v Stratstone Specialist Ltd (t/a Stratstone Cadillac Newcastle)* [2015] CTLC 206, the equitable remedy of rescission of a contract for the sale of a car was sought, and again the defence of delay was argued (unsuccessfully) on the grounds that there had been a period of four years between the sale and the claim to rescind.

Equity looks to the intent (or substance) rather than the form

This is one of the maxims that really goes to the heart of equity and the trust and demonstrates the essence of flexibility. It means that the courts will look at all the circumstances of a situation including spoken words, actions, the circumstances, as well as any written documents, in order to determine the intention of the parties to a claim.

The case of *Paul v Constance* [1977] 1 WLR 527 could be said to epitomise this maxim. Here the court declared the existence of an express trust over money held in a bank account on the basis that Mr Constance had said to Mrs Paul on a number of occasions, 'the money is as much yours as mine'. He had not drawn up a trust deed, he had not even used the word 'trust' and quite probably had no knowledge of trusts at all. The court focussed on trying to determine the intention of Mr Constance from the words he used, and also from his actions and the circumstances of the time when the events occurred, rather than insisting on a rigid formula for the creation of an express trust.

It is not intended to provide an exhaustive list of the equitable maxims here, but those listed above will be relevant and of interest to a student of equity and trusts. Throughout this book, where a maxim is applicable it will be highlighted and explained further if necessary. For example, in relation to constitution of trusts in **Chapter 2**, the maxims '**Equity will not assist a volunteer**' and '**Equity will not perfect an imperfect gift**' will be relevant.

1.5 What is a trust?

The law of trusts forms a large part of the law of equity, and arguably the trust is the keystone of equity.

Under the feudal land tenure system introduced by William the Conqueror in 1066, the Crown claimed title to all land, granting estates to loyal followers and seizing the land of those found to oppose the King. In a pyramidal hierarchy of land rights, the great nobles and clergy who were granted estates in land – that is the right to live on and enjoy the land for as long as they had heirs or as long as the King allowed them – in turn granted lesser estates to the next social rank, and so on, down to those who had no interest in land but merely worked the land for others and were allowed to live on it. Within the hierarchical social structure which was closely tied to land and power, each rank had to pay taxes or tithes, originally in the form of services or produce, later in money. Included in these services were 'knights' service whereby a man would go to fight for his overlord (the person in the rank above), often taking a retinue of staff and equipment. From the King's perspective, the payment of taxes and tithes was often not enough to finance the royal expenditure, and so other taxes were also payable. If taxes were not paid or a landlord was found guilty of a felony, or died without an heir, then the land would 'escheat' back to the Crown. In combination, these circumstances meant that succession to estates was precarious – a man might die leaving minor children and a spouse (who would be ineligible to inherit the estate), or might have to perform a service away from his home – perhaps for years at a time – and others might move on to his land or take his harvests.

One of the first illustrations of the trust arose from a predicament faced by men taking part in the Crusades, leaving a spouse and minor children at home on their land. During the 12th and 13th centuries these military campaigns in the Middle East meant that English knights and their retinues would often be away from home for long periods. It was common therefore for a knight to transfer his land to, let us say, a trusted friend on the understanding that it would be looked after during his absence and returned to the knight when he came home. This would mean that while he was away, his land would not escheat to the Crown and hopefully he would return to reclaim it. If not, perhaps his eldest son would have reached majority and could succeed to the land. Unsurprisingly, given that knights could be away for years at a time and the possibility of the 'trusted' friend turning into an unscrupulous opportunist, there were occasions when the land was not transferred back to the knight upon his return.

The common law recognised the transfer of legal title from the knight to the trusted friend but not the underlying agreement for the property to be cared for and then returned to the knight at a later date.

So it was just this type of situation, where a common law claim could not be brought, that the aggrieved knight (or his heir) would petition the King directly and request that a decree or order be issued acknowledging the rights and interest of the knight and/or his children in the transferred land. This early form of trust was called a use, and the beneficiaries were called *cestui que use*.

This is probably the first example of equity stepping in and recognising the split of legal and equitable ownership. The King's equity demanded that the trusted friend should act in accordance with the initial agreement – which was binding on his conscience – and transfer the land back to the knight or his heirs if adult.

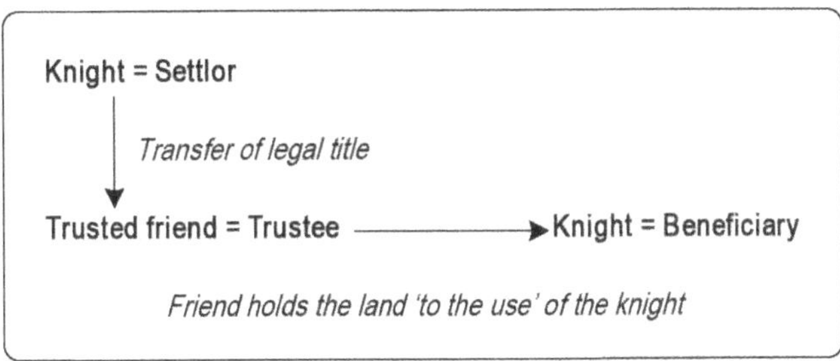

Figure 1.1 Use

This means that equity acknowledges the common law position, that the legal title to the land has been transferred, but then adds in an additional layer of beneficial or equitable title that is held by the knight. This equitable interest allows the knight to assert his rights before the King and obtain redress for breach of the initial agreement.

Although the Crusades ceased to draw men away from their lands, other wars followed and fighting men were always in demand, so this institution continued to be useful and the Chancellor continued to uphold the 'use'. The person who was less pleased with the popularity of this legal development was the King. While tax was payable on transfer of legal title, the common law did not recognise the 'use' and so there was no tax payable on the transfer of beneficial title. In 1535 Henry VIII passed a statute abolishing the use of this device (the Statute of Uses), choosing to recognise that the *cestui que use* would be regarded as legal (rather than equitable) owners of the land. This did not deter clever lawyers who simply added another limb to the device so that it was 'for the use' of X 'on trust for' Y.

After a while the first use fell away – not least because Henry VIII had to capitulate and allow land to be left by will (1540). The result is that today we have a trust device in which the legal title is held by trustees on trust for beneficiaries who have an equitable or beneficial interest.

1.6 The trust today

The diagram above (**Figure 1.1**) outlines the trust structure that continued to be used for over 700 years and still exists in the same format today. The basic elements of a trust are therefore as follows:

- There is **intention** on the part of the **settlor** to create the trust. The settlor is the initial owner of the property and he or she transfers it to the trustee.
- The **trustee**(s) is **compelled** to hold the legal title of the property in accordance with the instructions of the settlor while not being entitled to the benefit of the property in the capacity of trustee (he or she may also be a beneficiary).
- The **benefit** of the property accrues to the **beneficiary**.

The key word here is 'compel', because the trustee must hold the property and distribute it to the beneficiaries as instructed by the settlor.

Another fundamental aspect of a trust is the idea of conscience. The trustee's conscience is said to be bound so that he or she must follow the settlor's wishes and respect the rights of the beneficiary. The concept of conscience emanates from those early days of the ecclesiastical chancellors issuing moral decrees in order to remedy the deficiencies of the common law and continues to pervade the law of equity and trusts.

Let us take a more contemporary example to explore the position of the parties to a trust a little more deeply.

Robert has a holiday cottage and he wants Caroline, his solicitor, to hold it on trust for the benefit of Jenny, his daughter, until she reaches the age of 21.

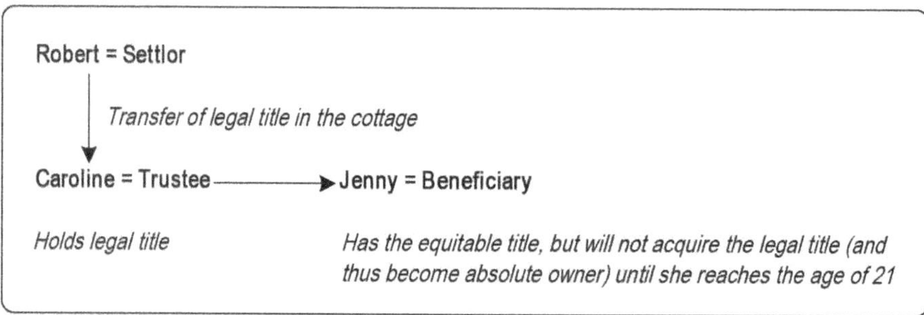

Figure 1.2 Trust today

The ideal course of action is for Caroline to draw up a trust deed setting out the terms upon which the trust is to be set up. The deed will clearly specify Robert's **intention** as **settlor** and he must transfer the legal title in the cottage to Caroline.

Caroline is the **trustee**; she will be the **legal owner** of the cottage and must deal with it accordingly. She may, for example, let it out so that it produces a rental income for the trust. Caroline is not entitled to the benefit of the cottage; she owns the cottage subject to the equitable interest of Jenny. Caroline may not, for example, keep the rent or live in the cottage. She will have positive duties towards Jenny, which are onerous and include acting in Jenny's best interests and distributing the cottage to Jenny when she reaches 21.

Jenny is the **beneficiary**; she has an **equitable interest** in the cottage. She is entitled to acquire the cottage when she is 21 along with any rental income earned. She may also be entitled to receive some or all of the income before she reaches 21. Jenny also acquires rights as a beneficiary. For example, if Caroline were to allow her friends to use the cottage and she received rent from them but kept it for herself, Caroline would be in breach of her duty as trustee and Jenny could bring a claim against her for payment of the rent monies to the trust fund. She could also, if she was really dissatisfied with Caroline as a trustee, go to court to seek her removal.

In practice, for a valid trust to exist, there must be (as described by Romer J in *Green v Russell* [1959] 2 QB 226):

(1) certainty of words – that is, show a clear intention to create a trust;
(2) certainty of subject matter – that is, be clear what assets are to form the trust fund;
(3) certainty of objects – that is, demonstrate clarity as to the beneficiaries who are to benefit from the trust.

1.6.1 Distinguishing the trust

At first sight the trust may look like other legal devices, and so it is important that it is distinguished from the following:

- *A gift* – under which the legal and beneficial title is transferred from a donor to a donee. The donee becomes absolutely beneficially entitled to the property. The donee gives no consideration for the gift. A gift is marked by transfer and the intention to give.
- *A loan* – this is usually governed by contract but may be informal and/or gratuitous. Under a loan there is transfer of the property from the lender to the borrower but the intention is different. The lender retains ownership of the property; he or she only transfers possession/control and usually for a limited time. An example would be the loan of a book or borrowing someone's car to pop to the shops.
- *A mortgage* – this is a form of loan generally secured against land/buildings. In the past the property was actually transferred (conveyed) to the lender with the contractual understanding that the property would be re-conveyed back to the borrower on redemption of the mortgage. Today this transfer does not occur.

Instead the borrower remains legal owner of the property and is allowed to remain in possession of it, and the lender secures the mortgage loan as a charge on the property. In the case of default of the loan arrangements – usually failure to keep up with repayments – the lender has the right to come into possession of the property and sell it. Equity has an important role to play in the law of mortgages but an examination of this topic is beyond the remit of this book.

- *A pledge* – a pledge is the transfer of property (usually personal property) as security for a loan or other benefit. A typical example would be the pledge of goods to a pawn broker or money lender for a loan with the intention of reclaiming those goods when the loan can be paid off. Pledges are governed by the law of contract. The pledgor parts with possession and ownership of the property but has a right to redeem the property. The pledgee has a duty to look after the property and a right to sell it if the debt is not repaid.
- *Bail* – bail or bailment arises where property is in transit or being kept safe for the owner. The keeper, the bailee, has a duty of care to the bailor to look after the goods and to ensure their safe arrival – a typical example would be where goods are being shipped by a third party or stored, as in a furniture depository. The bailee acquires no property interest in the goods even while in control of them. The issues that usually arise in bailment concern the passing of risk and who is to insure against that risk.
- *Agency* – this is where a person (or persons) is authorised to act as the agent of the owner and may exercise all the powers (or some of the powers) of the legal owner in relation to those assets – an example of agency would be the use of a power of attorney.

Foreign jurisdictions which do not have a tradition of using trusts struggle with the concept of what a trust is and how it operates. For example, many of the countries in the European Union have legal systems based on a civil code, and have never known the division between law and equity. The concept of fiduciary is understood, as is the law of contract, but civil law systems find it hard to accommodate the concept of the trust with its division of rights between the trustee(s) and beneficiaries.

1.6.2 Trusts and powers

We should also distinguish between a trust and a power. A power is the authority to do something with property conferred by the donor of the power on the donee of the power. Trustees have a number of powers (see **Chapter 5**) but an instrument that confers a power may fall short of being a trust. There are different types of powers.

- *A bare or mere power* – this arises when the donee of the power is simply given a power with no obligation to exercise it. Such powers may be further sub-divided into general powers, in which case the donee of the power can exercise it or not as they wish – including in favour of themselves – and special powers, in which case the power can only be exercised according to its terms, if it is exercised at all.

- *A discretionary power* – this arises when the donee of the power may exercise the power but does not have to do so. These kinds of powers are common in trust deeds (and therefore overlap with trust powers) and also arise under statute, such as the trustee's power of maintenance and advancement under ss 31 and 32 of the Trustee Act 1925.
- *A fiduciary power* – if a person is in the position of a fiduciary then if they choose to exercise the power, they must do so in good faith and in the way fiduciaries are expected to conduct themselves (see **Chapter 5**). An example would be a power of attorney.
- *A trust power* – this is mandatory insofar as the donee of the power, the trustee, must consider whether to exercise the power, and if they decide to exercise it, to do so in good faith and intra vires (ie within the scope of the powers given to them for the administration of the trust) (see **Chapter 5**).

1.7 Modern uses

The inherent flexibility of the trust means that it now occurs in many modern contexts. There is an obvious link between all of these uses, and that is the control of assets, the protection of the beneficiaries and often the minimisation of tax liability.

1.7.1 Private (family) trusts

The private family trust developed in the context of the preservation of family wealth, usually with the objective of manipulating control over assets, protecting beneficiaries and avoiding inheritance tax (and its predecessors). Prior to the end of the 19th century, they were also used to secure beneficial property rights for women when they married and for their children (marriage settlements), as on marriage women lost control over their own property until the passing of the Married Women's Property Act 1882.

These trusts might be found in a will (a testamentary trust) and so arise on the death of the settlor (referred to as a testator in the case of a will) or have been made during the settlor's lifetime by the drafting of a trust deed (an inter vivos trust).

The scenario at **1.6** concerning Robert and Jenny is a simple illustration of a family property trust. These are private trusts for the benefit of one or more individuals, often family members, and may be set up as:

- *fixed trusts* – where the settlor specifies the shares of the beneficiaries; or
- *discretionary trusts* – where the settlor specifies a class of beneficiaries but the trustees have the discretion to decide which beneficiaries will benefit and what their share will be.

Fixed trust – eg in equal shares. The settlor specifies the shares of the beneficiaries in advance.

Discretionary trust – the power is given to the trustees to decide which beneficiaries from the class will benefit and by how much.

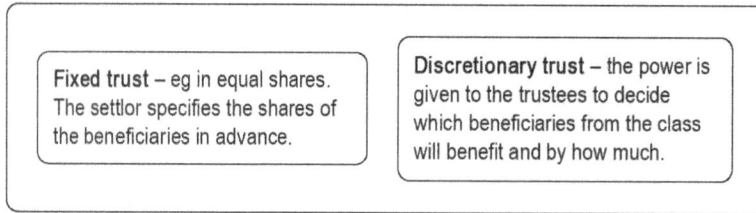

Figure 1.3 Methods of distribution within a typical family trust

It was and still is common for people to provide for children and to specify that the beneficiaries will not receive their share until they reach a certain age (a condition precedent). This allows the trustees to look after the assets for the children until they are old enough to deal with the property themselves.

From 1975 until 2006 these types of trusts were known as Accumulation and Maintenance trusts (A&Ms). A&Ms were a special hybrid of both discretionary and fixed interest trusts affording particularly useful tax breaks. Sadly, A&Ms were abolished by the Finance Act 2006 and replaced by the much more restrictive Bereaved Minor Trusts (BMTs) (which must vest at age 18) and Aged 18–25 Trusts (18–25) (where the vesting age can be no greater than 25).

These new trusts can only be created by the parent, step-parent or person with parental responsibility for the bereaved child and are only available on death. A&Ms could have been created by anyone for a class of children who all enjoyed common grandparents; they could also be created on death or during lifetime and the beneficiary had to get a vested interest by the time they reached 25, but this could be restricted to simply gaining a vested interest in income; whereas, the new trusts have to vest absolutely in both income and capital by either 18 (BMTs) or 25 (18–25).

Another popular trust construction, particularly in wills, is for a testator to leave his or her estate to his or her spouse for the spouse's lifetime and thereafter to their children. This is a successive interest trust and when included in a will is called an 'immediate post death interest'. Typically, the testator leaves his house, investments and cash on trust to his executors as trustees 'to his wife for life and thereafter to his children in equal shares provided they reach the age of 21'.

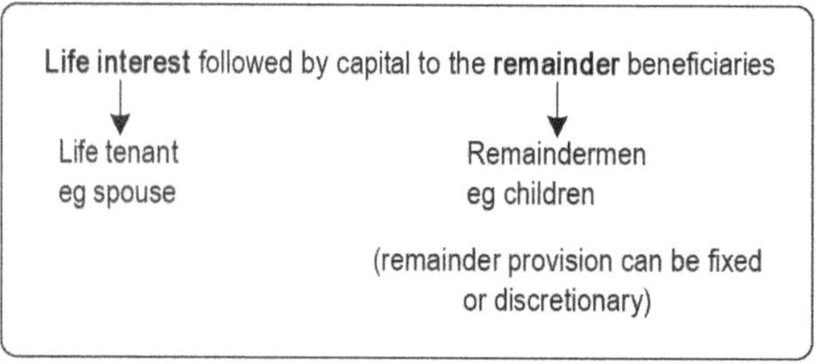

Figure 1.4 Successive interest trusts

The wife and the children are all beneficiaries of the trust with a guaranteed or 'vested' interest but their interests do not run concurrently. The wife's interest is referred to as 'vested in possession' as she has immediate enjoyment of it, whereas the interest of the remaindermen (ie the beneficiaries who take after the death of the wife) will not 'vest in possession' until their mother is dead. They have an interest 'vested in reversion'. If one of the remaindermen satisfies the age condition but pre-deceases the mother, that remainder interest vests in the deceased child's next of kin or passes by way of a will if the deceased child leaves a will. The original settlor/testator may stipulate that the shares of the children are to pass *per stirpes* and/or may stipulate in what circumstances any beneficiary may forfeit his or her interest – for example if the surviving spouse remarries.

1.7.2 Other types of trust

Within private trusts we also find:

- *Protective trusts* – under which a beneficiary is entitled to benefit from the trust unless or until an event happens, such as bankruptcy or criminal prosecution, at which point the beneficiary forfeits his or her entitlement and becomes a mere object under a discretionary trust. These are governed by s 33 of the Trustee Act 1925.
- *Disabled trusts* – where the prime beneficiary qualifies as a disabled person under Sch 1A of the Finance Act 2005 and receives most of the distributions from the trust whilst alive. In return these trusts are given certain tax benefits (Inheritance Tax Act 1984, ss 89–89B).
- *Secret trusts* – these are intentional testamentary trusts but are not evident from the will. They arise where a testator, prior to death, has asked a third party to hold property on trust for a beneficiary, who may be named or whom the settlor will make known to the intended trustee. If the intended trustee accepts then his or her conscience is bound. On the face of the will, the testator will have made an outright gift to the intended trustee and there will be no mention of the trust or the beneficiary. Typically this might arise where the testator wishes to keep the identity of the intended beneficiary secret from his or her family – for example a mistress, illegitimate child, second family etc. It might be thought that there is little need for such trusts in today's more liberal society but they still arise – see, for example, *Gold v Hill* [1999] 1 FLR 54; *Davies v Revenue and Customs Commissioners* [2009] UKFTT 138 (TC) – and may overlap with other implied trusts, as in *AM v SS* [2014] EWHC 2887 (Fam) (see **Chapter 4**).

  Clearly there may be evidential issues here to demonstrate that the conscience of the donee is bound (see for example *McCormick v Grogan* (1869–70) LR 4 HL 82).
- *Half-secret trusts* – these are also intentional trusts but the existence of the trust is evident on the face of the will where property may be left as follows: 'To

James, on those trusts which have been communicated to him.' Here it is self-evident that James is not intended to be the beneficiary of the property but to hold it for another, unnamed beneficiary. There must have been communication to James and acceptance of the obligation prior to the testator's death (given the possibility of the testator changing his or her will at any point up until death).

There are a number of guiding principles emerging from case law which govern both secret and half-secret trusts. The leading case here is *Blackwell v Blackwell* [1929] AC 318, and a recent case is *Rawstron v Freud* [2014] EWHC 2577. Secret and half-secret trusts are not common in practice.

- *Personal injury trusts* – the expression 'personal injury trust' is simply a legally binding arrangement, where funds are held by trustees for the benefit of another or others upon the terms of a trust, but where the funds which are held on trust have come as a result of a claim for compensation for injury. Damages for personal injuries may be awarded to a variety of claimants with different needs for the management of their award. The trust could therefore be a bare trust created by an adult who is mentally competent but who needs help with managing the use of those funds. The trust could be either for life or discretionary and created by a court to manage the compensation of a minor or mentally incompetent person.

1.7.3 Public trusts – charities

Trusts have been used for centuries to provide a structure for the administration of charitable funds. Charitable trusts fall within the category of purpose trusts; in other words they are set up for a purpose rather than for human beneficiaries. It will be seen in **Chapter 3** that there are detailed rules regarding the registration of a charity. Once registered, an organisation is eligible to take advantage of many benefits, not least the significant tax privileges available to charities.

1.7.4 The commercial sector

The following examples of modern commercial trusts are types of private express trusts.

1.7.4.1 Pensions

One way in which a pension scheme can be operated is via a trust. This might be a private pension fund or an occupational pension scheme. There are statutory provisions regulating this area and the duties on pension trustees are particularly onerous.

A pension trustee must have the requisite knowledge and understanding of the law relating to pensions, trusts and the principles of scheme funding and investment, whereas there is no restriction on who may act as the trustee of a family trust. Pension trustees also may not exclude their liability for negligence, although other trustees may be so excused in the trust deed.

With an occupational pension scheme, there is the attraction of having the pension funds placed in a trust pot separate from the rest of the company's assets, thereby not forming part of the company's assets for the purposes of insolvent liquidation, for example. However, a pension trust fund is still vulnerable to misappropriation by the trustees, as highlighted by the Robert Maxwell scandal in the early 1990s (see *Bishopsgate Investment Management Ltd (in liquidation) v Homan* [1995] 1 WLR 31).

1.7.4.2 Collective investment schemes

These schemes, administered by professional fund managers, offer investors the opportunity to pool their resources and spread the risk across a wide portfolio of investments. One way in which these schemes are run is by using a trust structure called a unit trust. Investors purchase units in the trust and the value of the units increases or decreases depending on how well the investments are performing. The units can be bought and sold like shares in a limited company.

Barlow Clowes International Ltd (in liquidation) v Vaughan [1992] 4 All ER 22, referred to in the context of tracing in **Chapter 6**, involved a collective investment scheme that went into liquidation following a fraud on the part of its managers. The court was involved in sharing out the remaining funds amongst the investors. See similarly *National Crime Agency v Robb* [2014] EWHC 4384 (Ch), where, although not initially set up as a trust, a number of defrauded investors who collectively had invested in a property development scheme were able to trace their investments under a constructive trust (see **Chapters 4** and **6**).

1.7.4.3 Company insolvency

In the past 40 years or so, there has been a noticeable trend towards claims of express trusts in cases of company insolvencies.

Some have been successful, such as in *Re Kayford Ltd (in liquidation)* [1975] 1 WLR 279, where the directors of a mail order company, realising it was in financial difficulties, sought to protect customer money by placing it into a separate bank account. The company went into liquidation and the court held that the money was held on trust for the customers, thereby giving them priority over other creditors of the company.

Others have not, such as in the unfortunate case of Farepak in 2006 (*Re Farepak Food and Gifts Ltd (in administration), Dubey v HM Revenue & Customs* [2006] EWHC 3272 (Ch)).

These issues will be developed further in **Chapter 2**. As we will see there is some debate as to whether these are express trusts or implied trusts which arise when the purpose of the intended transfer of beneficial interest fails – eg the goods which are paid for are not dispatched owing to the company's liquidation, or where money is loaned for a particular purpose which is not carried out (*Barclays Bank Ltd v Quistclose Investments Ltd* [1970] AC 567).

1.7.5 Implied trusts – division of the family home

The previous sections have involved express trusts, ie situations where someone has created a trust intentionally.

However, trusts can be implied from the circumstances, even though the parties involved may not be aware of this fact unless the situation comes under the scrutiny of the court.

Implied trusts fall into two categories: resulting trusts and constructive trusts. These trusts arise in a variety of situations and will be dealt with in **Chapter 4**.

An excellent modern-day example of the use of implied trusts occurs when a cohabiting couple separates and there is a dispute over the division of the home they shared together. Many such cases involve a house being purchased in the name of one partner (as happened in the case of *Oxley v Hiscock* [2005] Fam 211), but the principles have also arisen in joint names cases (as in the case of *Stack v Dowden* [2007] 2 AC 432). The claimant is the partner who argues that he or she is entitled to a share even though he or she is not on the title deeds, or where he or she is a joint owner (and therefore on the title deeds) but claims a larger share in the property than initially either expressly or impliedly agreed. That claim may be raised against the other partner or against a bank seeking to obtain vacant possession where there has been a mortgage default. Possession may be resisted by the claimant asserting an overriding interest based on actual occupation derived from a proprietary interest.

In such cases the courts may declare the existence of an implied trust, such as a constructive trust, to resolve the dispute, specifying that, for example, the sole owner holds the house on trust for the two of them as beneficial owners, or that both partners hold the house on trust for themselves as beneficiaries but in some unequal proportion. This will be explored in detail in **Chapter 4**.

1.8 Future developments

At the time of writing there are two relevant projects being undertaken by the Law Commission. First, a consultation completed in 2017 on reform of the law governing the making of wills is expected to be published as a report in 2019. The consultation brief refers to statistics from the Family Court in 2016 indicating that around 40% of adults die without making a will. The remit of the consultation was:

(a) to gain an understanding of why people may not make a will and how this could be addressed;

(b) to update the 19th century laws governing wills;

(c) to modernise the rules around capacity to make a will in light of medical advances in understanding mental health and dementia; and

(d) to address changes in societal behaviour such as cohabitation and digital technologies.

Chapter 2 looks at issues of capacity to make a will and a trust, and **Chapter 4** addresses the complex law on cohabitation and ownership of the family home.

Secondly, the Commission has embarked on a potentially broad-ranging project proposal entitled 'Modernising Trust Law for a Global Britain'. This is still at the 'initiation' stage and the problem is identified as follows:

> English trust law hasn't been comprehensively reviewed since 1925. Meanwhile, places like Singapore and New Zealand have updated their laws and been creative in maintaining a healthy trust market.
>
> A number of leading stakeholder groups have outlined various technical problems and limitations with our current trust law. Other countries have also come up with new trust and trust-like structures to meet demand.
>
> Not all of these structures may be suitable for this jurisdiction, but there is a strong argument that their advantages and disadvantages should be evaluated.

The proposal states that there will be an initial scoping exercise to identify areas for review and potential reform. This is definitely a project to keep an eye on.

1.9 Further reading

Greg Allan, 'Case Comment: AM v SS: Fraud and Flexibility' (2015) 4 *Conveyancer and Property Lawyer* 340–8.

Emma Challinor, 'Debunking the myth of secret trusts?' (2005) *Conveyancer and Property Lawyer* 492–500.

Sarah Hayden, 'Gifting chattels: the available methods considered' (2014) (3) *Private Client Business* 119–24.

Peter Jaffey, 'Explaining the Trust' (2015) *Law Quarterly Review* 377–401.

Margaret Halliwell, 'Equitable property rights, discretionary remedies and unclean hands' (2004) *Conveyancer and Property Lawyer* 439–52.

David Hayton, 'The development of equity and the "good person" in common law systems' (2012) *Conveyancer and Property Lawyer* (Editorial) 263–73.

William Batstone, 'One day all this will be yours', TEL & TJ, 2015, 170 (Oct), 18–21.

Lesley King, 'Detrimental move?', LSG, 25 October 2012, 109(40), 26.

Equity developed in response to the shortcomings of the courts of common law, and although today equity and common law are administered in one unified court system, there remain distinctions between these two branches of law. The impact of equity ranges further than the law of trusts but the focus here is on the trust, an equitable institution which evolved to meet a social need and has continued to demonstrate a remarkable flexibility to survive and be applicable in contemporary circumstances.

test your knowledge

1. An appreciation of the maxims of equity helps us to understand the way in which equity works. Would you agree?
2. The trust is distinct as a legal institution because it separates legal from beneficial interests in respect of the same property. Explain how it does this and what the consequences are for the trustee and the beneficiary.
3. How is the trust used today and what advantages does its use have for the settlor?

chapter 2

Creation of Express Trusts

After reading this chapter, you will be able to understand:

- the distinction between an inter vivos express trust and a testamentary trust
- the requirements for creating a valid trust
- the relationship between the various parties involved in the trust
- the role of formalities and constitution
- the ways in which incompletely constituted trusts and imperfect gifts might be saved.

2.1 Introduction

There are two basic categories of trusts: public and private. Within the latter there are those which are the consequence of a conscious decision to choose the institution of the trust as a way of transferring and managing interests in various forms of property; and there are those which are implied in the circumstances of the case, sometimes in line with the assumed intention of the transferor, sometimes in the absence of or contrary to the intention of the transferor (for example as in the case of resulting and constructive trusts considered in **Chapter 4**). This chapter is concerned with the former situation – the conscious choice to use the institution of the trust (as opposed to, for example, transferring interests in property by way of gift or sale).

However, whilst considering the rules for the creation of express trusts, this chapter also looks at cases and scenarios involving gifts, partly because there is a crossover between the rules for valid creation of both types of provision and partly because sometimes if a trust fails it may be construed as a gift. So, it is important to understand the distinction between a gift and a trust.

This is straightforward and simply involves a transfer of the whole of the title from the donor to the donee; there is no separation of legal and equitable title.

Figure 2.1 Gifts

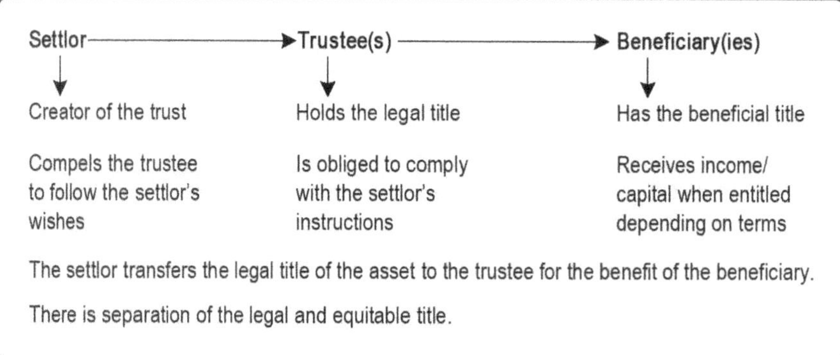

Figure 2.2 Trusts

Express trusts may be created in writing by deed, in a will or even quite informally through some other written expression of the requisite intention (for example in a letter or memorandum). It is also possible to create a trust using spoken words or via the conduct of the settlor (*Paul v Constance* [1977] 1 WLR 527) although inevitably such assertions will be more difficult to prove if the matter goes to court. The exception to this flexibility is where the subject matter of the trust is land, in which case the declaration of trust must be evidenced in writing in some way (Law of Property Act 1925, s 53(1)(b)). This is further explained at **2.4.2.1**.

Express trusts might take the form of a private family trust where, for example, money is set aside for the benefit of children, or they could arise in a commercial context where perhaps a company wishes to set aside customer funds to protect them from other creditors upon insolvency. Charitable and any non-charitable purpose trusts would be forms of express trust too, although you should note that some of the requirements for the creation of purpose trusts differ slightly, and on this point see **Chapter 3**.

The same instrument may make a number of bequests, which could include a mix of gifts and trusts (both private and public/charitable), so, for example, a will might include the following:

> *I leave my collection of pictures of the Lake District to my niece Ann knowing how much she loves that area.* [a gift]
>
> *I leave a third of the remainder of my estate to be divided equally between the following charities: the RSPCA, the Dogs Trust and the local animal rescue centre for cats.* [charitable trusts]
>
> *The remaining two-thirds of my estate I leave on trust for those of my grandchildren who reach the age of 25, and appoint my children, Jim and Sally, as trustees.* [private express testamentary trust]

There are four requirements for a valid express trust and these are:

- capacity to make the trust;
- the three certainties: intention, subject matter and objects;
- compliance with legal formalities; and
- constitution of the trust.

These rules also broadly apply to the making of a valid gift.

2.2 Capacity

In order to have sufficient capacity to make a trust, **the settlor** – that is the person who decides to use the trust to dispose of his or her property – must have the necessary mental competence. In other words the person must have the requisite ability and understanding to create a trust.

2.2.1 Age

The general rule is that a settlor must be aged 18 or over. However, minors can make a trust but the trust remains revocable until a reasonable time after the child reaches the age of majority. The age of majority is currently 18 years old but you should note that it was 21 years until 1969 (Family Law Reform Act 1969). *Edwards v Carter* [1893] AC 360 is an example of a trust created by a father during his son's minority. When his son tried to repudiate the trust after turning 21, the House of Lords held that he was bound by the deed of covenant undertaken on his behalf due to the amount of time that had passed since he had reached the age of majority. (A deed of covenant is a promise made in a formal document. The latter makes the former enforceable.)

2.2.2 Mental capacity

The test for mental capacity differs depending on the specific task being undertaken. The level of capacity required to get married is lower than that for making a gift or making a will. For a gift, the value of the asset being given away compared to the overall size of the settlor's estate will be relevant, and the larger the asset, the greater degree of understanding required.

In the case of *Re Beaney (Deceased)* [1978] 1 WLR 770 it was held that a level of understanding equivalent to that required for making a will was necessary when a mother, Maud, transferred her home (her main asset) to her daughter, thereby depriving her other two children of a share in her estate when she died. Maud was suffering from advanced dementia at the time of the transfer and on the facts did not therefore have the necessary capacity. *Williams v Williams* [2003] EWHC 742 (Ch) provides another good illustration of this rule.

One of the ways of making an express trust is in a will – a testamentary trust. In relation to making a valid will, the requirements for capacity are regarded as the highest standard – the same as was applied in *Re Beaney*. The testator must, subject to exceptions for those serving in the forces, be over 18 and have the relevant mental capacity in accordance with the test set out in *Banks v Goodfellow* (1869–70) LR 5 QB 549. Although our understanding of mental health has advanced considerably since the late 19th century, the dicta in this case remains the test for testamentary capacity – *Walker v Badmin* [2015] WTLR 493.

In *Banks v Goodfellow* it was held to be essential that a person making a will:

- understands the nature of his or her act and its effects – for the practising solicitor, this is probably the least difficult element to determine when the solicitor meets the client. If the initial contact comes from someone other than the intending testator, then additional care is needed in establishing whether the testator will be able to understand the basic nature of what he or she is about to do;
- understands the extent of the property of which he or she is disposing – the testator must remember and be aware of the extent and character of his or her assets;
- shall be able to comprehend and appreciate the claims to which he or she ought to give effect, and he or she should have no disorder of mind which would upset those objects.

A will must also be in writing and signed and witnessed in accordance with s 9 of the Wills Act 1837.

Note that, as mentioned in **Chapter 1**, the Law Commission is expected to report on the results of its 2017 consultation on wills, which is likely to include recommendations affecting the law on capacity and the signing and witnessing of wills, amongst other things.

This topic also raises the question of how incapacity can be dealt with practically. There are a number of possible solutions:

- If someone anticipates their lack of competency, for example due to ill health, they may execute a lasting power of attorney giving a trusted relative, friend or adviser control over their estate once they become incapacitated.
- The Court of Protection has wide powers to manage the affairs of any person whom the judge considers incapable of dealing with their own estate due to mental incapacity; this can even extend to preparing a will for the individual.

Capacity goes to the decision to use the trust as a way of disposing of property interests. It applies whether the trust is one made during the settlor's lifetime – an inter vivos trust – or on his or her death as a result of wishes expressed in a will – a testamentary trust. In addition, with gifts into trust, a practitioner drafting a will or a trust deed needs to be aware of whether the instructions are tainted by undue influence. If a person has capacity to make the gift, is their freewill overborne by the influence of those – often close family members who may also be carers – who seek to benefit? For gifts made in a will, this type of influence has to amount to coercion. For lifetime gifts, in addition to coercion, there is a presumption of undue influence if there is a relationship of trust between the parties and no independent advice on the nature and effect of the gift on the donor.

The issue of capacity can be problematic, especially where solicitors are dealing with elderly clients, with clients whose capacity may be impaired in some way, or with clients who may appear to be vulnerable. It is dangerous to make assumptions about people on the basis of apparent age or frailty and it is important to respect privacy and autonomy, so the solicitor has to tread a careful line between making appropriate and sufficient enquiries to ensure that there is capacity and reaching any conclusions that there is a lack of capacity.

in practice

The job of drafting a will for a vulnerable person is a high-risk activity and fraught with potential breaches of duties of care, leaving a firm open to claims in negligence. Most of the sources of potential negligence are nothing to do with the actual drafting of the will, but the surrounding circumstances, and the task requires both sensitivity and objectivity.

2.3 The three certainties

The settlor is just one of the components of the trust. The others are the trustee(s) – who may be the settlor him- or herself and/or others; the beneficiaries – of whom the settlor may be one; and the trust property. While the equitable maxim states that '**a trust will not fail for want of a trustee**' (see **Chapter 5**), it is necessary for other elements to be certain.

There are three certainties which must be present for a valid trust to be created and, as stated by Lord Langdale in *Knight v Knight* (1840) 49 ER 58, these are:

- *Certainty of intention* – which means that the settlor must intend to create a trust (as opposed to using some other legal institution to manage or dispose of his or her property – see **Chapter 1**). Clearly, it is important to ascertain the intentions of the person who created the provision and to reflect those, but a trust also imposes onerous legal obligations on the trustees so it is essential to be sure that a trust was intended because of the consequences that flow from this.
- *Certainty of subject matter* requires that the nature and extent of the trust property is clear and that the interests (or shares) of the beneficiaries can be ascertained, because, as we shall see, once property is placed in a trust it is treated distinctly from that of the settlor and the trustee.
- Finally, there must be *certainty of objects*, in other words it must be clear who the beneficiaries are. This is necessary so that the trustees are able to make a

distribution to the beneficiaries, but also so that there are identifiable individuals with the right to complain to the court in the event of a breach of trust. The reason why the term 'objects' is used is that in certain trusts, notably discretionary trusts, the trustees have discretion as to whom will benefit, and so it would be misleading to refer to these people as beneficiaries until we can be sure that they have been selected to benefit.

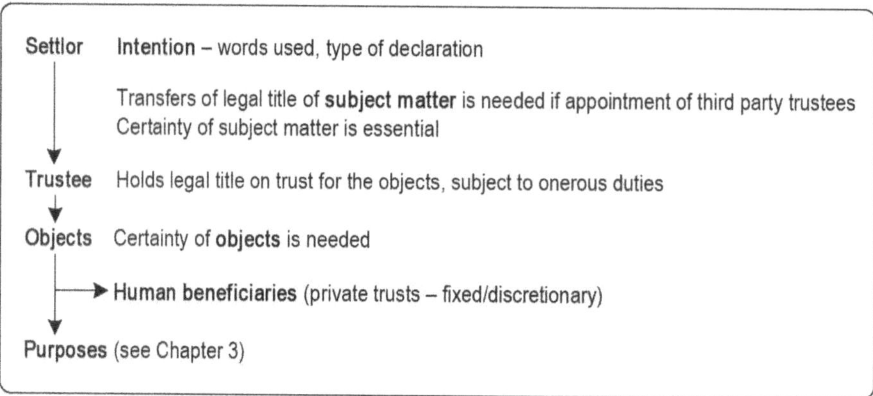

Settlor
Intention – words used, type of declaration
Transfers of legal title of subject matter is needed if appointment of third party trustees
Certainty of subject matter is essential
Trustee
Holds legal title on trust for the objects, subject to onerous duties
Objects
Certainty of objects is needed
Human beneficiaries (private trusts – fixed/discretionary)
Purposes (see Chapter 3)

Figure 2.3 The three certainties

Although *Knight v Knight* (above) remains good law, it is rarely cited today, and it may well be that the courts adopt a more holistic view of the settlor's intentions and where possible seek to bring certainty to possibly unclear provisions. For a recent discussion on the three certainties, the case of *North v Wilkinson* [2018] EWCA 161 provides an interesting, modern example. As David Richards LJ summarises:

> The creation of a trust has significant, and generally irreversible, consequences. The settlor, by creating the trust, ceases to be entitled to the benefit of the property subject to the trust. ... he holds it, to the extent of the interest created by the trust, for the benefit of the beneficiaries of the trust and becomes subject to exacting fiduciary duties owed to the beneficiaries in relation to the trust property. The law therefore requires certainty on three crucial elements: the intended beneficiaries, the property to be subject to the trust and the intention of the settlor to create the trust. These elements must be established objectively by reference to the documents, words or conduct relied on as creating the trust.

Practitioners use precedent templates to draft trusts, and therefore the three certainties are automatically covered unless a mistake occurs. However, in practice, the problem of validity usually arises in trusts created, intentionally or unintentionally, in homemade wills, and also where a trust arises by conduct, spoken words or other circumstances.

2.3.1 Certainty of intention

The settlor must have used words which impose a duty on the trustees to act in accordance with his or her instructions, rather than words which simply allow a discretion whether to act or not. This certainty goes to the heart of the definition of a trust; in other words, there is compulsion on the trustee to hold the trust property for the benefit of the beneficiary and to carry out the duties placed upon him or her as trustee. If this compulsion is lacking, then there is no trust (see **Chapters 1** and **5** in respect of powers).

A court will look, therefore, for evidence of the intention to create a trust, and in most cases this means looking at the words used by the settlor, whether written or spoken, to see if a trust is imposed. However, it is important to note that no particular form of words is required, and it is not necessary to use the word 'trust' provided the intention is clear (*Paul v Constance* [1977] 1 WLR 527, followed in the more commercial circumstances of *Shah v Shah* [2010] EWHC 313 (Ch)). The court will also take into account relevant conduct and other circumstances if appropriate. In *Revenue and Customs Commissioners v Annabel's (Berkley Square) Ltd* [2009] EWCA Civ 361, cash tips from customers looked after by one individual were said to be held on trust until shared out amongst the other staff.

The Court of Appeal in *Ong v Ping* [2017] EWCA Civ 2069 accepted the cumulative evidence of an incomplete trust deed and supporting letters as evidence of the settlor's intention to create a trust. This can be contrasted with the earlier Court of Appeal case of *Singha v Heer* [2016] EWCA Civ 424 where letters written between former business partners were not enough to demonstrate the requisite intention. Even though the word 'trust' had been used, the court was not convinced that this had been used in a legal sense.

It should be noted, of course, that the intention must be genuine and not fraudulent, as in the case of *Midland Bank v Wyatt* [1995] 1 FLR 697. Here the husband made a declaration of trust over the family home in favour of his wife and daughters, ie he wanted to retain the legal title to the house but declare that the beneficial interest belonged to them. His real intention was to ensure that the house was not available to his creditors in the event that he became bankrupt. Despite the declaration of trust, he continued to act as if the transfer had not taken place and even borrowed money for his business, using the house as security. The court held that the trust was a sham and it failed for lack of certainty of intention.

More recently in *Sparkasse Koln Bonn v Cutts & Anor* [2018] EWHC 1879 (Ch), the High Court found that an express trust over land, purported to have been created in writing in 2003, was invalid as it had clearly been drawn up much more recently in an attempt to protect the interests of the defendants.

Broadly speaking the cases on intention can be divided into two parts – those older cases dealing with poorly drafted will provisions, from which most of the principles relating to intention flow, and the more recent, commercial cases, often in the context of insolvency.

2.3.1.1 Wills cases – precatory words

When scrutinising the words used by a potential settlor, it is necessary for those words to convey compulsion on the intended trustee to act. Words demonstrating merely a hope, wish or desire that the recipient of the property will deal with it in a certain way will not suffice for a trust. These words of hope, etc are known as precatory.

The historical development of the rules on intention provides a useful and interesting background to the present state of the law. During the 18th and 19th centuries, the Court of Chancery was willing to construe precatory words as sufficient to create a trust. This was partly because, at that time, if property was not disposed of by a provision in the will, then the executors would keep the asset. In order to avoid this outcome, which may not have accorded with the intentions of the deceased, the courts were willing to find a valid trust from precatory words.

The attitude of the court changed towards the end of the 19th century, with the case of *Lambe v Eames* (1870–71) LR 6 Ch App 597. Here the testator had left his estate to his widow 'to be at her disposal *in any way she may think best*, for the benefit of herself and her family' (emphasis added). The court held that the words used were not sufficient to create a trust and instead there was an absolute gift of the estate to the widow. There was insufficient evidence that the gift to the widow was intended to 'be cut down' in any way. She may have felt morally obliged to follow the wishes of her late husband but she was not under any legal obligation to do so. There are plenty of other cases from around the same time illustrating that precatory words will not suffice – such as *Re Diggles* (1888) 39 Ch D 253 and *Re Hamilton* [1895] 2 Ch 372.

However, there are always examples of cases where slightly differing approaches are taken, depending upon the particular circumstances. It is interesting to compare the following two cases.

In *Re Adams and Kensington Vestry* (1884) 27 Ch D 394, a testator left his estate to his wife '*in full confidence* that she will do what is right as to the disposal thereof between my children either in her lifetime or by her will after her decease' (emphasis added). The court held that this provision was an absolute gift to the wife, and Cotton LJ commented that the word 'confidence' may create a trust but only if other wording in the will demonstrated that a trust was intended. In this case, no such intention was evident.

Then in *Comiskey v Bowring Hanbury* [1905] AC 84, the words '*in full confidence*' were again used in a will provision where a husband left his estate to his wife, but the provision went on to say 'that she will make such use of it as I should have made myself and that at her death she will devise it to such of my nieces and nephews as she may think fit'. In this case there was an additional clause known as a gift over in default of appointment (ie provision for an alternative disposition of the property should the first not be implemented), specifying that the estate must go to the nieces and nephews in the event that his wife did not create the necessary gift in her will. The court held, considering the wording as a whole, that the testator had intended to create a trust. Lord Davey commented that the use of the words 'in full confidence' was relatively neutral to the outcome of the case – they may or may not create a trust but whether they do so will depend upon the context.

2.3.1.2 Commercial cases – the insolvency context

In commercial cases the same principles are at play, ie working out the intention of the individuals involved by scrutinising the words used and actions taken.

Re Kayford Ltd (in liquidation) [1975] 1 WLR 279 provides a relatively straightforward starting point. Kayford was a mail order company that got into financial difficulties, and in order to protect its customers, the directors placed customer money into a separate bank account. The account was labelled the 'Customers' Trust Deposit Account', and the intention was to keep that money separate from the company's general funds in anticipation of a potential winding up of the company. The company was subsequently wound up and the court held that the money in the account was held on trust for the customers. Consequently the money did not form part of the company's assets and so was not available to other creditors; it was therefore returned to the customers. *Kayford* was applied with approval in *Brazzill v Willoughby* [2009] EWHC 1633 (Ch), a case concerning the security of monies deposited in a bank during the financial crisis of the period, and again in *Re Crown Currency Exchange Ltd (in liquidation)* [2015] EWHC 1876 (Ch) but with a rather less happy outcome for bank customers.

It should be noted, however, that simply setting money aside into a separate account will not necessarily be sufficient to demonstrate intention to create a trust (*Re Multi Guarantee Co Ltd* [1987] BCLC 257). It is worth reading the judgment in *Re Farepak Food and Gifts Ltd (in administration), Dubey v HM Revenue & Customs* [2006] EWHC 3272 (Ch), where placing money into a separate account, coupled with evidence of relevant intention on the part of the directors, was not sufficient to protect customers' money from the other creditors of the company. It is evident from *Farepak* that some judges place the interests of creditors generally on liquidation in priority to the claims of customers whose money is being held by a company pending delivery of their goods.

Another relevant factor in this context is where restrictions are placed on the recipient's ability to use the money freely. In *Freeman v Customs and Excise Commissioners* [2005] EWHC 582 (Ch), £693,000 was advanced by a purchaser of commercial premises to the vendor's solicitors on the condition that it was to be used only for the purposes of paying any VAT due on the transfer of the premises. The court held that a trust arose in this situation because the purchaser clearly intended to restrict the solicitor's freedom to deal with the money advanced other than in the manner specified. *Twinsectra Ltd v Yardley* [2002] 2 AC 164 is another good example of the point.

The case of *Barclays Bank Ltd v Quistclose Investments Ltd* [1970] AC 567 involved a similar restriction on the use of money loaned for one purpose only. There was no mention of the existence of a trust, but the money was loaned on the understanding that it was to be used only for the payment of a dividend by the borrower to its shareholders. The borrower became insolvent before the purpose could be carried out and the House of Lords concluded that the money was held on trust for the lender. However, this case is not straightforward and there is no clear agreement as to what type of trust existed in *Quistclose* – was it simply an express trust in favour of the lender (as in *Freeman* and *Twinsectra*), or did the purpose make it an invalid non-charitable purpose trust (see 3.4), or could it actually be a type of implied trust – a resulting trust (dealt with at 4.2)?

2.3.1.3 Different trust constructs

The examples considered so far have largely involved trusts where the trustees are different people from the settlor, ie the appointment of third party trustees. However, it is also possible for the settlor and the trustee to be the same person; this is referred to as a self-declaration of trust.

The case of *Paul v Constance* (above) involved such a self-declaration:

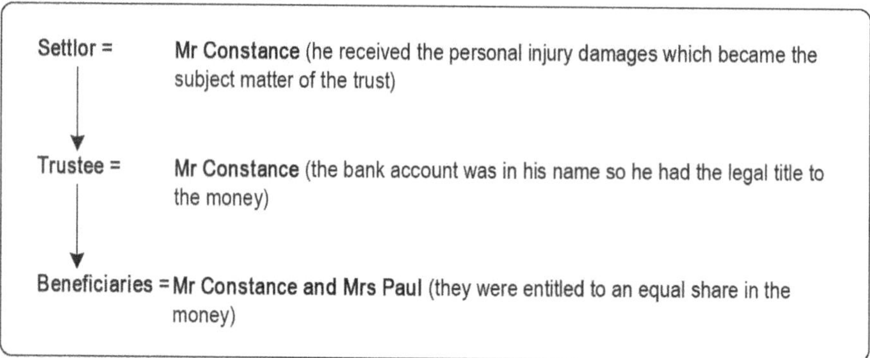

Settlor = **Mr Constance** (he received the personal injury damages which became the subject matter of the trust)
Trustee = **Mr Constance** (the bank account was in his name so he had the legal title to the money)
Beneficiaries = **Mr Constance and Mrs Paul** (they were entitled to an equal share in the money)

Figure 2.4 Self-declaration

(Note that in fact Mr Constance was also one of the beneficiaries in this case.)

The important point to note is that, regardless of the trust construct, the court still strives to find the intention of the settlor and to reflect this in its decision. Also, if the intention was to appoint third party trustees then the courts will not construe it as a self-declaration in order to save it (see for example *Milroy v Lord* (1862) 45 ER 1185 per LJ Turner: 'if the settlement is intended to be effectuated by one of the modes to which I have referred, the court will not give effect to it by applying another of those modes'). In the case of *Jones v Lock* (1865–66) LR 1 Ch App 25, the court refused to construe a failed gift as a self-declaration of trust as there was insufficient evidence that this was the intention of the donor, who had died shortly after purporting to transfer a cheque to his baby son.

2.3.2 Certainty of subject matter

The rules on certainty of subject matter fall into two parts: first, the property which is to form the subject matter of the trust must be clearly defined; and, secondly, the beneficial interests or shares in the trust fund must be capable of ascertainment.

2.3.2.1 The description of the subject matter

Cases in which the issue of certainty of subject matter is raised fall into a number of categories:

Ambiguous descriptions

In many cases the subject matter will be clear. For example in *Paul v Constance* (above) it was the money in the bank account and in *Midland Bank v Wyatt* [1995] 1 FLR 697 it was the house.

The problem tends to arise where the settlor or testator has described the property in an ambiguous or subjective manner and it is not possible for the trustees or the court to ascertain which assets ought to be subject to the trust.

In *Re Kolb's WT* [1962] Ch 531, the trustees were directed to retain in the trust certain 'blue chip securities'. 'Securities' is just another word for shares in a company but the difficulty lay in the meaning of 'blue chip'. The court sought expert evidence from a member of the stock exchange who confirmed that although there were a number of investments that some stockbrokers would class as blue chip, there were other equally competent stockbrokers who would disagree with the definition. The court held that the term did not have a sufficiently objective meaning and so there was no certainty of subject matter.

Anthony v Donges [1998] 2 FLR 775 is another case where the trust failed for lack of certainty of subject matter. The testator left the following provision for his wife – 'such minimal part of my estate … as she might be entitled to under English law for maintenance purposes'. The court held that this was void for lack of certainty because it was not possible to identify any entitlement of a widow under English law for maintenance purposes.

These cases can be contrasted with *Re Golay's Will Trusts* [1965] 1 WLR 969. In this case the testator, Adrian, directed his executors to allow Florence Bridgewater to live in one of his flats during her lifetime and in addition to receive a 'reasonable income' from his other properties. The court had to consider whether there was sufficient certainty in the second part of the provision. Ungoed-Thomas J held that it was certain and that the testator had provided an objective yardstick that could be used to measure the income to be provided to Florence. He said that the amount that was reasonable could be gauged by Florence's previous standard of living.

In the case of *Ong v Ping* (above), the trust deed did not specify the trust property and the space for identifying the property in the schedule was left blank. However, the court was convinced, having looked carefully at contemporaneous correspondence between the settlor and her solicitor, that the trust property was indeed the house in question, despite the defendant's submissions to the contrary.

Remainder provisions

Residue or remainder clauses at the end of a will are commonly used and refer to anything that is left in the deceased's estate once all liabilities (including tax), the specific bequests and trusts in the previous clauses have been removed or paid out. If any of the gifts or trusts in the will were to fail, the assets in those provisions would simply fall into the residue, if there is an effective trust gift of residue; or they are dealt with in accordance with the intestacy rules. The reason that will estates as a whole can be dealt with in this way is that they are essentially big trusts, ie the executors hold the deceased's estate on trust until it is distributed to the beneficiaries of the will. The executors therefore have control over the estate and for the most part its contents do not fluctuate (unlike a lifetime estate), although there may of course be changes to the value of the assets and income arising from them.

There are a number of different types of remainder provisions:

- residue clauses in wills;
- successive interest trusts; and
- 'anything that is left over' provisions.

The first two are generally not problematic if properly drafted; it is the third which causes problems.

Successive interest trusts were described in **Chapter 1**. In practice, such trusts are usually called 'interest in possession' trusts and they are a well-established trust structure to provide for the spouse of the deceased during the spouse's lifetime, and then passing the property to the children of the couple or other relatives following the death of the surviving spouse. They are not limited to this use – anyone can enjoy an interest in possession, but when it is a spouse or civil partner there is a tax exemption.

The third type of remainder provision could be viewed as a badly drafted successive interest trust and usually fails (as a trust). In *Palmer v Simmonds* (1854) 61 ER 704, the testator left her residuary estate to her husband 'for his own use and benefit', and on his death he had to leave 'the bulk of my estate' to certain relatives. This was held to amount to an absolute gift to the husband rather than a trust because the description of the subject matter was not clear. The term 'bulk of my estate' was too subjective and it was not clear how much would be left by the husband to the other relatives when he died.

Similarly, in *Sprange v Barnard* (1789) 29 ER 320, the testator left investments to her husband 'for his sole use, and all that is remaining that he has not use for' should be divided between other relatives. This again failed as a trust for lack of certainty of subject matter because it was unclear how much would be left at the date of the husband's death. It was held to be an absolute gift to the husband.

The cases of *Palmer* and *Sprange* are examples of provisions that leave property to A, and then 'anything that is left' goes to B. The problem arises when the part that will be left for B is not certain; then the provision will fail as a trust and operate as a gift to A.

If the provision is worded correctly, for example 'All my estate to A for life, remainder to B', then it can be a valid trust. In the case of *Re Last* [1958] P 137, the facts were similar to those in *Palmer* and *Sprange*, but the court held it to be a successive interest trust because the proper construction of the clause indicated that it was not up to A to make provision for B in his will; rather the testator had made provision in her will that the property must go to B after A's death. Clearly, each case will depend upon its own facts.

Trusts over unallocated assets

The general rule for certainty of subject matter is that assets must be clearly defined and segregated from the rest of the settlor's estate; otherwise it will not be clear which assets are to be in the trust. Problems occur therefore if the settlor states that a portion of similar assets from his or her estate are to form the subject matter. For example, the settlor has 50 paintings in his house and says that 20 of them are to be held on trust but without specifying which 20.

When considering the issue of unallocated assets, the law appears to treat tangible and intangible assets differently.

Tangibles

In *Re London Wine Company (Shippers)* [1986] PCC 121, the company held stocks of wine at a number of warehouses and, when a customer purchased wine, it would often store the bottles on behalf of the customer, for a fee, until he or she was ready to take delivery of them. The company went into liquidation and the customers tried to argue that they were the beneficiaries of a trust in relation to the bottles of wine they had purchased, and this gave them priority over creditors. Unfortunately the company did not segregate customers' wine from its general stock of similar wines and so it was not clear which bottles actually belonged to each customer. Accordingly it was held that a trust did not exist in favour of the customers because there was a lack of certainty of subject matter.

The rationale behind the decision was partly due to the fact that each bottle of wine, a tangible item, was unique and could differ from other bottles from the same source and year. Also, it was acknowledged that the general stock of wine held by the company would fluctuate from time to time, and so at any given point it was possible that there might not be sufficient bottles of a particular vintage to satisfy all the customers' deliveries if they all asked for their bottles at the same time. It was not therefore possible to say there was certainty of subject matter for a trust.

A similar approach was taken in relation to gold bullion in *Re Goldcorp Exchange Ltd (in receivership)* [1995] 1 AC 74, a Privy Council case on appeal from New Zealand, where it was held that the claimants could not claim title to unascertained goods – here gold bullion and gold coinage.

One way of avoiding the problem is, rather than declaring the trust over a specific number of items – for example 20 bottles of my wine – the subject matter is described as a fraction or percentage of the whole, eg one quarter of my bottles of wine. This possibility was discussed in the *London Wine* case (above) and results in the subject matter of the trust being a 'chose in action', ie a legal right to bring a claim – which is a form of intangible property. The basis for this is that the claimant is a tenant in common of a proportion of the mass of stock, rather than a purported owner of a number of particular items. The Sale of Goods Act 1979, s 20, as amended by the Sale of Goods (Amendment) Act 1995, provides a statutory authority for this right in a retail context.

Intangibles

The approach of the court has been different in relation to intangible property, which by definition could include many things such as intellectual property rights, bonds or even money potentially, but the cases in question relate to shares in a limited company.

Hunter v Moss [1994] 1 WLR 452 is the landmark Court of Appeal case on this point and involved a self-declaration of trust over 50 out of the settlor's 950 shares, but without specifying which 50. This was an inter vivos trust as opposed to a will trust and did not arise in the context of the bankruptcy of the settlor, rather upon the falling out of the settlor and beneficiary.

The trust was held to be valid and to have certainty of subject matter even though the individual shares were not identified. *Re London Wine Company* was distinguished as being confined to tangible property. There was an important difference with the shares in this case: the company was precisely defined and all the shares were identical so there was no difference between each of the settlor's 950 shares.

It seems therefore that the rule from *Hunter v Moss* is that, provided all the intangible items are identical, it is possible to create a trust over a portion of them without specifying each individual item. The following reasoning was given by Dillon LJ:

> Just as a person can give, by his will, a specified number of shares in a certain company, so equally he can declare himself trustee of 50 of his shares … and

that is effective to give a beneficial proprietary interest to the beneficiary under a trust.

However, this line of reasoning is not universally accepted, partly because this approach appears to overlook the distinction between inter vivos and testamentary dispositions. Upon the death of an individual, title to the assets passes to the personal representatives of the deceased, and so it is straightforward for the personal representatives to choose the required number of shares and transfer them to the beneficiary, subject to any provisions in the articles of association or shareholders' agreement. With inter vivos trusts, the beneficiary acquires a proprietary interest in the particular shares as soon as the trust is declared, and so it is crucial to identify which shares form the subject matter of the trust at the outset. If this has not been done, what would happen if the settlor sold some of his shares? Would this include the shares held on trust or not?

In any event, *Hunter* remains a good authority and has been followed in subsequent cases, such as *Re Harvard Securities Ltd (in liquidation)* [1998] BCC 567 and *Shah v Shah* [2010] EWHC 313 (Ch).

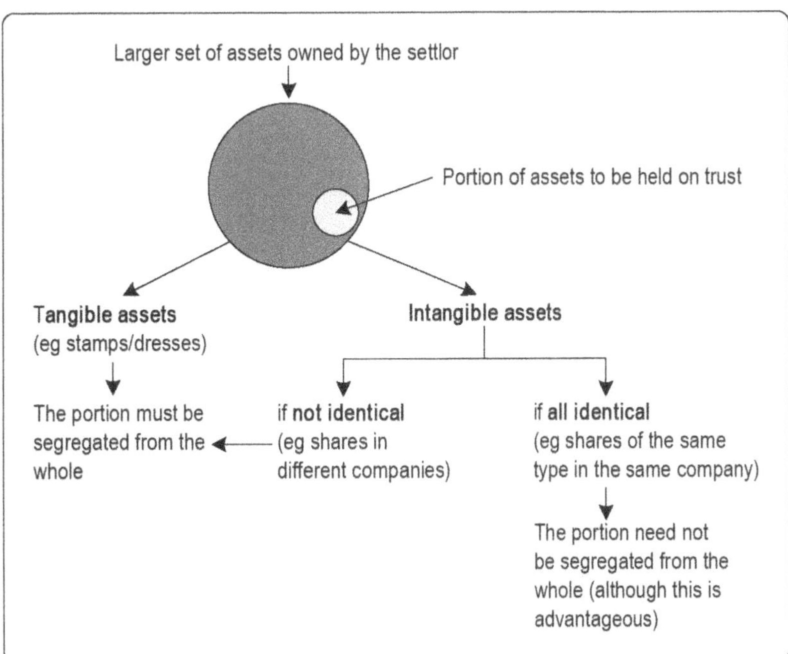

Figure 2.5 Tangible and intangible assets

2.3.2.2 Certainty of the beneficial interests

The second issue relating to the subject matter of a trust is that it must be possible to ascertain the interests or shares that the beneficiaries will receive.

It may be that the settlor has done this by specifying a fixed share, eg equal shares (this would be called a fixed trust), or the decision as to size of share may be given to the trustees (this is called a discretionary trust). These structures are both fine, but the difficulties arise where the settlor sets out a method of ascertainment that relies on, for example, a choice to be made by a beneficiary.

In *Boyce v Boyce* (1849) 60 ER 959, the testator left a number of houses to his trustees for his wife for her lifetime, and thereafter one house was to go to Maria and the remaining houses to Charlotte (ie the successive interest-type trust). The provision stated that Maria must select whichever house she would like but, unfortunately, Maria died before she made the choice. The court held that the gift to Charlotte was not ascertainable as it relied upon Maria's selection, which had not taken place, and therefore Charlotte received nothing. The houses were held on resulting trust and passed to the testator's residual beneficiary under his will.

The case of *Boyce* is considered to be a harsh example, but the difficulty for the court was that the settlor had been so specific about the method of determination that it was impossible for it to be carried out. Some might say that the court could have made the decision instead, and perhaps a modern court might be more willing to step in.

In *Re Knapton* [1941] Ch 428, the testator was less prescriptive and simply listed the beneficiaries and stated that each was to receive one property. The court took a pragmatic approach and allowed each beneficiary to choose a property, and the right of selection followed the order that they were named in the will.

2.3.3 Certainty of objects

Objects, in the context of trusts, can mean human beneficiaries or a purpose, and in both cases the objects must be clearly defined in order for the trustees to carry out their obligations, although there are exceptions for charitable purposes. In relation to purpose trusts, see **Chapter 3**.

This section relates to objects as human beneficiaries and, again, in many cases there will be no issue. So, for example, a trust of £100,000 for 'my brothers Andrew and Jack' has certainty of objects.

The problem tends to arise where the settlor sets out a class (or group) of beneficiaries and the description of the class is ambiguous or subjective. For example, a trust of £50,000 to be divided amongst 'my best friends' will not be valid unless I specify whom my best friends are (note, however, that where the obligation to distribute property is framed as a power rather than a trust, the class 'any of my best friends' may be valid – *Re Gibbards's Will Trusts* [1967] 1 WLR 42).

A body of case law has developed over the years providing guidance on the correct tests to be applied. It is crucial, first of all, to identify the type of provision in question and this will then determine the appropriate test:

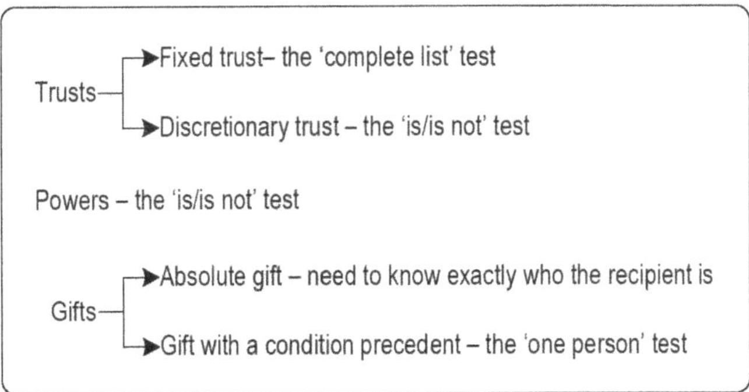

Figure 2.6 Tests

2.3.3.1 Fixed trusts

The definition of a fixed trust is one where the entitlement or share of each beneficiary has been fixed by the settlor. For example: '£500,000 to be divided equally between my children upon them reaching the age of 21'. Here, assuming the settlor has four children, they will each receive one quarter of the trust fund.

In order for the trustees to divide the trust fund up equally in accordance with the settlor's wishes, the trustees need to know how many beneficiaries there are, and so it makes sense that it must be possible to draw up a complete list of the beneficiaries (*Re Eden* [1957] 1 WLR 788; *IRC v Broadway Cottages* [1955] Ch 20).

The test can be referred to as the list test, the listing principle or the class ascertainability test.

In order to satisfy the test and create a list of beneficiaries, it is essential to have both conceptual and evidential certainty in the description of the class.

Conceptual certainty

The words used to describe the class must be clear and unambiguous. It must not be the type of term that could be interpreted in different ways. So 'siblings' or 'children' would be certain, but 'friends' or 'good customers' without further contextual elaboration would be conceptually uncertain.

Evidential certainty

Even though the concept is clear, there might still be difficulties evidentially. For example, although 'the members of my scout brigade in Gainford village in 1978' might seem conceptually quite certain, it might not be possible to draw up a list of the members due to fact that the records have been destroyed or lost. It is possible to use oral evidence but this may not be reliable, particularly if there is a lot of money at stake.

Although it is necessary to draw up a list of the beneficiaries, this does not mean that the trustees need to be able to locate them. If, for example, one of the beneficiaries were estranged from the family, his share could be paid into court by the trustees until such time as he comes forward to claim his share. If it turns out that the beneficiary is no longer alive then his share would be distributed according to his will or the rules on intestacy. This is known as the rule in *Re Benjamin* [1902] 1 Ch 723.

2.3.3.2 Discretionary trusts

> *'£100,000 to be held on trust and divided amongst such of my grandchildren and in such shares as my trustees shall see fit.'*

In this type of the trust, the trustees are given the discretion to decide which grandchildren will benefit and by how much. This can be attractive to a settlor because it allows the trustees to make the decision about who needs financial help at a later date. The use of a discretionary-type trust means that no beneficiary is entitled as of right to any part of the trust fund, with the result that no share or any part of the trust's value will be added to the beneficiary's estate on death and be taxed at the rates applicable at that time. Instead, there is a special inheritance tax regime for discretionary trusts that results in a lower rate of tax, which is applied on a periodic basis and when assets are distributed from the trust.

Another way to put it is that the trustees have the power to select who gets what. In fact a discretionary trust is a hybrid, a mixture of a trust with a power to select. The trustees are still under an obligation to distribute the fund; they have to give it to at least one of the beneficiaries; they cannot simply do nothing (as would be the case where a bare power of appointment is conferred on a person – see **Chapter 1**). This ties in with the idea of the element of compulsion on the trustees, which is the essence of a trust. You can spot that it is a trust by the mandatory or obligatory words used, so 'shall' or 'must' or 'will' distribute/divide indicate the compulsion.

So the discretionary trust involves a duty to distribute, coupled with a power (or discretion) to decide who is to benefit from a specified class of potential beneficiaries (objects), and how much those who are chosen to benefit should get.

It is also interesting to note that, unlike with a fixed trust, the potential beneficiaries in the class do not own any part of the trust fund unless and until they have been selected. They do have rights to complain to the court in certain circumstances – for example if the trustees are clearly choosing beneficiaries who do not fall within the nominated class, or if the trustees are refusing to even address their minds to the matter – but they cannot require the trustees to pick them, for example. The court is usually reluctant to interfere with the discretions given to trustees although it will, of course, impose liability for breach of duties.

Historically, the test for certainty of objects for a discretionary trust was the same as that for fixed trusts. For example, in *IRC v Broadway Cottages Trust* (above), the trustees were to hold a fund for such members of a class of beneficiaries as they saw fit, ie a discretionary trust. The class was extremely wide, consisting of remote relatives of the settlor and two charities. The trust was held to be void for uncertainty because it was not possible to draw up a complete list of all the possible beneficiaries. The reasoning given was that if the court had to distribute the fund, it would use the maxim '**equity is equality**' as a default method of division, and so in order to share the money out equally amongst the beneficiaries, the number of people and identity of each one would need to be known.

However, in the early 1970s, the test for discretionary trusts changed to the 'is or is not test', also known as the 'individual ascertainability' test. This change was made by the House of Lords in the case of *McPhail v Doulton (Re Baden's Deed Trusts No 1)* [1971] AC 424, and the *Broadway Cottages* case was overruled.

In *McPhail*, the settlor, Bertram Baden, set up a discretionary trust for the benefit of the current and previous employees of a company plus their relatives and dependants. The court had to decide whether this description of the class of potential beneficiaries was sufficiently certain. The House of Lords considered the list test and rejected it as inappropriate for the following reasons:

- It was not necessary to rely upon 'equity is equality' and to make an equal distribution amongst all the beneficiaries. In a case such as this, as in many discretionary trusts, that would make a nonsense of the settlor's intention when setting up the trust, and with such a large class, each person would receive only a small sum. The court accepted that it could exercise the necessary discretion itself if it had to and make a selection from amongst a class.
- The law should take a practical and sensible approach to the test for discretionary trusts. The distinction between a discretionary trust and a power was often very narrow and could turn upon the finest point of construction. It made sense for such trusts to have the same test as for powers rather than the same test as for fixed trusts, which was a very different provision.

As a result of this, the test for powers was therefore introduced to discretionary trusts – the 'is or is not test' (*Re Gestetner Settlement* [1953] Ch 672). In order for there to be certainty of objects, it must be possible to say of any given postulant (individual) that they are either in the class or not in the class. It is not necessary to draw up a list, but the trustees need to be able to work out whether any given person is a member of the class of beneficiaries or not. For this reason it is sometimes also called the 'any given postulant' test.

In *Re Baden No 1*, Lord Wilberforce gave the leading judgment and focussed on the importance of conceptual certainty when applying the test.

The case was then referred back to the Chancery Division so that the correct test could be applied to the Baden trust deed. This second part of the case is known as *Re Baden's Deed Trusts (No 2)* [1973] Ch 9. This time it was appealed to the Court of Appeal and although the three judges agreed that the trust was valid and had sufficient certainty of objects, each gave a differing opinion about the interpretation of the individual ascertainability test.

- Stamp LJ took the strictest approach and insisted that both conceptual and evidential certainty was required.
- Sachs LJ was of a similar view to Lord Wilberforce in saying that conceptual certainty was the key to the validity of the provision. In other words, are the words used to describe the class clear enough to determine whether someone is in it or not? In terms of evidence, he said that the person coming forward as a potential beneficiary had the burden of proof to substantiate his or her claim. So, whereas with a fixed trust the burden is on the trustees to be able to satisfy the evidential certainty, here the burden shifts to the beneficiary.
- Megaw LJ applied the least stringent interpretation. He said the important question was whether it could be said with certainty that a substantial number of people fall within the class, and it does not matter that, as regards other persons, it cannot be determined whether they fall in the class or not. This approach has been criticised as setting too low a bar and possibly diluting the test.

The approach taken by Lord Wilberforce and Sachs LJ would seem to represent the sensible middle ground, and due to a lack of subsequent case law involving certainty of objects in discretionary trusts, the issue remains undeveloped.

Administrative workability

Another issue to consider in the context of discretionary trusts is that of administrative workability. Although the trustees do not need to draw up a complete list of all the beneficiaries, they do have a duty to 'survey the field'; in other words they need to be able to look at the potential class of beneficiaries and then consider whether making a particular distribution is appropriate. This was discussed by Lord Wilberforce in *Re Baden No 1* but the class in that case was not so large as to cause the failure of the trust.

A good example is *R v District Auditor, ex p West Yorkshire CC* [1986] RVR 24, where the class consisted of all or some of the inhabitants of West Yorkshire, amounting to around 2.5 million people. The court described the class as 'hopelessly wide' and so large that the trustees could not effectively fulfil their duties nor exercise their discretions properly under the trust.

2.3.3.3 Powers

Powers come in a variety of forms and are essentially an authorisation to act. Powers, unlike duties, are not obligatory and it is up to the donee (or recipient) of the power to decide whether they should act or not (see **Chapter 1**).

Trustees are given many powers to act, which may include the power to select beneficiaries, in a discretionary trust, or the power to maintain an infant beneficiary before he or she receives his or her share of the capital (see **Chapter 5** on trustees' powers).

However, powers may be given independently of a trust, for example, '£10,000 to my brother to be divided amongst such of my children as he *may* decide and, if he does not so decide, then to my wife absolutely'.

Notice the use of the word 'may' instead of 'shall' or 'must'. This indicates a power or discretion rather than an obligation or trust. It is evident that there is a fine line between the drafting of a power and a discretionary trust, and it can difficult to distinguish the two. Another feature of a power is the last part, the 'gift over in default', ie what happens to the money if the trustees do not give it to the children? It goes to the wife. The presence of a gift over in default of the exercise of the power is construed as evidence of an intention to confer a power rather than a trust if there is uncertainty.

Although the donee of a power is not obliged to make the distribution, if he is also a fiduciary (for example, a trustee is a fiduciary) then he must periodically consider whether to exercise the power to select a beneficiary and he must not act capriciously or ultra vires (*Mettoy Pension Trustees Ltd v Evans* [1990] 1 WLR 1587).

The test for certainty of objects for powers is the 'is or is not test', as outlined in the previous section on discretionary trusts (*Re Gulbenkian Settlement Trusts (No 1)* [1970] AC 508, *Re Gestetner Settlement* [1953] Ch 672).

2.3.3.4 Gifts with a condition precedent

At its simplest, a gift is a transfer of an asset, such as piece of jewellery, from one person to another where no consideration is provided in return and no obligations are attached (see **Chapter 1**). For an absolute gift, with no conditions attached, the rule for certainty is that the recipient must be identifiable, which is purely common sense.

A gift with a condition precedent could involve one or possibly a series of gifts to a class of people who satisfy a particular condition specified by the donor, for example '£1,000 to each of my nephews who obtains a first class bachelor's degree'. The subject matter is the money, the objects of the gift are the nephews, and they will receive it when they satisfy the condition of graduating with a first.

This should be contrasted with trusts which can also have conditions attached, for example a very common trust provision is money left on trust for children who will receive their share when they attain a particular age. The difference with a trust is that the settlor places a specified amount of money or group of assets into the trust and instructs the trustees to divide it up amongst the beneficiaries in a particular manner.

The test for certainty of objects for a gift with a condition precedent was applied in the case of *Re Barlow's Will Trusts* [1979] 1 WLR 278. Here a will provision stated that 'any friends of mine who may wish to do so' could purchase one of the testatrix's paintings at its probate value. The court viewed this as a series of gifts in the form of options to purchase a painting, exercisable by anyone who satisfied the condition of being a friend of the deceased. Judge Browne-Wilkinson stated that if it had been a trust, then the term 'friends' would not satisfy the relevant tests because it is too subjective and lacks conceptual certainty. However, for a series of gifts, the 'one person' test applies, and all that is required is to be able to say with certainty that at least one person falls into the description. The judge was satisfied that there would be someone who could be classed as a friend of the testatrix, however this was defined.

In practice, gifts in wills can cause difficulty if there is a lack of practicality involved, such as who makes the decision if a choice is involved (the beneficiaries, and if so in which order; or the executors or a third party) and when must the decision be taken (within a specified period of time from date of death or without time limit).

Sometimes, a client may want what appears to be a simple gift in his or her will, eg £100,000 to my great-niece Lucy at 25. However, this is fraught with problems. This is a contingent pecuniary legacy and so the executors have to ensure they retain sufficient funds to be able to transfer exactly £100,000 to Lucy when she reaches 25. However, in the meantime, the estate will need to be managed and any investments which generate an income will result in that income falling into residue because it does not belong to nor can it be used for Lucy. Similarly, if Lucy is only three years old at the testator's death, that means that the executors have to find a way of guaranteeing that their investment of the estate's assets will ensure there will be £100,000 available to give to Lucy when she is 25. Who knows what to invest in that would provide this exact outcome in 22 years time?

A far better solution would be to put £100,000 into trust until Lucy is 25 and enable the executors and trustees to manage that fund for her benefit in the meantime, so that income or capital can be used for her maintenance, education or other benefit until she satisfies the age contingency.

2.3.3.5 Creative ways to avoid uncertainty

There have been attempts made to include additional guidance in order to avoid uncertainty of objects. One method, employed in the case of *Re Tuck's Settlement* Trusts [1948] Ch 747, was to appoint an expert who could give an opinion as to whether the conditions stated in the provision had been met. In *Re Tuck*, the principal beneficiary had to marry a wife who was of the Jewish faith, and the court agreed that, as stated in the trust document, a Chief Rabbi could be consulted to determine whether this condition had been satisfied. Lord Denning stated that the conceptual uncertainty around the provision had been 'cured' by the inclusion of the Chief Rabbi clause.

Of course, the matter upon which the 'expert' is asked for an opinion must be one that is capable of being given an objective definition. If the 'expert' simply gives another subjective opinion then this will not assist in finding certainty.

2.4 Formalities

The final requirements for the creation of an express trust are compliance with the necessary formalities for the declaration of trust and then constitution of the trust. These requirements operate quite closely with each other.

The first issue to consider is what type of provision you are dealing with, and for these purposes we can divide the provisions into two categories:

- a self-declaration of trust (commonly known as a declaration of trust) – here the settlor and the trustee are the same person (see *Paul v Constance* above and **Figure 2.4**); and
- an appointment of third party trustees, via a trust deed, settlement deed or created orally, and outright gifts, created orally or by a deed of gift. With this type of provision the transferor and the transferee are different people (although the body of trustees may still include the settlor). In a trust the settlor transfers the property to the trustees, and with a gift the donor transfers the property to the donee.

2.4.1 Self-declaration of trust

With this type of provision, the settlor does not need to transfer the property (or subject matter of the trust) to anyone; he or she simply holds it as trustee rather than for him- or herself as before. The legal title remains with the settlor, but he is now the trustee of it and so holds the legal title to the property but is not entitled to the beneficial interest anymore. All that is needed in this situation is an effective declaration of trust, demonstrating that the legal and equitable title has been split between the settlor/trustee and the intended beneficiary.

As we have already seen, where the property is personal, eg chattels, shares, money, there are no formal requirements for the declaration of trust (*Paul v Constance* (above); *Rowe v Prance* [1999] 2 FLR 787). It can be done in writing, orally or arise from the circumstances – although there may be evidential difficulties if the declaration is purely oral unless there are witnesses prepared to attest to this. However, if the subject matter is land then s 53(1)(b) of the Law of Property Act 1925 requires that 'a declaration of trust respecting any land or interest therein must be manifested and proved by some writing …'. This does not require the drafting of a trust deed but can take another form of writing, such as a letter, and may even have occurred after the transfer of the land. In *Ong v Ping* (above) the relevant letter was written some three years after the signing of the defective trust deed.

Failure to comply with this rule does not result in the trust being void but just that it would be unenforceable by the beneficiary.

One aspect that has caused some difficulties in the case law is the provision in s 53(1)(c) which requires 'a disposition of an equitable interest or trust subsisting at the time of the disposition' to be in writing, signed by the person making the disposition (or his or her lawfully authorised agent).

It is possible to place an existing beneficial interest on trust. So, for example, the settlor may be a beneficiary under an existing trust and wish to put that interest on a further trust. The settlor's interest in this case is an equitable interest, and this becomes the subject matter of the new trust. The problems that have arisen in the case law focus on the question of whether or not there has been an effective disposition of a beneficial interest, usually for tax purposes. If the beneficial interest has not been entirely disposed of to the extent that the settlor has severed all rights to the beneficial interest, then the settlor may still be liable for tax on the benefit. An area of some controversy is the assignment of intangible property, such as the benefits of an insurance policy.

From a practical perspective, insurance has an important part to play in personal financial planning, both as a means of providing protection and as an investment. Life assurance products designed more as an investment include endowments or investment plans (if you pay regular premiums) or investment bonds or single premium bonds (if you pay in one or more lump sums).

The policy proceeds of a life policy mature on the death of the life assured or, where there is more than one life assured, on the death of the last of the lives assured. Where that person remained the beneficial owner of the policy, it will form part of the deceased estate and be subject to inheritance tax (IHT) like any other asset in the deceased's estate.

There will also be provision for the payment of a surrender value on the surrender, in whole or in part, of the policy at any time up to the maturing of the policy on the death of the life assured.

By using whole life policies written into trust, large IHT-free funds can be left to heirs on death, and the funds can be used to pay the liability to IHT on other assets arising on the death whilst themselves not being charged to IHT because they do not form part of the deceased's estate. Existing policies assigned into a trust will be treated as a transfer of value for IHT purposes.

Declarations of trust are usually used to place policies of assurance into trust. The person who benefits from the policy declares that, from the date of the declaration, the proceeds of that policy no longer remain in the donor's estate but are now held in trust for the benefit of the beneficiaries.

2.4.2 Appointment of third party trustees/making an outright gift

As acknowledged above, this requires a transfer of the property from settlor/donor to trustee/donee. How the formalities are complied with depends upon the type of property in question. The following are the most common types of property that will be encountered.

2.4.2.1 Land

The legal title to land must be transferred by deed (Law of Property Act 1925, s 52(1)). Once signed, the deed must be sent to the Land Registry, and legal ownership passes to the trustee/donee when the register is amended to show the transferee as the new proprietor or, in the case of land that has previously been unregistered, once the land is registered in the name of the new legal owner (Land Registration Act 2002, ss 7 and 27).

For a gift, the transaction is then complete.

For a trust, the requirement under s 53(1)(b) of the Law of Property Act 1925 still needs to be met (as set out above), ie the declaration of the trust must be manifested in writing. In fact there is a space to do so on the Land Registry form that is used to transfer land.

Richards v Delbridge (1874) LR 18 EQ 11 provides an example of a failed transfer of an interest in land. The case involved a lease, and the correct method of transfer is by deed of assignment. The transferor simply wrote a memo on the back of the deed of lease, and this was insufficient. The court held that the gift of the lease failed as the correct mode of transfer had not been used.

In practice, it would be more usual to create a trust using a deed and putting in only say £10 at the start to properly constitute the trust. Subsequently, assets, such as land, could then be transferred to the trustees to hold on the terms of the trust.

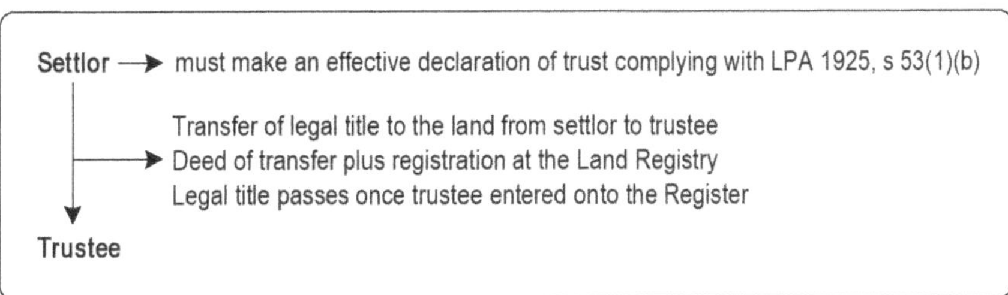

Settlor
must make an effective declaration of trust complying with LPA 1925, s 53(1)(b)
Transfer of legal title to the land from settlor to trustee
Deed of transfer plus registration at the Land Registry
Legal title passes once trustee entered onto the Register
Trustee

Figure 2.7 Declaration of trust over land involving third party trustee

2.4.2.2 Shares

Under s 1 of the Stock Transfer Act 1963, the transferor must execute a stock transfer form and hand this over to the transferee along with the share certificate. The trustee or donee then applies to the company asking to be registered as a member (or shareholder). Again, transfer of the legal title is not complete until the transferee's name is entered onto the register of members (*Re Rose* [1952] Ch 499). For companies listed on a stock exchange there is an electronic system for the transfer of shares, known as CREST, which replaces the paper-based stock transfer form. In the case of private companies, where the number of shareholders is usually limited, the consents of other shareholders may be required before transfer can take place, and in the case of some forms of business there may be citizen and resident requirements attaching to shareholders.

Milroy v Lord (above) is one of the leading cases on formality and constitution and involved shares in a bank. The settlor executed a deed purporting to transfer the shares to Lord to hold as trustee for Milroy. However, the form used was incorrect and the shares were never registered in Lord's name. The trust failed as the correct formalities for transfer of the shares had not been used.

2.4.2.3 Chattels

Chattels include most forms of personal property, such as jewellery, paintings and antiques. Passing title in a chattel can be achieved by simply handing the item over to the trustee or donee. In other words, physical delivery of the chattel, coupled with the relevant intention to make a gift or trust, is sufficient (*Re Cole* [1964] 1 Ch 175). In some cases symbolic transfer might be sufficient if the object is too large to hand over physically.

It is possible to execute a deed of gift to evidence the transfer in writing if this is desirable. One example might be if the chattel was very large and the transferor did not want to move it.

In *Jaffa v Taylor Gallery* (1990) *The Times*, 21 March, a trust of a painting was held to be valid even though the painting was never physically delivered to the trustees. Indeed works of art which are on loan to national galleries, museums, etc may change hands several times without being moved, especially where these are the property of family trusts.

Some chattels, such as cars, require the completion of formalities to effect transfer. This is not so much about determining ownership as determining liability should the vehicle be involved in an accident or infringe a road traffic rule.

2.4.2.4 Equitable interests

Examples of equitable interests are a beneficial interest under a trust, or a chose in action such as a debt. According to s 53(1)(c) of the Law of Property Act 1925, the transfer of an equitable interest must be effected by written assignment. For a debt, notice must also be given to the debtor.

A classic type of transfer of equitable interests is used in tax planning. This is where the remainder beneficiary under a fixed interest in possession trust does not want to inherit the reversion on the death of the person enjoying the interest in possession (known as the' life tenant'), as this would increase the value of their estate for IHT purposes. Instead, whilst the life tenant is alive, the remainder beneficiary may assign their equitable interest in the remainder to a beneficiary or beneficiaries of their choice or in trust for them. This interest is 'excluded property' for IHT purposes and is therefore not brought into charge to IHT even if the remainder beneficiary dies shortly after making the assignment.

Also, property which is co-owned may be owned as tenants in common such that each co-owner owns a fixed interest in the equity. This enables each co-owner to transfer that equitable interest under a gift or trust to others. It is common to find such an equitable interest being transferred into trust on the death of the first of the co-owners, such that the surviving co-owner (usually a spouse or civil partner) can continue to live in the property as provided by s 12 of the Trusts of Land and Appointment of Trustees Act 1996 but the value of the deceased's equitable interest does not form part of the co-owner's estate on their death.

2.5 Constitution

A trust or gift is fully constituted if, in the case of the appointment of a third party as trustee, the legal title to the property has been vested in (ie 'transferred to') the trustee or donee, or, where the settlor declares him- or herself trustee, declaration has been properly made. In the case of a trust, the trustee must become the legal owner of the asset and then will hold it on trust for the beneficiary as equitable owner. With a gift it is much more straightforward: the title must pass from donor to donee and there must be the intention to make a gift.

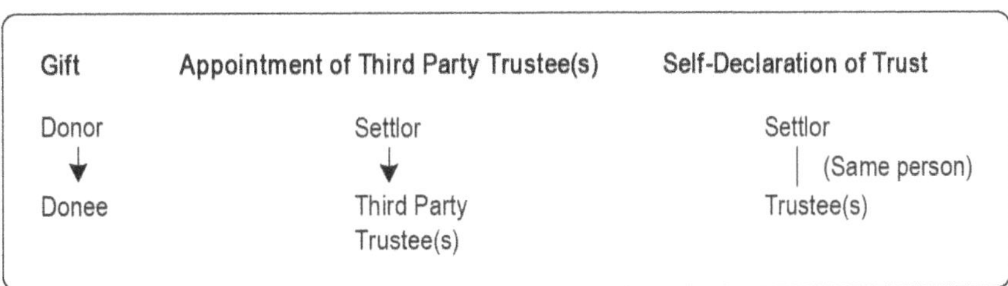

Figure 2.8 The three modes

If constitution has taken place then the trust or gift becomes valid and irrevocable, ie the settlor or donor cannot change his or her mind – *Paul v Paul* (1882) 20 Ch D 742, CA. In a trust context, the trustees become obliged to act in accordance with the terms of the trust and their other duties, and the beneficiaries acquire rights of enforcement.

If constitution has not happened then the general rule is that the trust or gift fails and the equitable maxim '**equity will not perfect an imperfect gift**' applies (*Milroy v Lord* above).

As set out earlier in this chapter, the courts strive to adhere to the intention of the settlor or donor when determining the type of provision in question. For example, if the settlor intended to create a trust with a third party trustee, as *in Milroy*, the court will not construe this as a self-declaration in order to rescue the provision:

> *If the settlement is intended to be effected by one of the modes to which I have referred, the court will not give effect to it by applying another of those modes.* If it is to be intended to take effect by transfer, the court will not hold the intended

> transfer to operate as a declaration of trust, for then every imperfect instrument would be made effectual by being converted into a perfect trust. (*Milroy v Lord*, per Turner LJ)

Similarly in *Jones v Lock* (above), a father placed a cheque in his baby's hand and said, 'I give this to baby, it is for himself.' The court took this as a clear intention to make a gift, but the father did not take any further steps to transfer the money into the child's name as required by the nature of the property – a cheque. When the father died, the court declared that the gift had been ineffective and refused to construe the provision as a self-declaration of trust in order to save it.

More recently in *Choithram International SA v Pagarani* [2001] 1 WLR 1, the court considered quite a unique set of facts overlapping the two ways in which a trust can be established during the settlor's lifetime (self-declaration and transfer to trustees together with declaration). The settlor established a philanthropic foundation of which he was one of seven trustees. He signed a trust deed declaring that he was giving various monies to the trust. The funds were already vested in the settlor but were never transferred into the joint names of all seven trustees. Following the death of the settlor, the court had to decide whether the trust had been properly constituted.

Lord Browne-Wilkinson stated that the fact that the settlor was one of the trustees was relevant, and his words effectively acted as a self-declaration which did not require any transfer of legal title. The court saw no distinction in principle between a case where the settlor declares himself the sole trustee and one where he declares himself as one of the trustees. In both scenarios the conscience of the settlor is affected and so the trust is enforceable. Interestingly, his Lordship went as far as to say that 'equity will not strive officiously to defeat a gift', possibly indicating a less stringent approach in the context of constitution and creating a new equitable maxim. It could also be argued that *Choithram* identifies a fourth mode, effectively an overlap between the self-declaration and appointment of third party trustees, as set out above.

2.5.1 Exceptions to the general rule on constitution

Although there are case examples of the court taking a strict approach with regard to constitution, there are in fact various exceptions to the maxim **'equity will not perfect an imperfect gift'** (or intervene to constitute an incompletely constituted trust), and it could be argued that the courts have been quite generous in assisting the constitution of trusts and gifts where there is evidence of a clear intention, or where the situation calls for the flexibility of equity to intervene. It should be noted that in the following sections some of the cases relate to gifts and some to trusts, but, in theory at least, there is no reason why all of the exceptions should not apply to either provision. It would also appear that little distinction is made today between trusts/gifts made during the settlor's/donor's lifetime and those made in a will, although clearly some exceptions are limited in application to where a donor/settlor dies.

2.5.1.1 The doctrine of every effort

In *Re Rose (Deceased)* [1952] Ch 499, a settlor executed a share transfer form and handed it to the trustee along with the share certificate during his lifetime. The transfer of title was not registered on the books of the company until two months later. The question for the court was to ascertain at what point the transfer of the shares was effective in equity. If the relevant date was when the form was executed then no estate duty would be payable, but if it was effective upon registration then the tax would be payable as the disposition would be seen as an attempt to evade tax prior to death. It was held that the transfer was valid in equity as soon as the settlor had done everything he could, ie filling out the form and handing it to the trustee with the certificate. *Re Rose* was applied in *Curtis v Pulbrook* [2011] EWHC 167 (Ch) but with a different outcome, as here the attempted divesting of beneficial interest in shares by the settlor was held to be incomplete – and illegal, and subject to be set aside under s 423(3) of the Insolvency Act 1986, which can be used even if the principle in *Milroy* is successfully applied if the purpose is to defeat the claims of creditors.

This rule applies when the transferor (settlor or donor) has done what is required of him or her, and the only reason the transfer has not been completed is that the transferee (the trustee or donee), or the company if the share transfer form has been sent directly to the company, has yet to carry out the final stages of the transaction. It lends itself well to transfers of land and shares, where there are a number of stages to the process.

Mascall v Mascall (1984) 50 P & CR 119 is a good example involving registered land. The father executed a transfer deed in favour of his son and handed this over along with the land certificate. However, before the son sent the documents off to the Land Registry, the father changed his mind. The court held that the gift was already complete in equity, even though the son had not acquired the legal title, and so the father's gift was irrevocable.

In cases such as these, the transfer is immediately valid in equity and, until the legal title passes, the transferor will hold the property on trust for the transferee.

More recently, in 2002, the every effort doctrine was applied in the controversial case of *Pennington v Waine (No 1)* [2002] 1 WLR 2075. The donor, Ada, was a director and shareholder of a company. She wished to transfer 400 shares to her nephew, Harold, who would also become a director in the company. She signed a stock transfer form, handed it to her assistant to deal with but he did not arrange for the transfer to be completed properly and merely filed the form. However, the assistant did write to Harold informing him of the share transfer and inviting him to become a director, which he duly agreed to do. Harold was assured that there was nothing further he needed to do.

Following Ada's death, it came to light that the 400 shares were still registered in her name, and the court had to decide whether the purported but incomplete transfer to Harold was valid or not. If it was not then the shares would form part of Ada's estate. If it was, then the shares were held on trust for Harold pending registration on the company's books.

Lady Justice Arden explored the rationale for the every effort doctrine and said that existing case law did not reveal any consistent single policy on the test. She took into account a number of relevant facts, including:

- Ada's intention was clear, she did not change her mind and thought she had nothing further to do. In particular she had made no provision for the 400 shares in her will. The court ought to give effect to, rather than frustrate, the clear and continuing intention of the donor. This is reminiscent of the *Pagarani* case and the, possibly new, maxim 'equity will not strive officiously to defeat a gift'.
- Harold's agreement to become a director – one requirement of which was that he held at least one share in the company – and the assurances given to him that everything was settled made it unconscionable not to proceed with the transfer of the shares. This could also be framed as preventing the donor (or more correctly here, Ada's executors) from acting in a way that is unconscionable.

It was held that the gift was valid and the transfer to Harold should go ahead. This appears to be a very generous approach, especially compared to cases such as *Re Fry (Deceased)* [1946] Ch 312. It could be argued that the decision goes too far and has changed the every effort test to 'equity will perfect a gift if it would be unconscionable not to do so'.

However, *Curtis v Pulbrook* (above) is a case where it was held not to be unconscionable to hold that the transfer failed, and it could be argued that *Pennington* is an exceptional case, confined to its own facts or at least to cases involving reliance and detriment by the transferee (to this end see the next section on proprietary estoppel). In any event, subsequent cases such as *Zeital* v *Kaye* [2010] EWCA Civ 159 confirm that the transferor must have done all he or she could do in order for the equitable title to pass to the transferee using the every effort test.

2.5.1.2 Proprietary estoppel

The requirements for estoppel in this context are generally agreed to be as follows:

- **assurance** given by X to Y that Y has an interest in the property (this could be express or implied);
- **reliance** by Y on the assurance; and
- Y suffers a **detriment** as a result, not only because of relying on the assurance but because the expectation is frustrated.

For example, in *Dillwyn v Llewelyn* (1862) 45 ER 1285, the father gave a memo to his son, purporting to transfer a piece of land. With the father's approval, the son built a house on the land and moved in. Unfortunately the father never took any steps to formally transfer the land to his son. When the father died, the court ordered that the land should be transferred to the son. The father's conduct had amounted to a promise or assurance (ie the memo and the permission to build), which the son had relied on and consequently had acted on to his detriment by spending money to build the house, believing that the land was his.

In *Re Basham (Deceased)* [1986] 1 WLR 1498, the court confirmed that the doctrine could be applied to an interest someone believed they would receive by will. The claimant helped to run her stepfather's business without any salary on the understanding that she would receive the business. She also looked after him when he was elderly, having been given repeated assurances that she would receive the house too. It was held that she should receive the business and the house.

The court clarified, in *Gillet v Holt* [2000] Ch 210, that promises to leave property in a will are revocable until the testator dies, but where assurances are given over many years and it is clear that the other party relied on that to their detriment then the doctrine of proprietary estoppel may apply on the basis that repudiation of the promise would be unconscionable (see *Thorner v Major* [2008] EWCA Civ 732). More recently in *Davies v Davies* [2014] EWCA Civ 568, the court scrutinised the dealings between the parties carefully in order to determine whether sufficient assurance and detriment had occurred in order to justify the estoppel. There must be a causal link between the assurance given and the detriment incurred. In other words, the court may ask whether the applicant would have taken the steps they did regardless of whether they believed they were getting an interest in the property or not.

It is important to note, however, that, with estoppel, the court has discretion to award a range of remedies based on the nature of the assurance and bearing in mind the guiding principle that the court will award the minimum equity in the circumstances. Also if third parties are likely to be affected by any remedy, this might influence the court's decision – as with any equitable remedy. So rather than ordering the transfer of the property to the claimant, it may award damages to compensate for the detriment suffered. An example of this can be seen in the case of *Dodsworth v Dodsworth* (1973) 228 EG 1115. Other remedies found in estoppel cases include the award of a licence for life, the conveyance of the fee simple and the grant of temporary occupation rights.

Interestingly, in a second appeal from *Davies v Davies* (above) in 2016 ([2016] EWCA Civ 463) the court reduced the claimant's award from £1.3 million to £500,000 on the basis that the trial judge had taken far too much of a broad brush approach, rather than analysing the facts with 'sufficient rigour' in order to quantify the appropriate compensation. Lewison LJ reiterated the importance of balancing the expectation of the claimant with the detriment suffered.

As in the *Davies* case, family farms are often the subject of disputes over ownership, partly due to the potential value of the land involved but also because it is quite common for one of the children from the family to stay on the farm and work there for little salary on the understanding (justified or otherwise) that they will one day inherit the whole lot. In 2018 there was a spate of farming cases in the High Court including *Thompson v Thompson* [2018] EWHC 1338 (Ch) and *Habberfield v Habberfield* [2018] EWHC 317 (Ch).

2.5.1.3 The rule in *Strong v Bird*

This rule is often referred to as 'automatic constitution' and arises where the following criteria are satisfied:

- the transferor makes an immediate imperfect inter vivos transfer (ie attempted gift or transfer to trustees);
- the transferor's intention continues until his death; and
- the transferee (donee or trustee) is appointed executor of the transferor's (settlor's or donor's) estate upon death.

In these circumstances, the transfer is said to be perfected as the legal title to the property reaches the hands of the intended recipient upon the death of the transferor.

The case of *Strong v Bird* (1874) LR 18 Eq 315 actually involved a loan. Bird borrowed money from his stepmother, who was at the time living in his house and paying rent. They agreed that he would repay her gradually by a reduction in her monthly rent. However, after six months, even though the debt was not repaid, the stepmother insisted on paying the full rent and continued to do so for four years until she died. Bird was appointed as executor of her will and thus acquired title to her estate. The court held that the debt was extinguished.

Re Stewart [1908] 2 Ch 251 confirmed that the rule applied to an ineffectual gift and Neville J stated:

> Where a testator has expressed the intention of making a gift of personal estate to one who upon his death becomes his executor, the intention continuing unchanged, the executor is entitled to hold the property for his own benefit.

In *Re Freeland* [1952] Ch 110, the importance of the intention of the donor was highlighted. Despite the fact that the claimant was appointed as executor, there was contradictory evidence regarding the intention of the deceased to make a transfer of a car to the claimant.

Trusts

As stated, there is no reason why the rule in *Strong v Bird* should not apply to trusts, as with the other exceptions, and the case of *Re Ralli's Will Trusts* [1964] Ch

288 provides some authority for this. The facts of the case are a little complicated and some question its authority. There were two trusts involved as follows:

- The father's will trust left his estate to his wife for life, remainder to his two daughters in equal shares.
- One of the daughters, Helen, made a marriage settlement promising to transfer into the trust any money she inherited under the trust set up in her father's will.

Helen died before her mother and so did not inherit her share. Helen's share therefore resulted back to her father's estate and fell into the hands of the trustee of her father's will. It just so happened that this trustee was also the same trustee of Helen's marriage settlement. As we know, trustees hold the legal interest of the subject matter, and so this trustee now had the correct property for Helen's trust, albeit via a route that had not initially been anticipated.

The court had to decide whether the property could be held by the trustee under the terms of Helen's marriage settlement, ie was this trust properly constituted now? Judge Buckley stated that it was irrelevant how the property reached the trustees, and accidental or automatic constitution was possible in this way. The trust was constituted and therefore valid.

Some consider this case to have pushed the limits of the rule in *Strong v Bird* too far, and it is clear that the requirement for the trustee to be appointed as the settlor's executor was not met. On the other hand, Helen did not change her mind about her intention to transfer the property into the marriage settlement and so the requirement for continuing intention would appear to be present.

It has been pointed out though that the first criterion from *Strong v Bird* is for an intention to make an immediate lifetime gift, and that in *Re Ralli* it was not possible for Helen to do this as she did not have the property at the time she made the marriage settlement. However, it could also be argued that she knew she was going to receive her share under her father's trust, as this was specifically provided for in his will – she was to receive a half share when her mother died. She had therefore what is sometimes referred to as a 'floating equity' insofar as her interest had not yet vested in possession but would do so in due course.

The same point was considered in an earlier case, *Re Brooks Settlement Trusts* [1939] Ch 993, which was not cited in *Re Ralli* (although it probably ought to have been). The facts were similar except that the son in that case did not have a guaranteed share in the remainder; rather it was for his mother to select which of the children would receive a share. So at the time he made his covenant, he only had a hope of receiving a share of his father's estate (this in known as future or 'after acquired' property). The son was selected by his mother, and when his share was paid out he changed his mind and did not want to place it into the trust. However, the trustees of his father's will and his trustees were the same – Lloyds

Bank. The court decided that he was entitled to change his mind and that Lloyds were not obliged to hold the property in the terms of the son's settlement.

Arguably the significant difference between *Ralli* and *Brooks* is the fact that in *Brooks,* the son changed his mind and so there was no continuing intention. Some commentators would also reiterate the point that he did not have an interest in the property at the time he promised to transfer it into the trust, and therefore he was not attempting to make an imperfect, immediate lifetime transfer so that criterion is not met either. In other words, they dispute whether the rule in *Strong v Bird* could be applied to future property.

Both cases were decided in the Chancery Division and so are of equal weight, and neither has been overruled, but *Ralli* has received rather less favourable mention than *Brooks* in subsequent cases.

Administrators

The final issue regarding the rule in *Strong v Bird* is whether it could be applied to situations where the transferor did not make a will but died intestate, and therefore administrators are appointed to distribute the estate in accordance with the intestacy rules. There are two contrasting authorities on this point, again both Chancery Division decisions.

In *Re James* [1935] Ch 449, it was held that a housekeeper acquired the house and furniture of the deceased after being appointed as his administrator. The deceased had made repeated promises that she should have these assets and the court was convinced of his continuing intention in this regard.

However, in *Re Gonin* [1979] Ch 16, the court doubted whether *James* was correct because an administrator is not chosen by the testator, as an executor is in a will. Therefore the link with the settlor's intention is weaker. On the facts of *Gonin,* the court did allow the administrator to acquire part, but not all, of the estate in accordance with evidence available regarding the intentions of the deceased. Walton J stated:

> The appointment of an administrator is not an act of the deceased but of the law. It is often a matter of pure chance ... why, then, should any special tenderness be shown to a person so selected by law? ... In spite of these doubts I shall follow *Re James.*

2.5.1.4 Donatio mortis causa (DMC)

Also known as deathbed gifts, such gifts commonly take place when someone is terminally ill and is unable to make the necessary arrangements to transfer an asset properly.

The criteria for a valid DMC were set out by Lord Russell in *Cain v Moon* [1896] 2 QB 283:

- an attempted lifetime gift made in contemplation of death;

- delivery of the subject matter to the donee; and
- a gift made in circumstances where it is clear that the property is to revert to the donor if he recovers, ie it is conditional on death.

Contemplation of death

Most of the cases involve a donor who is very poorly, often with a terminal illness. It is not enough to be simply reflecting on the fact that 'everyone dies one day' or that we are all mortal. It is possible that the definition of contemplation might extend to activities such as going into battle in a warzone or setting off on a hazardous journey, such as climbing Mount Everest. The important point is that the donor considers that death is a real possibility.

In *Wilkes v Allington* [1931] 2 Ch 104, the donor had been diagnosed with cancer but the cause of his death was pneumonia. The court held that the gift was a DMC and the fact that the donor died from another cause did not affect the validity. This suggests that the test for contemplation is subjective. However, in *King v Dubrey* [2015] EWCA Civ 581, it was clearly held that this requirement of contemplation of death is not satisfied in a situation where an elderly donor was approaching the end of his natural lifespan, but did not have a reason to anticipate death in the near future from a known cause.

Delivery of the subject matter

The donor must have parted with dominion of the gift, ie handed the property over to the donee or given a means of access to the property. This must be coupled with intention to part with dominion rather than, for example, handing it over for safekeeping (see **Chapter 1**).

In *Woodward v Woodward* [1995] 3 All ER 383, handing over the keys to a car and saying 'I won't be driving it anymore' was sufficient. It did not matter that the donor had the spare set as he was too ill to drive in any event.

There is no need to comply with the legal formalities for transfer of assets. The leading case of *Sen v Headley* [1991] Ch 425 involved a DMC of unregistered land. Shortly before he died, the donor gave the donee a key to a box containing the title deeds to his house and said 'the house is yours'. The box was in the donor's house, and the donee also had access to the house as she had a key. This was held to be sufficient delivery of title. This would not have been possible in the case of registered land insofar as there would be no deeds to hand over and, since the abolition of land certificates under the Land Registration Act 2002, no documents of title at all to hand over.

The approach in *Sen* that land can be transferred by DMC by handing over the deeds and key has been confirmed in the recent case of *Vallee v Birchwood* [2014] Ch 271. *Vallee* was, however, held to be wrongly decided in *King v Dubrey* (above) on other grounds.

Conditional upon death

Generally speaking, if the other two conditions are satisfied, this requirement will be implied. In *Re Lillingston (deceased)* [1952] 2 All ER 184, the donor, aged 78, was very ill and confined to bed. She said she was 'done for' and would not be leaving the room again. She handed over the keys to a trunk where she kept her jewellery to a member of her family and said 'I want you to have all my jewellery'. The court held that a DMC had taken place, and Wynn-Parry J stated:

> It must be taken as part of our law that a DMC remains to the end subject to the condition that, in the event of the donor's recovery, the property shall be given back, yet I agree ... that such a condition in the general case would be very easily presumed.

It follows that, if the donor recovers, there will be automatic revocation of the gift (*Staniland v Willott* (1852) 42 ER 416).

The cases on DMCs involved gifts but there is no reason why the principles should not apply to a trust.

2.5.2 Scrutinising the covenant

In the context of trusts, there are further issues that may be considered when dealing with an incompletely constituted trust.

2.5.2.1 The trust of a promise

This rule is derived from the case of *Fletcher v Fletcher* (1844) 67 ER 564, where the settlor covenanted with his trustees that, after his death, his executors would transfer £60,000 out of his estate and into the trust for the benefit of his surviving illegitimate sons until they reached the age of 21 (truly a case of its time). Following the death of the settlor, the executors refused to transfer the money and then one of the sons came forward to enforce the promise and claim his share. It was held that the trust had been constituted at the time of the covenant, but rather than the money being the subject matter of the trust (which incidentally the father did have at the time), it was the settlor's promise or the right to sue to enforce the promise that was the subject matter. In other words the subject matter of the trust was the chose in action.

Unfortunately this rule cannot be applied to every failed trust, and the court would look for clear wording in the deed/covenant setting out the settlor's intention for the trustees to hold the right to enforce the promise on behalf of the beneficiaries (*Re Schebsman (Deceased), ex p Official Receiver* [1944] Ch 83).

Few cases seemed to have followed *Fletcher*, and the court has cast doubt on whether the rule in *Fletcher* could be applied to money or assets that the settlor does not have at the time of the promise. In *Re Cook's Settlement Trusts* [1965] Ch 902, the money to be held in trust was to be raised from the sale of paintings at a later date. However, the more recent case of *Don King Productions Inc v Warren*

(No 1) [1998] 2 All ER 608, regarding boxers' promotional agreements, suggests that it might be possible.

What seems more likely to apply is that a proprietary estoppel is raised to assert that certain assets have been 'gifted' during a deceased's lifetime (on proprietary estoppel, see **Chapter 4**).

2.5.2.2 Equitable consideration

The maxim '**equity will not assist a volunteer**' means that if someone is a volunteer, ie they have not provided any consideration in return for receipt of their interest, then such a person is generally unable to enforce the promise. It is linked with the maxim '**equity will not perfect an imperfect gift**' (*Milroy v Lord* above).

A good, clear example of how this works is provided by the case of *Re Ellenborough* [1903] 1 Ch 697, where the settlor made a promise to transfer any property she might receive from a will in the future (future or 'after acquired' property). When she inherited the property, she decided not to transfer it into the trust. The court held that there was nothing the beneficiaries could do as they were volunteers, and until the settlor transfers the property into the trust, the beneficiaries have no rights in relation to it.

Consideration at common law would include, for example, money or money's worth, and this is also accepted as consideration in the law of equity. Where a beneficiary has paid for his or her interest then he or she may obtain specific performance and compel constitution of the trust (*Holroyd v Marshall* (1862) 11 ER 999). In these circumstances equity follows the law. The claim is based in contract although the remedy is one from equity.

However, equity also recognises marriage consideration. This occurs when a settlement is created in consideration of marriage (an example of a marriage settlement was seen in the case of *Re Ralli*, above). It was common during the 19th century and early part of the 20th century for wealthy families to use these trusts to provide security for the new couple and any future children, especially where the fortunes of the spouses were unequal or in order to provide for a daughter, as women lost any rights to property on marriage until 1882. In this context, the spouse of the settlor, the children of the couple and possibly also the grandchildren would be deemed in the eyes of equity to be encompassed by the consideration of marriage and thus be in a position to enforce the promise if the settlor failed to transfer property in. This would not apply to other family members (*Re Plumptre's Marriage Settlement* [1910] 1 Ch 609).

For example, in *Pullan v Koe* [1913] 1 Ch 9, a husband and wife covenanted to settle future property, but when the wife received relevant assets, she did not transfer them to the trustees. Several years later, the children of the marriage successfully secured constitution of the trust in court.

It should be noted that where the assets in question are future property, as was the case in *Pullan*, there can be no enforcement of the trust unless and until the settlor receives title to the property. Today such settlements would be rare as not only do married women retain their own property rights, it is also permissible for a couple to make pre-nuptial agreements in respect of their property.

2.5.2.3 Parties to the contract

Trustees

Usually the trust deed is signed by the settlor and the trustees. As party to the agreement, trustees have on occasion attempted to enforce the trust at common law. However, the courts have generally given this approach short shrift. For example in *Re Pryce* [1917] 1 Ch 234, Eve J reasoned that since the beneficiaries could not obtain relief directly (ie they were volunteers), there was no reason for the courts to give them relief indirectly via the trustees.

Even if the trustees were able to bring such an action, there are further problems regarding damages. Damages should reflect the amount of the loss suffered by the claimant. If it is acknowledged that the trustees are not entitled to the beneficial interest then the court may only award nominal damages, in which case bringing an action would be a waste of time.

If, on the other hand, it is argued that the common law does not recognise the separate beneficial interest, then the trustees may be entitled to substantial damages. There is some case authority for this, such as *Re Cavendish-Brown* [1916] WN 341. However, that is not the end of the story as the question to be answered is, 'Where does that leave the beneficiaries?' Payment of damages is not the same as constitution of the trust, the beneficiaries are volunteers and unable to enforce and the trustees cannot keep the money for themselves. Theoretically this is a can of worms and another good reason for the courts to disallow such claims by trustees.

Beneficiaries

It is relatively uncommon for a beneficiary to sign the trust deed, but if he or she were to do so then the beneficiary would have the right to sue for breach of covenant and obtain damages at common law under the law of contract. The case of *Cannon v Hartley* [1949] Ch 213 provides an illustration of this. A husband, wife and daughter signed a deed of separation whereby the father promised to settle property he hoped to inherit from his parents. When he received his inheritance, he refused to transfer it. The daughter was a volunteer and so had no rights in equity, but she was a party to the deed and so was able to sue for damages to the value of the interest she would have received under the settlement.

The Contracts (Rights of Third Parties) Act 1999

The final possibility for a beneficiary would be to rely on the 1999 Act. Section 1 provides as follows:

(1) Subject to the provisions of this Act, a person who is not a party to a contract (a 'third party') may in his own right enforce a term of the contract if—

  (a) the contract expressly provides that he may, or

  (b) subject to subsection (2), the term purports to confer a benefit on him.

(2) Subsection (1)(b) does not apply if on a proper construction of the contract it appears that the parties did not intend the term to be enforceable by the third party.

...

Thus, where a contract bestows a benefit on a third party, such as a beneficiary in a trust context, then it is possible for the third party to bring an action to enforce the terms of it. The likely remedy would be damages payable to the beneficiary.

There are some limitations to the scope of this provision. First, it only applies to contracts made after 11 May 2000, and, secondly, if it is clear from the agreement that the parties did not intend for it to be enforceable by the third party then the action will not be allowed. For example, if the deed excludes the operation of the Act, this would be a clear indication of the latter point.

In practice it would be highly unusual for a beneficiary to sign a trust deed. The fundamental relationship between settlor, trustees and beneficiaries is predicated on a trust existing and containing assets which have to be administered. It is not a contractual relationship. If the settlor does not supply any assets to the trustees and does not take steps to fund the trust further than the initial £10 with which it was constituted, then it is not likely that a trustee would succeed in obtaining any further assets to populate the trust unless the settlor intended this to happen by his or her actions.

Beneficiaries of a trust, as opposed to a promise, can only ask the court to review decisions of the trustees; or, in fixed trusts, ask the court to enforce their entitlement as against the trust at the relevant time of vesting. It is hard to see how they can seek to enhance their position as against the settlor by pursuing the trustees as there is no contractual position between them and the trustees, nor between them and the settlor.

2.6 Further reading

Juliet Brook, 'Case Comment: King v Dubrey – a donatio mortis causa too far?' (2014) 6 *Conveyancer and Property Lawyer* 525–34.

Hugh Cumber, 'Case Comment: Donationes mortis causa; a doctrine on its deathbed? King v Chiltern Dog Rescue [2015] EWCA Civ 581; [2015] WTLR 1225' (2016) 1 *Conveyancer and Property Lawyer* 56–61.

IM Hardcastle, 'Administrative unworkability – a reassessment of an abiding problem' (1990) *Conveyancer and Property Lawyer* 24–33.

Margaret Halliwell, 'Perfecting imperfect gifts and trusts: have we reached the end of the Chancellor's foot?' (2003) *Conveyancer and Property Lawyer* 192–202.

Jonathan Garton, 'The Role of the Trust Mechanism in the Rule in Re Rose' (2003) *Conveyancer and Property Lawyer* 364–79.

Joseph Jaconelli, 'Problems in the rule in Strong v Bird' (2006) *Conveyancer and Property Lawyer* 432–50.

Judith Morris, 'Questions: when is an invalid gift a valid gift? When is an incompletely constituted trust a completely constituted trust? Answer: after the decisions in Choithram and Pennington' (2003) 6 *Private Client Business* 293–403.

Patrick Parkinson, 'Reconceptualising the express trust' (2002) 61(3) *Cambridge Law Journal* 657–83.

Nicholas Roberts, 'Donationes mortis causa in a dematerialised world' (2013) 2 *Conveyancer and Property Lawyer* 113–28.

Chee Ho Tham, 'Careless share giving' (2006) *Conveyancer and Property Lawyer* 411–31.

Christopher Whitehouse & Lesley King, *A Modern Approach to Lifetime Tax Planning for Private Clients (with precedents)* (Jordans, 2014), Chapters 4 and 5.

David Hayton et al, *Underhill & Hayton Law of Trusts & Trustees*, 19th edn (LexisNexis, 2016).

Lynton Tucker et al, *Lewin on Trusts*, 20th edn (Sweet & Maxwell, 2018).

The law relating to the creation of express trusts and gifts requires compliance with the rules on capacity, certainty, formality and constitution.

The three certainties have developed and adapted over the last century and a half, from their beginnings in the context of interpretation of will provisions to the more contemporary scenario involving claims by creditors of insolvent companies. This evolution of the rules demonstrates again the flexibility of equity to adapt to changing trends in society. It is clear that although each case comes before the court with a unique set of facts, there are sets of principles that have emerged from the case law in relation to the three certainties. For each of the certainties, clarity in the words and expressions used is essential when drafting provisions. Intention can be demonstrated in a number of ways, including written and spoken words and from the acts of the people concerned. Subject matter and beneficial interest in it must be ascertained or ascertainable, and care must be taken to identify the property clearly. The objects of a trust or gift should be clearly defined, and the courts take different approaches depending on the type of provision in question.

Constitution of trusts and gifts essentially requires the transfer of the legal title to an asset from the settlor or donor to the trustee or donee. Although the maxims underpinning this rule might seem to be set in stone, the courts of equity have strived to deliver a just solution where it would not be fair to ignore the claims of a would-be beneficiary. Each of the exceptions to the general rule has a fairly well established set of criteria that must be shown by a claimant if they are to be successful. A wide variety of issues can be taken into account, including promises or attempts to transfer made during the donor's lifetime, continuing intention and detriment suffered by the purported recipient.

test your knowledge

1. What criteria would need to be satisfied to demonstrate capacity to make a gift or trust? Is there any difference between capacity to make an inter vivos provision and a clause in a will?
2. Why is it difficult for the courts to interpret will provisions? What type of words will not be sufficient to create a trust?
3. In a commercial context, what factors would a court take into account when deciding whether there is sufficient evidence to demonstrate intention to create a trust in favour of creditors?
4. Make a list of the issues that can arise in relation to certainty of subject matter. Can you see any overlap with certainty of intention?
5. What are the different modes of transfer, as set out in *Milroy v Lord*?
6. Transfer of which assets requires completion of forms followed by registration?
7. Can you name the two maxims that underpin the general rule on constitution? And what is meant by the word 'volunteer'?
8. Which of the exceptions to the rule on constitution requires satisfaction of three criteria? Can you remember the criteria for each?
9. What does equity recognise as good consideration?
10. Why is it significant when the beneficiary has signed the trust deed?

chapter 3

Purpose Trusts

After reading this chapter, you will be able to understand:

- the distinction between people trusts and purpose trusts
- how charitable trusts are defined and determined
- why equity has problems with non-charitable purpose trusts
- what these problems are
- in what circumstances these non-charitable purpose trusts will be upheld
- how these non-charitable purpose trusts are relevant to unincorporated associations
- why the revised law on charities might assist
- how Community Interest Companies might be the answer.

3.1 Introduction

The trusts encountered so far have been private express trusts in which there are clear human beneficiaries. It is also possible for trusts to be created for purposes. Some of these purposes are directly beneficial to humans, for example a trust to help those who are blind; others may be more indirectly beneficial to humans, for example a trust to preserve ancient monuments. The scope of the benefit of these trusts can be extensive or may be fairly limited. The approach of the law to these purpose trusts is twofold:

(1) to recognise them as charitable trusts;

(2) to hold that they are non-charitable trusts.

3.2 Distinguishing people trusts and purpose trusts

The law of trusts requires beneficiaries in whose interests the trust can be enforced, either on their own initiative, for example through the beneficiaries holding the trustees liable to account, or on whose behalf the court can intervene. This is true of private trusts and purpose trusts which have charitable status (charitable trusts), the only distinction being that in the case of the latter it is the Attorney General who intercedes on behalf of the those members of the public who should be benefitting from the charitable trust. This 'beneficiary principle' as it is referred to (*Morice v Bishop of Durham* [1805] 10 Ves 522) has been upheld by the courts in rejecting the validity of trusts which lack identifiable beneficiaries. The importance of the beneficiary principle is clear in the following quotation:

> [F]or if the purposes are not charitable then it is clear in my view that the trust must fail, both because it is designed to go on for ever – and therefore would fall foul of the rule against perpetuities – and also because no individual beneficiaries are ascertainable and so the purposes can only be enforced by the court, if within the ambit of charity. (Goulding J in *Re Bushnell* [1975] 1 WLR 1592)

In private trusts, the identity of the intended beneficiary is not usually a problem, provided that the description of the beneficiaries is certain (see the creation of express private trusts in **Chapter 2**). In the case of charitable trusts, it may be less clear who exactly will benefit, but the Attorney General and the Charity Commission have the power to enforce the trust. The following diagram illustrates the options.

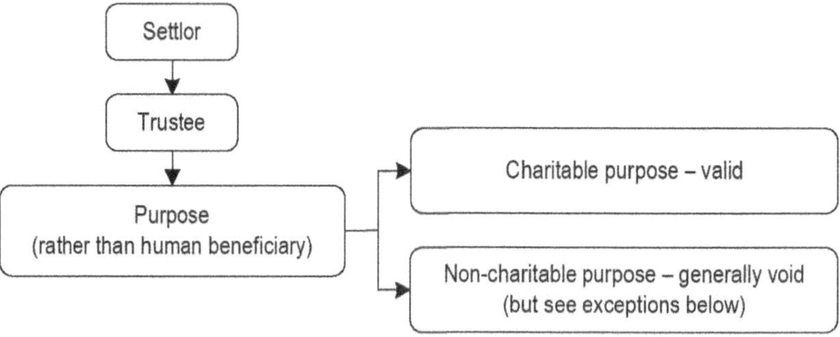

Figure 3.1 Purpose trusts

3.3 Charitable trusts

Charitable giving and acts of charity have their origins in religious practices and were encouraged not only for personal spiritual benefit, but also to provide for those in need when there was no state welfare and when the presence of the poor, needy, infirm and destitute might become a burden on parishes and a possible threat to public order. Elizabeth I was therefore quite astute when she approved of the Statute of Charitable Uses 1601, encouraging the wealthy to set up 'uses' (the old term for what are today 'trusts') and offering incentives for them to do so. The 1601 Act was repealed in 1960 but the objects set out in its Preamble (the introductory words of the Act) became enshrined in case law and are still referred to by academics and the judiciary alike.

Today the law that governs charitable trusts is found in the Charities Act 2011, which consolidates a number of statutes including, importantly, the Charities Act 2006. The 2006 Act was the culmination of decades of reviews and reports on the law of charity and purported to address the huge body of case law that had developed over the previous centuries. Whilst the 2006 Act did clarify the law to some extent, it relied considerably on previous laws, especially the decisions of the courts in interpreting what is a charity.

As in the past, the present law of charities offers advantages to donors as well as to recipients of charitable giving. Donors may offset charitable donations against income for taxation purposes, or reduce inheritance tax on capital donations from estates, while the recipient charity may claim back gift aid from taxpaying donors and is itself exempt from the payment of various taxes. The fiscal advantages of charities therefore act as a motive for charitable giving and a privilege for charities themselves.

There are three basic criteria that must be satisfied if a purpose trust is successfully to claim charitable status:

(1) The purpose must be charitable and therefore fall within one of the heads of charities listed in the legislation.
(2) The charity must confer a public benefit.
(3) The purpose must be wholly charitable.

3.3.1 Charities – general requirements

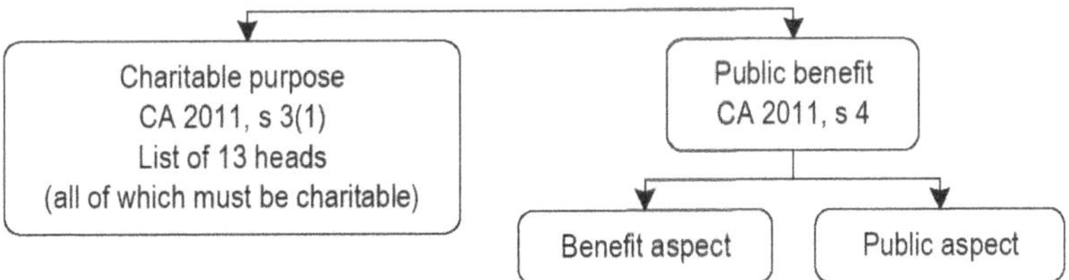

Figure 3.2 Charities

3.3.2 Charitable purposes

A purpose will be charitable if it comes within one of the headings listed in s 3(1) of the Charities Act 2011. There are 12 specific headings:

(a) the prevention or relief of poverty;
(b) the advancement of education;
(c) the advancement of religion;
(d) the advancement of health or the saving of lives;
(e) the advancement of citizenship or community development;
(f) the advancement of the arts, culture, heritage or science;
(g) the advancement of amateur sport;
(h) the advancement of human rights, conflict resolution or reconciliation or the promotion of religious or racial harmony or equality and diversity;
(i) the advancement of environmental protection or improvement;

(j) the relief of those in need because of youth, age, ill-health, disability, financial hardship or other disadvantage;

(k) the advancement of animal welfare;

(l) the promotion of the efficiency of the armed forces of the Crown or of the efficiency of the police, fire and rescue services or ambulance services;

and a final catch-all heading:

(m) any other purposes.

These are defined as:

(i) any purposes that are not listed in the Act but are recognised as charitable purposes under existing charity law; and

(ii) any purposes that may reasonably be regarded as analogous to, or within the spirit of, any of the purposes listed in the Act or those already recognised as charitable purposes under existing charity law.

So the list is not closed but neither is it entirely open-ended, as reference must be made to some form of authority – most usually existing case law – to justify the claim to charitable status. There is therefore room for limited expansion to reflect contemporary society and its concerns.

3.3.2.1 The development of the law on purposes

The reference to analogous purposes in s 3(1)(m) above relates to a process used by the courts throughout the development of the law on charity. This approach allowed the law to evolve over the years in light of changing social circumstances.

An example of this can be seen in *Scottish Burial Reform and Cremation Society Ltd v Glasgow City Corporation* [1968] AC 138, where the issue arose as to whether a trust for the provision of cremation facilities was charitable. The House of Lords held that it was charitable via a step-by-step approach as follows:

- the starting point was the Preamble, which included the 'repair of churches';
- by analogy, a trust to repair a churchyard was held to be charitable in *Re Vaughan* (1886) 33 Ch D 187;
- then followed a secular trust to maintain a cemetery, held to be charitable in *Re Eighmie* [1935] Ch 524; and
- finally a cremation facility was held to be a charitable purpose in the *Scottish Burial* case in 1968.

The listed heads of charitable purposes contain the well established 'old' heads of charity. These are so called because, prior to the 2006 Act, the most widely used statement of charitable purposes came from the case of *Commissioners for Special Purposes of Income Tax v Pemsel* [1891] AC 531, referred to as *Pemsel's* case. In this case Lord Macnaghten set out a fourfold classification of charitable purposes:

- relief of poverty;
- advancement of religion;
- advancement of education; and
- trusts for other purposes beneficial to the community within the spirit and intendment of the Preamble.

This classification provided a working model for subsequent charity law. Under the 2011 Charities Act, clearly the first three remain in s 3(1)(a), (b) and (c) and then the fourth head from *Pemsel* is expanded into the remaining categories. Some of these reflect case law where the courts had previously recognised a purpose as charitable even where it did not fit easily into the *Pemsel* classification. A good example which pre-dates *Pemsel* is the advancement of animal welfare found in s 3(1)(k) which, although not mentioned in the Preamble, has been recognised as charitable since the 19th century (*University of London v Yarrow* (1857) 1 De G & J 72).

Some of the other purposes are thoroughly modern, such as s 3(1)(h): the advancement of human rights, conflict resolution or reconciliation or the promotion of religious or racial harmony or equality and diversity; and s 3(1)(i): the advancement of environmental protection or improvement. The new law also brings within its ambit purposes that had previously struggled to achieve charitable status, in particular associations aimed at promoting amateur sports (now covered under s 3(1)(g)).

Many of the headings listed in the 2011 Act require further clarification and this is provided by existing case law and by the Charity Commission (<http://www.charity-commission.gov.uk>), which issues opinions on applications.

However, it is important to highlight some of the particular requirements or definitions that have been established in relation to the long-standing heads of charity.

3.3.2.2 The relief of poverty

Although this is possibly one of the fundamental and indisputable charitable purposes, dating back to the Preamble, there is in fact no definition of 'poverty' in the context of charity law. Poverty is not restricted to absolute destitution and has been held to mean 'going short', relative to the person's situation in life (see, for example, *Re Coulthurst* [1951] Ch 661).

You can contrast the following cases for an illustration of how the courts have approached the question of poverty: in *Re Gwynon* [1930] 1 Ch 255, a testamentary gift of short trousers for boys in Farnham was held not to be charitable because the benefits were not restricted to poor boys; but in *Re Niyazi's WT* [1978] 1 WLR 910, a trust to build 'working men's hostels' was upheld as charitable although it was agreed that not all 'working men' would be poor – the inclusion of the word 'hostel' implied that it was for the relief of poverty because the proposed accommodation was modest.

3.3.2.3 The advancement of education

The Preamble referred to 'schools of learning, free schools and scholars in universities'; however, the meaning of education in charity is not confined to situations involving the traditional teacher–pupil relationship. It is now well established, for example, that research falls within the definition of education provided that the subject matter is considered to be useful and beneficial to the public and that the fruits of the research are disseminated in some way (*Re Besterman* (1980) *The Times*, 21 January). Museums would also be caught within this head (*British Museum Trustees v White* (1826) 2 Sim & St 594). Similarly, conferences aimed at promoting greater international understanding have been held to be charitable under this heading (*Re Koeppler Will Trusts* [1986] Ch 423).

3.3.2.4 The advancement of religion

As you would imagine in the context of the law of England and Wales, this heading was for a long time confined to the advancement of monotheistic religions, in particular Christianity (*Thornton v Howe* (1862) 31 Beav 14 serves as an interesting example). More recently, the courts and the Charity Commission have taken a broader view of religion and recognised a wider range of faiths such as Hinduism and Buddhism.

Now s 3(2)(a) of the 2011 Act clearly states that religion includes:

(i) a religion which involves belief in more than one god; and
(ii) a religion which does not involve belief in a god.

In fact, case law has also established that the key requirements are belief in a supreme being (as opposed to a 'god' as such) and worship of that being (*Re South Place Ethical Society* [1980] 3 All ER 918). In the case of the *Church of Scientology's Application for Registration as a Charity* [2005] WTLR 1151, however, it was held – approving *R v Registrar General, ex p Segerdal* [1970] 2 QB 697 – that English charity law required an organisation that advanced a religion to worship, not merely acknowledge a supreme being. The Charity Commission guidance further states that the religion concerned must have a degree of cogency, cohesion, seriousness and importance and an identifiable positive, beneficial, moral or ethical framework. The decision by the Charity Commission to grant charitable status to the Druid Network in 2010 provides a good example of the application of these criteria. This can be contrasted with the application for registration by the Temple of the Jedi Order in 2016, which was rejected by the Charity Commission.

3.3.3 Public benefit

Section 4 of the Charities Act 2011 explains what is meant by public benefit:

(1) In this Act 'the public benefit requirement' means the requirement in section 2(1)(b) that a purpose falling within section 3(1) (the list of

charitable purposes) *must be for the public benefit* if it is to be a charitable purpose.

(2) In determining whether the public benefit requirement is satisfied in relation to any purpose falling within section 3(1), *it is not to be presumed that a purpose of a particular description is for the public benefit.* (emphasis added)

This requirement has two interrelated parts: the charity must confer a benefit, *and* that benefit must be available to the public or a section thereof. This might seem straightforward but there are difficulties.

3.3.3.1 Benefit

The Charity Commission has issued guidelines on what is meant here. It has stated:

> In the modern law, the concept of public benefit as integral to a charitable purpose is regarded as having two principal aspects, namely that, for a purpose to be charitable:
>
> - it must be beneficial, and
> - any detriment or harm that results from the purpose must not outweigh the benefit ('the benefit aspect').

Whether something is of benefit or not may be quite subjective – although the subjective view of the settlor or testator will not be taken into account (*Re Shaw's Will Trusts* [1952] Ch 163 and *Re Pinion (deceased)* [1965] Ch 85). For example, while it might be presumed that advancing religion is generally beneficial to the public at large even if the majority of the population does not practice a religion, on the grounds that religions encourage positive social behaviour, we know that religious extremism can be dangerous to the public. Also it is very difficult to assess the spiritual benefit of religion. Indeed the Charity Commission has suggested that, 'In general, the benefit to the public should be a tangible and objective one'. If a non-tangible benefit is being claimed then it may be more difficult to show public benefit, and expert evidence might be required. Similarly, awarding charitable status to a particular cultural or artistic endeavour or heritage status to a particular site or building may not be widely supported by many members of the public. Indeed the courts and the Charity Commission have quite a lot of discretion in this area, and while experts may be called in (as happened in *Re Pinion* (above)), this will not always be done, especially if a good argument is made out by those who support the case for charitable status (*Re Delius* [1957] Ch 299).

3.3.3.2 Public

The public does not mean everyone, for example a charity to assist those with autism will not be useful to those without autism, but does mean that the charity must be potentially accessible to all members of the public. So even fee-paying schools attract charitable status on the grounds that any member of the public who can afford to attend such a school could do so (this claim will be assisted by the availability of scholarships, fee reductions and community use of some of the facilities, such as sports fields – *R (Independent Schools Council) v Charity Commission* [2012] Ch 214). The matter of fee charging is a contentious issue, with the charitable status of private schools and private hospitals at one end of the scale attracting significant criticism. On the other hand it is generally accepted that, for example, museums, conservation areas or art galleries might charge an admission fee and offer discounts to certain people, such as pensioners and students or those on benefits.

In *Oppenheim v Tobacco Securities Trust Co Ltd* [1951] AC 297 a trust was set up to educate the children of employees and former employees of the company, and the House of Lords set out the criteria for determining whether a proposed class constituted a section of the public. Lord Simmonds stated that:

(a) the possible beneficiaries must not be numerically negligible; and

(b) the quality which distinguishes those beneficiaries from other members of the public must not depend upon their relationship to a particular individual or entity.

The first part of the test is flexible and there is no predetermined threshold at which the number would become negligible: each case is decided on its own facts. It is acceptable to benefit people in a particular geographical location, for example a charity raising funds for a special care baby unit in a small town.

This second part is referred to as the personal nexus test. It is clear that the personal nexus test applies to cases involving the advancement of education. However, the approach of the court prior to the 2006 Act differed in relation to the relief of poverty, and there are case examples where a trust was upheld even though the number benefiting was very small and a personal nexus was present. The point was clarified by Lord Cross in *Dingle v Turner* [1972] AC 601 at 624, who said:

> In truth the question whether or not the potential beneficiaries of a trust can fairly be said to constitute a section of the public is a question of degree and cannot be by itself decisive of the question whether the trust is a charity. Much must depend on the purpose of the trust

Following the Charities Act 2006 it was widely believed that the personal nexus test would be applied equally to all heads of charity, but in 2012 it was confirmed that the law on this point had not changed. In *AG v Charity Commission for England and Wales* [2012] UKUT 420 (TCC) (paras 22, 35, Annex 2.1–2.3), which was a case referred to the Upper Tribunal (Tax and Chancery) for clarification purposes rather than litigation, it was held that in the case of a trust for the relief of poverty (as opposed to the prevention of poverty), the charitable status would not automatically be defeated by the fact that the class of potential beneficiaries was defined by their relationship to an individual, their employment by a commercial company or their membership of an unincorporated association. In all of these situations the trust was capable of being a charitable trust.

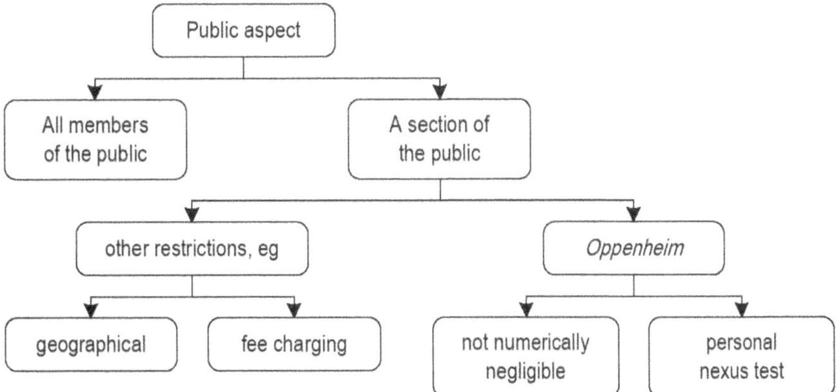

Figure 3.3 Public benefit

3.3.3.3 Application of the test

As seen above, s 4 of the 2011 Charities Act states that 'it is not to be presumed that a purpose of a particular description is for the public benefit'.

The apparent reason for this provision is that prior to the Act it appeared that certain heads of charity were presumed to be for the benefit of the public without the need to prove this (consider, for example, the Charity Commission decision regarding the Sacred Hands Spiritual Centre in July 2001 and the opinion of Lord Wright in *National Anti-Vivisection Society v IRC* [1948] AC 31). This included charities for the advancement of religion, those for the relief of poverty and those for the advancement of education. While some doubt has been cast on whether in fact the courts did make these presumptions, it is crystal clear that this presumption no longer applies. However, recourse to pre-2006 case law may be used to show that such charities have generally been held to be for public benefit or that they have not. For example, even before the forerunner to the present 2011 Act, the 2006 Charities Act, it was clear that religious worship could be for the advancement of religion, but if this was undertaken by cloistered religious orders then it could not be charitable (*Gilmour v Coates* [1949] AC 426). See similarly *Kings v Bultitude* [2010] EWHC 1795 (Ch), in which it was stated that the requisite element of public benefit might be evidenced by public worship and public administration of the sacraments.

Further clarification on this point has also been provided in the case of *AG v Charity Commission for England and Wales* [2012] UKUT 420 (TCC) (paras 30–39), where the question asked was whether it was still the case that charities and benevolent bodies whose objects were the relief of poverty for a restricted group of beneficiaries and which had, prior to 2006, been upheld as valid charities, would still be regarded as such, given the express requirement for public benefit. It was held that they would. The court held that

> The abolition of the presumption of public benefit in s.3(2) of the Act had had no impact on whether a trust for the relief of poverty was charitable or not. In deciding whether a trust was for the public benefit, a court would form its view on the evidence, not by way of assumption.

Therefore in the case of charities for the relief of poverty, not only is there a relaxation of the personal nexus test but also of the public benefit test.

3.3.4 Wholly charitable

Because of the advantages accruing to charities, the law requires that the entire purpose be charitable. This is often a question of semantics and interpreting the document of bequest. If a will, for example, includes a number of bequests, some of which are charitable and some are possibly not charitable, the test may be whether the testator has used the word 'and' rather than 'or'. For example, in the case of *Attorney General of the Cayman Islands v Wahr-Hansen* [2001] 1 AC 75, the Privy Council held that 'where general statements of benevolent or philanthropic objects were made, it would not be appropriate to limit the meaning of those statements to objects that were exclusively charitable'. If this cannot be done then the possibility of non-charitable purposes also benefitting renders the whole bequest void. See similarly *IRC v Baddeley (Trustees of the Newtown Trust)* [1955] AC 572, but compare *Re Sutton* (1885) 28 Ch D 464 in which the phrase 'charitable and deserving' was upheld.

The issue also arises that some of the activities of a charity may appear not to be charitable. For example, if the charity runs a shop selling various merchandise and second-hand goods, does this affect its charitable status? Charities are not permitted to make a profit but are permitted to raise money for their causes and to engage in what might appear to be commercial activities – such as advertising and paying employees. Below is an example of where an apparent charity overstepped the mark.

> **When is a charity not a charity**
>
> case example
>
> A charity may cease to be regarded as a charity if it is suspected of mismanaging funds to the extent that a substantial part of the donations and government grants that have been received are not used for the charitable purpose for which it was set up, or if its charitable status is being abused. An example in 2015 was the closure of the charity Kids Company which provided support for inner-city children and young people. This was quite a sizeable charity, set up in 1996, employing over 600 people, supporting thousands of children through outreach centres and school, with an annual funding from government and private donors of around £20m. Allegations of mismanagement and financial difficulties, as well as allegations of criminal abuse of children – which were subsequently not upheld – led to the charity closing down just a few weeks after the Government had given it a £3m grant, a large portion of which was used to pay wages including those of the founder. In 2015 the charity was the subject of a Charity Commission investigation and an inquiry by the House of Commons Public Administration and Constitutional Affairs Committee.

Purposes which seek to bring about a change in the law cannot be charitable – largely because the courts will not determine the charitable status of organisations that have a political aim, because to do so would imply that the court was taking a political standpoint and thereby offending the doctrine of the separation of powers. Whether the main purpose of an organisation claiming charitable status is political or not is not always clear. This includes purposes that potentially fall within some of the new heads of charity, such as: (k) the advancement of animal welfare; (e) the advancement of citizenship or community development; (h) the advancement of human rights; and (i) the advancement of environmental protection or improvement.

These are areas where the case law has been divided in the past. See for example *National Anti-Vivisection Society v IRC* [1948] AC 31 – advocating animal rights; *McGovern v AG* [1981] 3 All ER 493 – raising awareness of the plight of political prisoners; and *Baldry v Feintuck* [1972] 2 All ER 81 – Student Union campaign to restore free school milk, which were all held not to be charitable.

Separating political from non-political purposes can be a challenge. For example, if a testator left a large sum of money for research into the impact of fracking on a site of special natural interest, which happened also to be the breeding ground of a rare form of orchid and a certain endangered species of butterfly, with the additional request that this research be used to inform public opinion, would this be charitable or would it be too political to be charitable?

3.3.5 The doctrine of cy-près

Some charities are of ancient origin and it can happen that their purpose is no longer feasible or relevant in contemporary society. It may also be the case that some charities cease to exist – for example an orphanage is closed down – and so the question arises as to what is to happen to a donation to that charity or its existing assets.

Under this doctrine, if circumstances arise as outlined above, the assets or donation can be applied to a similar charity having 'as near as possible' the same purpose, provided there is no indication in the gift or the establishment of the trust that this was not intended. If there is such indication of intention then the doctrine cannot apply (see *Kings v Bultitude* [2010] EWHC 1795 (Ch), in which the court held that the testatrix intended the bequest to go to a particular church where she had worshipped and which disbanded shortly after her death). The application of the doctrine can be seen in the case of *Varsani v Jesani* [1999] Ch 219, in which the court held that the exercise of its jurisdiction (then under the 1993 Charities Act, s 13) was not limited to occasions when the objects had become impossible or impracticable. The test was whether the original purpose of the charitable gift had ceased to provide a suitable and effective method of using the property given, regard being had to the spirit of the gift.

A well drawn-up will might envisage this possibility and include a clause such as that found in *Phillips v Royal Society for the Protection of Birds* [2012] EWHC 618 (Ch):

> that if, before her death, any charitable body to which a gift was made had changed its name or amalgamated with another body or transferred all its assets, then her trustees would give effect to the gift as if it were a gift to the body in its changed name or which resulted from the amalgamation, or the body to which the assets had been transferred.

The Charities Act 2011, Pt 6 governs the duties of charitable trustees in respect of cy-près and s 61 reads as follows:

> **61 Duty of trustees in relation to application of property cy-près**
>
> It is hereby declared that a trust for charitable purposes places a trustee under a duty, where the case permits and requires the property or some part of it to be applied cy-près, to secure its effective use for charity by taking steps to enable it to be so applied.

The court and the Charity Commission may also make orders regarding cy-près or approve mergers of charities.

Practitioners should ensure that the correct name of a charity is specified in a will when a bequest is made and provide for the event that the charity is no longer in existence at the time of the testator's death. This can occur because of insolvency. *Berry & another v IBS-STL Ltd (in liquidation)* [2012] EWHC 666 (Ch) looks at the relationship between s 75F of the Charities Act 1993 (now s 311 of the Charities Act 2011) and the wording of the will. The will in that case included in clause 6 the following:

> 6.1 I give the residue of my estate … to my trustees upon trust to divide in equal shares between such of the following charities as shall to the satisfaction of my trustees be in existence at the date of my death namely …
>
> 6.2 If any charity or charitable organisation which I have named as a beneficiary in this Will is found never to have existed or to have ceased to exist or to have become amalgamated with another organisation or to have changed its name before my death then the gift contained in this Will for such charity or charitable organisation shall be transferred to whatever charitable institution or institutions and if more than one in whatever proportions as my trustees shall in their absolute discretion think fit

The International Bible Society UK (IBS) (one of the charities listed in the will) was at the date of the will an unincorporated registered charity, but it transferred all its assets to an incorporated registered charity before the date of the deceased's death, with IBS ceasing to exist on 5 February 2008. After the death of the testator, the incorporated charity became insolvent and was wound up. The case decided that clause 6.1 only enabled the trustees to transfer property to those organisations that were in existence at the date of the deceased's death, and so the trustees were not compelled to pay the funds to the merged company in liquidation.

However, contrast this with the decision in *Re ARMS (Multiple Sclerosis Research) Ltd* [1997] 2 All ER 679 where the incorporated charity went into liquidation but the court decided that, as the testator died after the date of the winding-up order but before the formal dissolution, the legacies had to be paid to the liquidator – something surely a testator would not have wanted.

It is therefore useful to give trustees discretion as to whether they have to apply the funds to a charity which is in liquidation but not yet formally wound up at the date of death, or whether they are able to ensure the funds are used for charitable purposes.

Cy-près, together with the power of the Attorney General to enforce charitable trusts and the power of the Charity Commission to intervene, means that property intended for charities rarely reverts to the donor unless the essential criteria for claiming charitable status are not met. Where there is a lack of clarity, it is possible that a cheaper method of ensuring a particular charity might benefit instead may be to use the Royal Sign Manual. This direction identifies the beneficiary whose identity was previously uncertain. It is used where there is a gift for charitable purposes but there are no particular objects selected. The Treasury Solicitor acts on behalf of the Attorney General in these cases and it is to the Treasury Solicitor that requests to use this method have to be directed.

Charities can also exist in perpetuity (that is they can go on for an indefinite period of time), and a number of contemporary charities date back many hundreds of years.

3.3.6 Setting up a charity

While many bequests in wills are likely to be for existing charities, a person may wish to set up a charity, either leaving it to executors to do so once they are dead, or wishing to do so during their lifetime, perhaps as a reaction to a personal experience – for example a rare disease in a child or a sudden need identified in the community, such as the repair of local heritage.

The Charity Commission website is a useful source for setting up a charity, but here are some tips:

- Clients should think carefully about the cost of setting up and administering a trust and note that it cannot be a charitable trust if it is to only benefit one person, such as their son or daughter.
- It is likely that a charity already exists with the objectives they wish to achieve with all the infrastructure already in place – it would be more cost effective to provide for a gift to that charity or give the executors discretion to choose charities like it, rather than setting up a new trust with similar objectives but which will need a considerable endowment to get it off the ground and be sustainable.
- In practice a charitable trust might usefully be set up during the testator's lifetime using Charity Commission precedent documents (or if funds to be committed are large, a bespoke document could be prepared) and to which a legacy may be left in the testator's will. Otherwise, there will be onerous responsibilities placed on the testators' executors and trustees to create the charity following the testator's death and get it registered, employ staff and fundraise to make the charity sustainable.

3.3.7 The regulation of charities

Because charities attract a number of fiscal benefits, and also because they may attract and control considerable sums of money and other assets, it is important that charitable status is not abused or misused. Those taking on the role of trustees of charities should be aware of the requirements of the Charity Commission, and they are recommended to look at the Charity Commission website for up to date information about their duties and liabilities – <www.gov.uk/guidance/charity-trustee-whats-involved>.

3.4 Non-charitable purpose trusts

As indicated at the outset of this chapter, considerable importance is attached to the **beneficiary principle**, and the law is reluctant to uphold trusts that seem to have, as their aim, a purpose which does not benefit any identifiable human beneficiary.

However, as with so much in the law, there are exceptions where the courts are prepared to uphold a trust that is neither for the benefit of identifiable humans nor for public benefit. These are referred to as non-charitable purpose trusts because it is evident from the wording of the trust that the settlor or author of the trust intended to promote or support a particular purpose or non-human beneficiary. Quite why these trusts are upheld is unclear. It would seem that equity is prepared to do so in order to give effect to the intention or wishes of the settlor – usually expressing a desire in a will, so these are essentially testamentary trusts – and because to do so does no harm and means that the legacy left by the settlor is used rather than left in a vacuum.

3.4.1 The anomalous exceptions

These non-charitable purpose trusts have been referred to as trusts of imperfect obligation, and as concession to human weakness or sentiment (*Re Shaw's Will Trust* [1957] 1 WLR 729).

Because they are exceptions to the general principle, their scope is limited to the following:

(a) trusts for the purpose of erecting and/or maintaining graves and monuments;
(b) trusts for the saying of masses for the deceased, ie private masses; and
(c) trusts for specified animals.

These will be considered shortly, but first there are some overarching general principles which need to be taken into account if a non-charitable purpose trust is to be upheld.

3.4.1.1 General principles

(1) The person expressing the desire to set up a non-charitable purpose trust must be competent to do so, in other words must have the legal capacity to do so (as outlined in **Chapter 1**).
(2) The purpose for which the non-charitable purpose trust is being set up must not be so capricious, offensive or extravagant as to be contrary to public policy.
(3) There must be sufficient certainty as to what is intended, ie certainty of the purpose (this is the same as the certainty of who is to benefit – see **Chapter 2** – and so requires clear, unambiguous wording).
(4) The duration of the non-charitable purpose trust must not offend the rule against perpetuities.

The rule against perpetuities

The rule against perpetuities applies to private express trusts and non-charitable purpose trusts. Although it is possible in trusts to provide for successive interests into the future, this cannot continue indefinitely. The benefit must vest or be enjoyed within a period of time, which is known as the perpetuity period. This period used to be specified in the trust instrument but is now governed by statute. The relevant statute is the Perpetuities and Accumulations Act 2009 in which the perpetuity period is stipulated as being 125 years for new wills executed and new trusts created on or after 6 April 2010. This Act specifically states that it does *not* extend to private purpose trusts (s 18). We must look elsewhere therefore for the law governing this point in the case of non-charitable purpose trusts. Here the law is as follows:

- either the length of time is determined by any human lives that are mentioned in the bequest plus a period of 21 years – so, for example, a bequest 'to my daughter Sally to look after my cat James' would mean Sally's lifetime plus a further 21 years; or
- it is determined by reference to 'royal lives' – for example 'for as long as the king shall reign'; or
- if no human lives are mentioned, then the period is simply 21 years from the date the bequest becomes effective.

The 2009 Act did not taken the opportunity to consolidate the law in this area so the outcome is that we have three separate sets of rules applying to perpetuities and accumulations:

- pre-1964 rules for instruments created on or before 15 July 1964;
- the Perpetuities and Accumulations Act 1964 (1964 Act) for instruments created between 16 July 1964 and 5 April 2010;
- the 2009 Act for instruments created on or after 6 April 2010.

In drafting testamentary trusts, the 'Trust Period' is often defined as 'the period ending on the earlier of the last day of the period of 80 years from the date of this Deed which period, and no other, shall be the applicable perpetuity period'.

Now this can be simplified to: 'the last day of the period of 125 years from the date of this Deed', as there is no need to talk about the possibility of any other period since there is no other choice. In fact, all interests to which the perpetuity rule applies now have a 125-year perpetuity period whether or not one is specified. It is not possible to specify a shorter or longer period. If the trust needs to be for a shorter period than the perpetuity period then the 'Trust Period' needs to be defined differently and its length stated.

The operation of the perpetuity rule becomes evident in the exceptions which follow.

3.4.1.2 Trusts for tombs, graves and monuments

The courts have upheld bequests for the purpose of erecting tombs and monuments to the deceased provided these comply with the general principles set out above.

So in *Re Endacott* [1960] Ch 232, where a gift of £20,000 was made to the parish council to provide a useful memorial to the deceased, this was held to be void for uncertainty, the bequest being worded so broadly as to make the actual intention of the deceased unclear.

Where the sum or purpose is regarded as being *capricious, excessive or contrary to public policy* (or plain good sense), the court may reject such a purpose, as in the two Scottish cases of *McCaig v University of Glasgow* (1904) 41 SLR 700 and *McCaig v Kirk-Session* (1915) SC 426, where the erection of statues of not less than £1,000 each, at various locations throughout Scotland, in memory of relatives of the deceased was held to be excessive and of benefit to nobody.

The erection of any such monument must itself be within the perpetuity period, and the likelihood of this happening will be determined by the wording. So, for example, in *Musset v Bingle* (1876) WN 170, the building of a monument to the wife's first husband was upheld even though no perpetuity period was set but the court accepted that it would take place within 21 years. However, there is a distinction between the initial erection of a monument or tomb and its maintenance. The former may be allowed, but the latter may fail if it offends the rule against perpetuities by not stipulating how long the maintenance is to continue (this was a problem in *Musset v Bingle* (above)). This may be avoided if the bequest includes the correct perpetuity period. An example of an inventive clause to ensure as long a period as possible is '21 years from the death of the last surviving descendant of King George VI living at the date of the Deed', which was used in the case of *Re Horley Town Football Club* [2006] EWHC 2386 (Ch).

There are also cases where the court has allowed a trust to run for 21 years where the wording makes some attempt to restrict the time frame. These are known as saving clauses, for example 'as long as the law allows', as used in *Pirbright v Salway* [1986] WN 86 Ch D and *Re Hooper* [1932] 1 Ch 38.

Alternatively, in the case of a tomb or monument, the deceased may have entered into a 99-year maintenance contract with the local authorities responsible for tombs and monuments under the Parish Councils and Burial Authorities (Miscellaneous Provisions) Act 1970, or the executors may do so. Today most burial sites have to be booked well in advance through contractual arrangements. This does not mean that monuments and memorials cannot be located outside graveyards. Indeed they can and they are found scattered all over the country, from park benches to magnificent monuments erected by public subscription.

3.4.1.3 Trusts for the maintenance of animals

An example of a bequest that raises this issue is as follows:

> I give to my trustees my eight horses and ponies (excluding cart horses) at *Littledown*, and also my hounds in the kennels there. And I charge my said freehold estates hereinbefore demised and devised, in priority to all other

> charges created by this my will, with the payment to my trustees for the term of fifty years commencing from my death, if any of the said horses and hounds shall so long live, of an annual sum of £750. And I declare that my trustees shall apply the said annual sum payable to them under this clause in the maintenance of the said horses and hounds for the time being living, and in maintaining the stables, kennels, and buildings now inhabited by the said animals in such condition of repair as my trustees may deem fit; but this condition shall not imply any obligation on my trustees to leave the said stables, kennels and buildings in a state of repair at the determination of the said term; but I declare that my trustees shall not be bound to render any account of the application or expenditure of the said sum of £750, and any part thereof remaining unapplied shall be dealt with by them at their sole discretion. And my will is that, so long as there shall remain any of my said horses, ponies and hounds living, they shall be kept in the stables, kennels and buildings which they now occupy. (*Re Dean* (1889) 41 Ch D 552 at 553)

The courts have upheld gifts for specific animals (*Mitford v Reynolds* (1848) 16 Sim 10; *Pettingall v Pettingall* (1842) 11 LJ Ch 176) and it is now not uncommon to come across provisions in wills providing for the care of a family pet. However, the issue of perpetuity must still be addressed, and unless a human life is specified in the bequest then a perpetuity period of 21 years will apply (*Re Kelly* [1932] IR 255). It has been suggested that this is more than sufficient (*Re Haines* 1952 WL 12533, (1952) *The Times*, 7 November) but of course there are animals that may outlive this period, in which case the statutory perpetuity period would be insufficient to ensure their maintenance. In some cases the courts seem to have been quite lenient here, as in *Re Dean* (above), in which the gift of £750 for the maintenance of the testator's horses and hounds for a period of 50 years was upheld, although the case has been criticised on this point.

It is also important that the animals can be sufficiently identified and that the bequest is not worded so loosely as to make it possible that future animals will be included, for example 'Bess and her puppies' would have the potential to take the period of maintenance beyond the perpetuity period.

3.4.1.4 Trusts for the saying of masses

In certain religions it is important that intercessionary prayers are said by the living for the dead. Money set aside for this purpose by the deceased has long been upheld as a valid purpose provided it does not exceed the perpetuity period (*Bourne v Keane* [1919] AC 815). Where such bequests do exceed the perpetuity period, they may be saved by being interpreted as charitable purposes provided the mass is open to the public (*Re Hetherington* [1990] Ch 1).

In practice

Non-charitable purpose trusts remain relevant in practice, not least because pet ownership has risen over the last few decades. Over 5.2 million households in the

UK are now estimated to own dogs; 6.1 million households own cats and 4.1 million households own fish (Pet Food Manufacturers Association, 2004). This has resulted in many clients asking solicitors about how to provide for the care of their dog or cat following their death. Perhaps the easiest way of dealing with this is to provide a legacy of a sum of money and the pet to a particular person and express the hope and wish that they will look after it. This results in the person being entitled to take the legacy even if the pet has died. It does not of course guarantee that the legatee (the person to whom the legacy is left) actually looks after the said pet.

It is rare for the maintenance of tombs or graves to be requested today.

Checklist

To decide if a non-charitable purpose trust might be upheld, apply the following test:

- Does it fall under one of the 'exception' headings?
- Does the testator/settlor have the requisite capacity?
- Will the interest 'vest' or be applied within the perpetuity period?
- Are there any concerns about public policy/capriciousness?
- Is the description of the purpose clear?

3.4.2 Unincorporated associations

The other area in which non-charitable purpose trusts arise is in the context of unincorporated associations. These are the type of associations commonly found in clubs and societies where people come together for a mutual purpose but are not registered as a company, co-operative society or a charity. They may be governed by a committee and certain rules of association and may hold a portfolio of property, for example a clubhouse, sports equipment, a bank account for subscriptions and so on. Often, long-term members leave bequests to such organisations, either to promote their functions or as a token of gratitude for the enjoyment they have derived from membership. The problem is that these societies and associations are often unincorporated, that is they have no legal personality which is independent of their members – unlike a company. As explained by Lawton LJ in *Conservative and Unionist Central Office v Burrell* [1982] 1 WLR 522 at 525:

> An unincorporated association is not a legal person and is not an entity capable of holding property. It has been defined as 'two or more persons bound together for one or more common purposes, not being business purposes, by mutual undertakings each having mutual duties and obligations, in an organisation which has rules which identify in whom control of it and its funds rests and on what terms and which can be joined or left at will'.

The question therefore arises as to how the law can uphold any such bequest. There are a number of options (initially outlined in *Neville Estates v Madden* [1962] Ch 823), but none of them provides a perfect solution.

3.4.2.1 The gift is regarded as being one to the members as trustees for themselves and future members or for the purposes of the club/society

This might succeed on the beneficiary principle provided there is sufficient certainty as to who the beneficiaries are. As explained by Viscount Simmonds:

> ... if a gift is made to individuals, whether under their own names or in the name of their society, and the conclusion is reached that they are not intended to take beneficially, then they take as trustees. If so, it must be ascertained who are the beneficiaries. If at the death of the testator the class of beneficiaries is fixed and ascertained or ascertainable within the limit of the rule against perpetuities, all is well. If it is not so fixed and not so ascertainable the trust must fail. (*Leahy v AG for New South Wales* [1959] AC 457 at 484)

The problem here is that as soon as future members are expressly or impliedly included, there is a danger of uncertainty as to the identity of the beneficiaries. There is also the danger of offending the rule against perpetuities by seeking to provide too far into the future, so the gift will be void. Even if this was not the case, the donor's intentions may be frustrated because there is the possibility that the trustees will use the gift for a different purpose.

3.4.2.2 The gift is to the members at a specific date

This may be what is intended by the donor/settlor, but the problem is that where the members are regarded as being joint owners in law (referred to as joint tenants), they have the right to claim their respective share through 'severance' and go off with it. If the settlor/donor has left money, for example for the purposes of the club or society, this is probably not what he or she intended. The effect of this is explained by Cross J:

> If this is the effect of the gift it will not be open to objection on the score of perpetuity or uncertainty unless there is something in its terms or circumstances or in the rules of the association which precludes the members at any time from dividing the subject of the gift between them on the footing that they are solely entitled to it in equity. (*Neville Estates v Madden* [1962] Ch 832)

3.4.2.3 The gift is to the members, not as joint tenants but subject to their respective contractual rights and liabilities towards each other as members

In such a case, individual members cannot sever their share, and if a member leaves or dies, that share accrues to the other members.

This line of reasoning has been followed in *Re Recher's Will Trust* [1972] Ch 526 – applied more recently in *Re St Andrew's (Cheam) Lawn Tennis Club Trust* [2012] EWHC 1040 (Ch) – and *Re Lipinski's Will Trusts* [1976] 3 WLR 522. There remains the possibility that the members may decide not to carry out the intended purpose of the testator and use the bequest for something else. Nothing can be done about this, as one of the criteria that has to be satisfied for the gift to succeed under this heading is that the members have the power to control the property under their membership rules or to gain control of the property by changing the rules. This includes the possibility that the members may decide to wind up the association. If the rules of the club do not confer this power on the members then the non-charitable purpose trust may fail (*Re Grant's Will Trusts; Harris v Anderson* [1980] 1 WLR 360).

Of course some of these problems would be avoided if the constitution of a club or society were drafted in such a way as to facilitate bequests or donations.

3.4.2.4 *Re Denley*

One way around the problems indicated above is for the testator or settlor to bequeath the gift to the members in language which indicates that there are identifiable beneficiaries. This would then satisfy the beneficiary principle. Such an approach was adopted by the court in the case of *Re Denley's Trust Deed* [1969] 1 Ch 373. In this case land was bequeathed to trustees for the use and enjoyment of employees of a company. Although at first sight this appeared to be for a purpose, the court held that it clearly benefitted identifiable individuals and so satisfied the beneficiary principle. The specific wording of the bequest also complied with the rule on perpetuities, and the identity of potential beneficiaries was easily ascertainable as there was reference to a particular company.

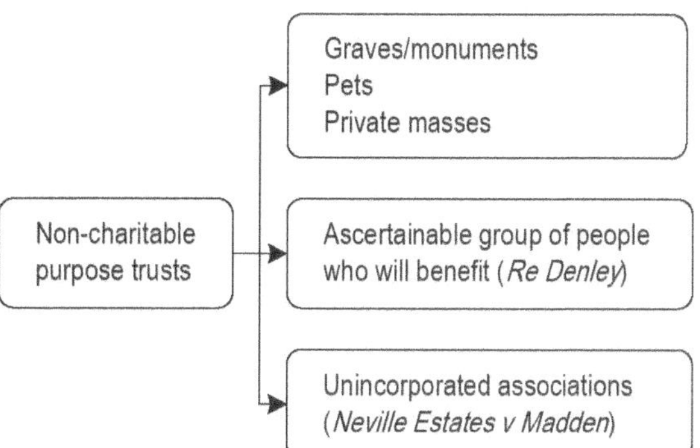

Figure 3.4 Non-charitable purpose trusts

3.4.3 Can the problems of non-charitable purposes trusts be avoided?

Clearly non-charitable purpose trusts can be problematic. There are two ways in which some of these problems might be avoided:

(1) the expansion of the scope of charities under the Charities Act 2011; and

(2) the development of Community Interest Companies.

3.4.3.1 A wider range of charities under the Charities Act 2011

Formerly, some organisations which applied for charitable status failed in their application and thus fell into the no-man's land of non-charitable purpose trusts which did not fit within the limited range of exceptions.

As has been indicated above, the current law on charities found in the 2011 Charities Act has expanded the heads of charity from the four broad heads of charity previously used.

Arguably, trusts for the purpose of maintaining tombs and monuments, or for the maintenance of animals, could be framed as charities, for example the charitable head of advancement of religion includes the maintenance of religious buildings (s 3(1)(c)) so that tombs and monuments within the fabric of a religious building, or its grounds, might attract charitable status (as was the case in *Re Hooper* [1932] 1 Ch 38 and *Re Vaughan* (1886) 33 Ch D 187).

Similarly, the saying of a mass, provided it is in public or in a venue to which the public has access, even if the mass is private, has been held to be charitable under the advancement of religion, so that where a testator leaves money for such a purpose, this may succeed as being charitable.

Trusts for the maintenance of animals in general may also be charitable – although those for a specific animal will not, unless perhaps that animal is of such national significance that this is deemed to be of public benefit.

However, the second main requirement for claiming charitable status may still prove an obstacle. This is that the purpose must be for public benefit. So, for example, while the facts of *Re Denley* (above) might fit within the charitable head of advancement of sport, the personal nexus between the company and the employees eligible to use the sports facilities might offend the public benefit test – discussed above and illustrated by such cases as *Oppenheim v Tobacco Securities Trust Co Ltd* [1951] AC 297 – unless it could be shown that non-employees were also permitted to use the facilities as well, as in the case of fee-paying private schools.

3.4.3.2 Community Interest Companies

Emerging from various working groups in 2001, Community Interest Companies (CICs) came on to the scene in 2005. Defined as 'a business with primarily social objectives, whose surpluses are primarily reinvested in the business or community', CICs are registered initially either as companies limited by guarantee or as companies limited by shares. They then have to apply to the CIC Regulator to be registered as a CIC and change their name to reflect this. Approval depends on sufficient evidence of community interest and benefit. Directors are accountable both to Companies House and the CIC Regulator. In this context, CICs are useful because they include 'asset lock' mechanisms to protect land and other assets and profits generated by these companies for the benefit of the community, and also to prevent demutualisation through the distribution of profits and assets to directors and/or members. CICs are regulated by the Companies (Audit, Investigations and Community Enterprise) Act 2004, the Community Interest Company Regulations 2005 and the Companies Act 2006.

Although the CIC is not charitable in status and so lacks the advantages accruing to a charity, it could prove useful for non-charitable purposes and in particular for associations which have as their purpose non-commercial and primarily social objectives. Although the initial take up of this type of organisation appeared to be slow, the register of CICs suggests that there are nearly 11,000 CICs currently registered, mainly by smaller local enterprises and large spin-outs from the public sector, especially the NHS and local authorities (see <www.thirdsector.co.uk>).

3.4.4 What happens if a bequest to a non-charitable purpose fails?

Where a bequest fails there are two possibilities:

(1) The bequest results, or goes back, to the estate and becomes part of the residue or remainder of the property of the deceased, which will either be distributed according to the terms of the will or, if there is no provision for the distribution of the undistributed part of the property but there is a valid will, this property will pass to next of kin under the rules of partial intestacy.

(2) If the testator has actually envisaged the possibility of a bequest failing or of there being property (usually funds) which is not used up, he or she may have made a provision called 'a gift over in default of appointment' – see **Chapter 2**. Under this, an alternative recipient is indicated. Where this is the case then that part of the bequest may be upheld. This is more likely to happen where the bequest is interpreted in such a way that the non-charitable purpose is read as being the motive for the gift. As such there is nothing other than a moral obligation on the donee. For example, 'To John in the hope that he will look after the trees planted in memory of my grandfather' can be construed as a gift with a motive. On the other hand, if the gift over is conditional on carrying out the non-charitable purpose and this is held to be void then the gift over may also fail – for example, a bequest of '£100,000 for the erection of a stunning monument in memory of me, with any remaining monies to go to my niece Alice' is likely to fail and Alice will get nothing.

Avoiding the problem

There are also ways in which a bequest might be drafted to avoid the problems associated with non-charitable purposes trusts:

(1) Draft the bequest as a power rather than a trust (see **Chapter 1**). This avoids the beneficiary principle problem because the exercise of a power is discretionary, although it may not escape problems of certainty or the rule against perpetuities.

(2) Draft the bequest as a mandate of agency to use the funds in a particular way. This may succeed provided there is sufficient certainty and the scope of the bequest falls within the power of the agent – for example the secretary of a club. However, the purpose may fail if the agent changes, because the mandate of agency is likely to be personal, unless the office itself is deemed to be a corporation sole (such as the Archbishop of Canterbury, or the Crown, which are posts which continue even when the human incumbent changes).

3.5 Further reading

James Brown, 'What are we to do with testamentary trusts of imperfect obligation?' (2007) *Conveyancer and Property Lawyer* 148–60.

Jonathan Garton, 'Justifying the cy-près doctrine' (2007) *Trust Law International* 134–49.

James Goodwin, 'Purpose Trusts: Doctrine and Policy' (2013) 24(1) *Kings Law Journal* 102–10.

Joseph Jaconelli, 'Adjudicating on charitable status – a reconsideration of the elements' (2013) *Conveyancer and Property Lawyer* 96–112.

Mark Pawlowski and James Brown, 'Testamentary trusts and the rule against capricious purposes: an underlying rationale?' (2012) *Trust Law International* 109–19.

Harriet Sergeant, 'How to judge a charity: the five questions no one asked Kids Company', *The Spectator*, 2 January 2016 (www.spectator.co.uk).

Lesley King, 'Probate: Drafting and construing charitable legacies', *LSG*, 10 May 2012, Legal Update, 17–18.

Lynton Tucker et al, *Lewin on Trusts*, 20th edn (Sweet & Maxwell, 2018).

The Charities Act 2011 provides a consolidation of the law on charities, but its interpretation relies heavily on prior case law and the guidelines of the Charity Commission. The basic requirements for achieving charitable status remain the same as previously: to fall under a recognised head of charity and to be of public benefit. Charities avoid problems with the beneficiary principle and the rule against perpetuities and attract considerable fiscal advantages for donors and charities alike, hence the need for regulation and monitoring, including the filing of accounts and the oversight of the Charity Commission.

Provided a bequest falls within one of the exceptions and does not offend the rule against perpetuities and is not deemed to be contrary to public policy, a non-charitable purpose trust may be upheld. Where a purpose does not fall within one of the exceptions, there may be ways around the problem of satisfying the beneficiary principle if identifiable beneficiaries can be found, or if the gift is deemed to be for the members within the ambit of their interpersonal contract under the rules of association of the club or society. In the latter case, there remains the possibility that the intended purpose of the donor may be frustrated, insofar as the members decide to use the bequest for other purposes.

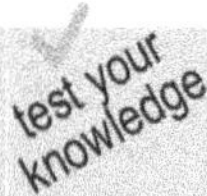

1 A testator proposes to make the following testamentary provisions:

- £50,000 to look after my dog 'Prince' for as long as he shall live, and any money remaining at his death shall be donated to the Dogs Trust.
- The land known as 'The Acres' to be used as a sports field for the benefit of the employees of Wooden Box Ltd.
- £250,000 for the purposes of securing a permanent football ground for the Brotton Ladies Football Club.
- The remainder to be used to erect some useful memorial in my name and thereafter to maintain that memorial.

(a) Which of these potentially falls under the exceptions pertaining to non-charitable purpose trusts?

(b) What perpetuity issues are raised?

(c) Are there any issues as to certainty, capriciousness or public policy concerns?

(d) Would the guidelines established in *Re Denley* help with any of these?

(e) What rephrasing might be wise if the testator's intentions are to be carried out?

2 In *Gilmour v Coates* (1949), Lord Simmonds said:

> ... it is, I think, conspicuously true of the law of charity that it has been built up not logically but empirically. It would not, therefore, be surprising to find that, while in every category of legal charity some element of public benefit must be present, the court had not adopted the same measure in regard to different categories ...

To what extent does the law after the 2006 and 2011 Charities Acts change this position, if at all?

(a) What changes does the new law make as regards public benefit?

(b) What contradictions are evident in the pre-2006 case law as regards public benefit?

(c) Are these permitted to continue under the most recent (2011) Act?

(d) What consequences might an illogical law have?

(e) Are then any ways of addressing this illogicality?

chapter 4

Non-express Trusts

After reading this chapter, you will be able to understand:

- the operation of resulting trusts
- the traditional use of the constructive trust
- the use of the constructive trust with reference to the shared home
- the relationship between constructive trusts and proprietary estoppel.

4.1 Introduction

The trusts encountered so far have been express trusts created during the settlor's lifetime or in a will (testamentary trusts). These, as we have seen in **Chapter 2**, may require compliance with certain formalities, and we need to be certain that the settlor had the intention to set up a trust.

In the case of the trusts considered in this chapter, first, in the case of land, they do not need to comply with formalities. Indeed, s 53(2) of the Law of Property Act 1925, which concerns 'Instruments required to be in writing', states that 'this section does not affect the creation or operation of resulting, implied or constructive trusts'. So non-compliance with these formalities, while it may be fatal for the validity of an express private trust, will not defeat these types of trusts. It would appear that s 53(2) is not limited to where the subject matter is land. In *Singh v Anand* [2007] EWHC 3346 (Ch) it was held that a constructive trust arose in the case of shares 'in respect of which writing was not necessary under s 53(2) of the Act' (see also *Neville v Wilson* [1997] Ch 144 concerning a constructive trust of shares).

Applying this absence of formality in the case of the resulting trust, Lord Denning MR in *Re Vandervell's Trusts (No 2)* [1974] Ch 269 at 320 explained as follows:

> A resulting trust for the settlor is born and dies without any writing at all. It comes into existence whenever there is a gap in the beneficial ownership. It ceases to exist whenever that gap is filled by someone becoming beneficially entitled. As soon as the gap is filled by the creation or declaration of a valid trust, the resulting trust comes to an end.

Secondly, the role of intention is slightly different. As will be seen, the courts will often infer an intention from the conduct of the parties or the surrounding circumstances, rather than from evidence of an express intention. Sometimes the way in which the court does this may seem rather contrived, especially when there appears to be a completely contrary intention, or no clear indication as to intention. As will be seen in some cases, one party appears to understand one thing and the other intends something rather different, especially in those cases that may be bracketed together as 'excuse cases' – see below.

Finally, when considering these types of trust, we need to remember the origins of equity (**Chapter 1**), as in a number of cases the court is essentially asking if it would be unconscionable for the legal owner of property to deny a beneficial claim by the other party.

The focus of this chapter will be on resulting and constructive trusts.

4.2 Resulting trusts

4.2.1 Resulting trusts based on presumptions of intention

In *Westdeutsche Landesbank Girozentrale v Islington LBC* [1996] AC 669, there is useful guidance from Lord Browne-Wilkinson, who stated:

> Under existing law a resulting trust arises in two sets of circumstances:
>
> 1. Where A makes a voluntary payment to B or pays (wholly or in part) for the purchase of property which is vested either in B alone or in the joint names of A and B, there is a presumption that A did not intend to make a gift to B: the money or property is held on trust for A (if he is the sole provider of the money) or in the case of a joint purchase by A and B in shares proportionate to their contributions. It is important to stress that this is only a *presumption*, which presumption is easily rebutted either by the counter-presumption of advancement or by direct evidence of A's intention to make an outright transfer ...
> 2. Where A transfers property to B *on express trusts*, but the trusts declared do not exhaust the whole beneficial interest ... (at 708)

In both of the above situations the resulting trust gives effect to the presumed intention of the settlor.

In some cases it has been argued that the beneficial interest has never left the settlor, for example because the purpose of the intended transfer is frustrated – such as where A transfers property to B on express trust, but the purpose is not carried out – as in *Barclays Bank Ltd v Quistclose Investments Ltd* [1970] AC 567. The '*Quistclose* trust' has been applied in a variety of situations and was described in the case of *Re Yarce (Adequate Maintenance: Benefits: Spain)* [2012] UKUT 425 (IAC) (an immigrant's benefits calculation case where monies had been provided by a third party) as arising where a person is paid money in order for it to be used for a particular purpose, on the condition that it would be returned if not used for that purpose on resulting trust for the payer. The payee had no beneficial interest in it. The courts have held that there must be sufficient evidence that a *Quistclose* trust was intended – see *Copper v Official Receiver* [2002] EWHC 1970 (Ch), where a father failed in his attempt to claim a *Quistclose* trust of a sum of money paid under an individual voluntary arrangement to his son in an ultimately unsuccessful effort to stave off the son's bankruptcy. Somewhat confusingly, the language of 'purpose trusts' appears to be used in some of the cases (see for example *Eleftheriou v Costi* [2013] EWHC 2168 (Ch)) – these should not be confused with non-charitable purpose trusts discussed in **Chapter** 3.

Alternatively, a resulting trust of this nature may arise because, despite appearing to part with the beneficial interest, this can in fact be traced back to the settlor (see *Re Vandervell's Trusts (No 2)* above). Lord Browne-Wilkinson in *Westdeutsche Landesbank* (above) has suggested that these types of resulting trust are traditionally regarded as examples of trusts giving effect to the common intention of the parties. A resulting trust is not imposed by law against the intentions of the settlor/trustee (as is a constructive trust) but gives effect to his or her presumed intention.

As we will see, Lord Browne-Wilkinson's view of the constructive trust is perhaps limited to the more traditional use of that trust, and not to the modern application of it to the cohabited home where we find intention playing a key role.

This application of the resulting trust should be distinguished from the situation where the intention of the settlor was to set up a trust but this fails. We have already encountered this form of resulting trust elsewhere in this book. For example, in the case of a trust failing to be completely constituted or proving to be administratively unworkable (see **Chapter** 2), the property intended for the trust 'results' back to the settlor's estate. A resulting trust may also be held to apply where a perfectly valid purpose is intended but fails to be achieved. This is one way of looking at the *Quistclose* case above, but it is not very satisfactory insofar as if there is an express trust then there is the intention that the beneficial interest be transferred (see *Freeman v Customs and Excise Commissioners* [2005] EWHC 582 (Ch), in which the express trust and *Quistclose* trust were argued in the alternative). A better approach is to hold that the beneficial interest will not transfer unless and until the intended purpose is achieved. See for example *Wise v Jiminez* [2014] WTLR 163, in which money was advanced for investment in a golf course which never materialised. The court held that the money was held on resulting trusts to be repaid by way of equitable compensation.

4.2.2 The automatic resulting trust

The above situations need to be distinguished from an automatic resulting trust, which arises in the following situations.

4.2.2.1 Initial failure

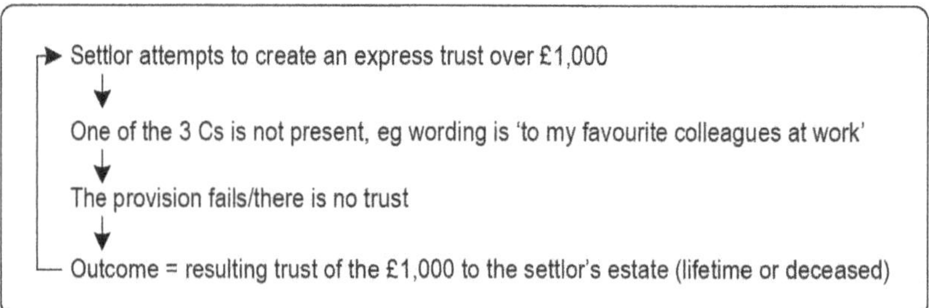

Settlor attempts to create an express trust over £1,000
One of the 3 Cs is not present, eg wording is 'to my favourite colleagues at work'
The provision fails/there is no trust
Outcome = resulting trust of the £1,000 to the settlor's estate (lifetime or deceased)

Figure 4.1 Initial failure

In this situation there is an initial failure to set up a trust, possibly due to failure of one of the three certainties (see **Chapter 2**), or non-compliance with the necessary formalities which cannot be saved by one of the exceptions (such as the rule in *Strong v Bird*, a donatio mortis causa or proprietary estoppel – see **Chapter 2**). In such cases the property goes back to the settlor.

Megarry J in *Re Vandervell's Trusts (No 2)* [1973] 3 WLR 744, Ch, expresses it thus:

> For the second category, there is no mention of any expression of intention in any instrument, or of any presumption of a resulting trust: the resulting trust takes effect by operation of law, and so appears to be automatic. What a man fails effectually to dispose of remains automatically vested in him, and no question of any mere presumption can arise.

In practice, a settlor who fails to include sufficient beneficiaries, including a default or longstop beneficiary, ie one that takes in the event that his or her preferred beneficiaries fail to attain a vested interest, will find that a resulting trust in his or her favour arises once the beneficiaries are exhausted. If the trust fund reverts back to the settlor then the funds will once again be in his or her estate for inheritance tax (IHT) purposes. The creation of the trust may have been to start the seven-year clock running for the settlor to get the value of the fund out of his or her estate on death for IHT purposes, so a reversion of the fund to the settlor will potentially frustrate this aim. (Currently if a person disposes of assets seven years prior to death, provided the donor/settlor survives for seven or more years from the date of disposal, those assets will be deemed not to fall into the estate of the donor/settlor for IHT purposes (that is the tax payable on the value of deceased's estate). Recipients of such disposals may be liable for capital gains tax however.)

A professionally drafted trust created during lifetime will not only ensure there is a longstop beneficiary, such as a charity, to ensure that the trust vests in someone or something other than the settlor, but will also exclude a settlor and his or her spouse or civil partner from benefit. This is so that HMRC cannot argue that from the outset the trust is at risk of reverting back to the settlor. If there is the prospect of a reversion to the settlor, however remote, HMRC will tax the income and capital gains of the trust as if they were received by the settlor rather than the trustees.

4.2.2.2 Subsequent failure of the trust

In some cases the settlor may have anticipated the trust fund not being exhausted, or drafted a power which allowed for non-exhaustion of the trust fund, and by way of a gift over in default of appointment made provision for what is to happen to this residual trust property.

The settlor may not always anticipate all the possible eventualities, however, so for example in the case of *Moor v Raisbeck* (1841) 59 ER 1078, the settlor made provisions for the children of a deceased relative living at her death. Unfortunately there were no children living at the death of the settlor, only grandchildren, whose claim failed and the money resulted back into the residue of the deceased settlor's estate. In other cases it may simply be that the trust fund was surplus to requirements, and there is then the question of what is to happen to this surplus. Different facts may give rise to different solutions. For example, in *Re Trusts of the Abbott Fund* [1900] 2 Ch 326, there were funds left over when the two intended beneficiaries had died. The funds had been raised by way of private subscription, and the court held that the surplus should go back to those who had contributed to the fund in this way. This may not always be very practical where money has been contributed anonymously by a number of people, as in *Re Gillingham Bus Disaster Fund* [1958] Ch 300, where Harman J explained:

> The general principle must be that where money is held upon trust and the trusts declared do not exhaust the fund it will revert to the donor or settlor under … a resulting trust. The reasoning behind this is that the settlor or donor did not part with his money absolutely out and out but only sub modo to the intent that his wishes as declared by the declaration of trust should be carried into effect. When, therefore, this has been done any surplus still belongs to him. This doctrine does not … rest on any evidence of the state of mind of the settlor, for in the vast majority of cases no doubt he does not expect to see his money back: he has created a trust which so far as he can see will absorb the whole of it. The resulting trust arises where that expectation is for some unforeseen reason cheated of fruition, and is an inference of law based on after-knowledge of the event.

If, however, the court finds that the settlor has expressly, or by necessary implication, abandoned any beneficial interest in the trust property, the undisposed-of equitable interest vests in the Crown as bona vacantia (see *Re West Sussex Constabulary's Widows, Children and Benevolent (1930) Fund Trusts* [1971] Ch 1). Note that in the case of charities (see **Chapter 3**), any surplus may go cy-près to another charity. It may well be the case that the court holds that the donors to a fund neither intended the surplus to result back to them or to go bona vacantia to the Crown. In the case of *Davies v Hardwick* [1999] CLY 5954, residents of a village had raised money to pay for specialist medical treatment in America for a child from the village. In the end, the treatment was available free of charge on the National Health Service in the UK so the funding was not necessary for the life-saving operation. In considering what was to happen to the funds raised, the court found that the motive for the donations were the health needs of the child and that he should be beneficially entitled to the whole fund (see also *Re Osoba (deceased)* [1979] 1 WLR 247).

In practice, in testamentary trusts, surplus funds will either fall into residue or, if it is the residuary estate which has failed, it will be dealt with under the intestacy rules. This is not without difficulty since the intestacy rules applicable at the testator's death apply, and this may result in a need to trace missing beneficiaries and re-open estates which were otherwise thought to have been wound up.

In the case of funds raised by public subscription, it will nearly always be necessary for the trustees to seek court directions as to what to do with any surplus funds if the reasons for the collection did not exhaust the fund. A trustee will want the comfort of following the court order so as to protect him- or herself from allegations of misuse of the funds.

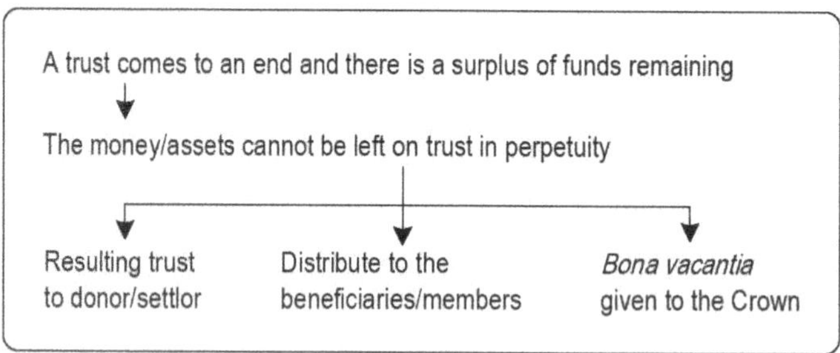
A trust comes to an end and there is a surplus of funds remaining
The money/assets cannot be left on trust in perpetuity
Resulting trust to donor/settlor
Distribute to the beneficiaries/members
Bona vacantia given to the Crown

Figure 4.2 Subsequent failure

4.2.3 Presumed purchase money resulting trusts

As seen in *Westdeutche Landesbank* (above), this form of resulting trust will in particular arise where property is purchased in the name of another. The presumption here is one of intention: would A put up the purchase price for a property to be registered in B's name (making B the legal owner) if A did not intend to retain a beneficial interest in the property? The presumption is rebuttable, for example by evidence that the transfer was intended as a gift. The law distinguishes between gifts of land and gifts of other property as far as this presumption is concerned.

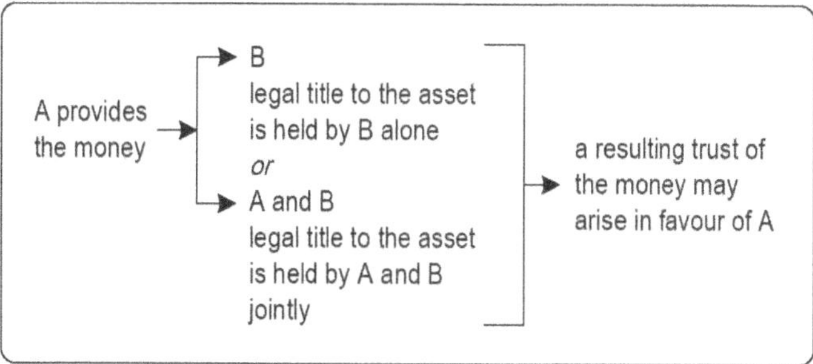

Figure 4.3 Presumed purchase money resulting trusts

4.2.3.1 Gifts of land

Section 60(3) of the Law of Property Act 1925 states that: 'In a voluntary conveyance a resulting trust for the grantor shall not be implied merely by reason that the property is not expressed to be conveyed for the use or benefit of the grantee.' This indicates that there is no presumption of a resulting trust in the case of land, although this does not mean that a resulting trust will not be found.

In the case of *Hodgson v Marks* [1971] 1 QB 234, CA, Mrs Hodgson transferred her property to her lodger, Mr Evans, on the understanding that she would retain a beneficial interest in the property. Mr Evans sold the property to Mr Marks without Mrs Hodgson's knowledge. The Court held that the property was held on resulting trust in favour of Mrs Hodgson. For a more recent example, see *Bank of Scotland Plc v Forrester* [2014] EWHC 2036 (Ch), in which a son had bought property belonging to his bankrupt father from the trustee in bankruptcy on the understanding with his father that he, the father, would be allowed to remain in occupation and would pay his son monies to meet the mortgage debt that his son had incurred in acquiring the property. The son tried to claim that the property was his to do what he like with (including remortgaging it), but the court found that the father had never intended to part with beneficial ownership. Note that in this case the son was not a volunteer but had paid the trustee in bankruptcy, not the father, and there were also elements of proprietary estoppel raised.

4.2.3.2 Gifts of other property

Where property other than land is transferred gratuitously to a third party, there is a rebuttable presumption of a resulting trust. In the case of *Sillett v Meek* [2007] EWHC 1169 (Ch), an elderly lady had transferred an investment account into the joint names of herself and her companion. When the elderly lady died, there was a dispute between members of her family and the surviving companion as to whether the deceased had intended the defendant companion to take the account beneficially after her death or whether the account formed part of the deceased's estate. The court held that the investment account (worth some £300,000) was held on resulting trust for the estate as there was insufficient evidence that a gift was intended (compare, however, the decision in *Fowkes v Pascoe* (1874–75) LR 10 Ch App 343, where there was insufficient evidence to rebut the gift).

Elderly people are vulnerable to financial abuse, which is on the rise. It is harsh to presume that all lifetime 'gifts' by an older person to a donee are the result of undue influence, but KPMG's Fraud Barometer in 2015 showed that the value of scams by younger relatives on older people rose by 384% compared to the same period in the previous year. Younger members of the family stole £1.7 million from elderly relatives.

Lifetime gifts between people in a relationship of trust are presumed to be the result of undue influence and are liable to be set aside as above unless there is sufficient evidence to rebut this presumption. The obvious relationship of trust is between parent and child. Sometimes, donees do not know of this rule and fail to arrange independent advice for the donor, which is a key way of demonstrating that the presumption should not apply.

In an increasingly technology driven banking world, elderly people struggle to access their own funds and quite commonly put their accounts into the joint names of themselves and their family, carers or friends to facilitate use of the bank account. However, not all such arrangements are benign, and the courts are increasingly having to consider whether a gift was intended or merely a nomineeship, with the funds at all times remaining in the ownership of the elderly person.

There are IHT ramifications too. For example in *Taylor v Commissioners for HMRC SpC 00704,* 18 June 2008, the deceased, Mrs Kathleen Boland, had no children but a sister Mary who was married to Peter Taylor. Mary and Peter had two children and various grandchildren. Mrs Boland lived with Philip King, and at various times during his life Philip indicated to Mrs Boland's nieces that he intended the money in two building society accounts to be ultimately used for the benefit of their children.

On Mr King's death the whole of his estate passed to the deceased by his will. At some point following Mr King's death, the deceased transferred the two accounts into the joint names of herself and Mr Peter Taylor. The operating instructions for both accounts were that any one signature was required and that on a death the whole account would pass to the survivor.

On the deceased's death, no mention was made in the IHT return of these accounts and therefore no IHT was paid in respect of them. In subsequent correspondence between the family and HMRC, it was suggested that the monies on the accounts belonged to Mr Peter Taylor and that there was a secret trust.

HMRC argued that the full value of both of the accounts belonged in the deceased's estate for IHT purposes on her death and should have been fully returned on the basis of s 5(1) of the Inheritance Tax Act 1984, which provides that a person's estate is the aggregate of all the property to which he or she is beneficially entitled other than excluded property.

In the alternative, HMRC said that the transfer of the accounts into joint names by the deceased was a gift of property subject to a reservation because Mr Peter Taylor was not exclusively entitled to use the account, given that the deceased had a general power to dispose of the whole of the accounts, and therefore that the gift was caught by s 102(1), (2) and (3) of the Finance Act 1986.

The Special Commissioner concluded that there was no evidence of any formal trust established in favour of Mr Taylor, given that Mr King left all his estate to the deceased absolutely. She also decided there was no secret trust either in favour of Mr Taylor since whilst Mr King was alive he was anxious to benefit the Taylors' children and grandchildren. The deceased did not apply all the money for those objects nor did Mr Taylor benefit from the accounts personally. On the deceased's death, the money on the accounts was used partly to pay her debts and funeral expenses and partly to benefit the grandchildren of Mr and Mrs Taylor.

As to whether the deceased had a general power over the accounts which enabled her to dispose of the whole of the accounts, the Special Commissioner agreed with HMRC's arguments that on the basis of *Sillars v IR Commissioners* [2004] STC 180, s 5(2) of the IHTA 1984 will apply to such a joint account because either holder was able to dispose of the balance in the accounts as he or she saw fit.

The result was that the Special Commissioner found that the deceased was to be treated as beneficially entitled to the whole of the money in the accounts at the date of her death for IHT purposes. She also confirmed that by the same token the transfer of the assets into joint names by the deceased in an account where the deceased was equally entitled to dispose of the balance as and when she saw fit prevented Mr Taylor from enjoying the joint accounts to the entire exclusion of the deceased, and therefore a reservation of benefit applied.

See also *Northall v Northall* [2010] EWHC 1448 (Ch) and *Matthews v HMRCC* [2012] UKFTT 658.

Therefore, practitioners have to be careful when dealing with joint accounts in the IHT 400 where the money was originally in the sole ownership of one party.

4.2.3.3 Presumption of advancement

It used to be the case that there was a presumption that where a husband put up the purchase price for property held in the name of his wife, or a parent put up the purchase price of property held in the name of a child, a gift was intended (*Dyer v Dyer* (1788) 2 Cox Eq Cases 29). This was known as 'the presumption of advancement' and was a rebuttable presumption. In the case of *Lavelle v Lavelle and others* [2004] EWCA Civ 223, Lord Phillips said:

> Where there is no close relationship between A and B, there will be a presumption that A does not intend to part with the beneficial interest in the

> property and B will take the legal title under a resultant trust for A. Where, however, there is a close relationship between A and B, such as father and child, a presumption of advancement will apply. The implication will be that A intended to give the beneficial interest in the property to B and the transaction will take effect accordingly.

Lord Phillips went on to conclude that: (a) the presumption of advancement can be rebutted by evidence; (b) evidence does not have to be contemporaneous with the arrangement in question, it can relate to matters after the transaction has taken place; and (c) the court's task overall is 'to search for the subjective intention of the transferor'.

Today the presumption of advancement may appear to be something of an anachronism and possibly contrary to principles of equality (see Equality Act 2010, s 199, which, however, is not yet in force), especially as historically this presumption did not apply in the situation where the wife/mother provided the purchase money (*Bennet v Bennet* (1879) 10 Ch D 474). Nevertheless we still find the presumption being raised, for example in *Chapman v Jaume* [2012] EWCA Civ 476, where it was held that the presumption did not apply between cohabitants (following *Stack v Dowden* [2007] 2 AC 432, discussed below); *Close Invoice Finance Ltd v Abaowa* [2010] EWHC 1920 (QB), where it was held that the presumption could apply between mother and daughter; and *Sansom v Gardner* [2009] EWHC 3369 (QB), where it was held in circumstances where the role of in loco parentis has not been assumed that the presumption could not apply (conversely it could where a person stood in loco parentis).

4.2.4 Illegality

The retention of a beneficial interest under a resulting trust or constructive trust (*O'Kelly v Davies* [2014] EWCA Civ 1606 held there should be no distinction) cannot be relied on to promote an illegal cause. This reflects the maxim that '**he who comes to equity must come with clean hands**' (see **Chapter 1**). For example, where a property is bought in the name of one party in order to allow the other to continue to claim social security benefits (*O'Kelly* above); or to defeat the claims of creditors (*Tinker v Tinker (No 1)* [1970] P 136); or to frustrate the claim of a former spouse (*Lowson v Coombes* [1999] Ch 373, CA); or for any other reason where it would be contrary to public policy, an applicant cannot then claim that they had a beneficial interest in the property.

The timing of the fraud or dishonest conduct is relevant. In the case of *Slater v Simm* [2007] EWHC 951 (Ch), the defendant had lied about certain property interests during the course of divorce proceedings. When he came to claim a beneficial interest in certain property, these lies were raised in opposition to his claim. The court found, however, that these lies had been told several years after the acquisition of the property and that the intention regarding the beneficial interest in the property had to be assessed at the time of acquisition – 'The lies that

D told in the divorce proceedings were not sufficient to rebut the presumption that he had acquired a share when the property had been acquired several years earlier.'

In this area, trusts law overlaps with contract law insofar as the court needs to be persuaded that the claim to a beneficial interest is dependent on the illegality. If it is then equity will not assist the claimant because to do so would be to condone the illegality. In the case of contract, a claimant cannot seek to rely on an illegal contract to then claim back monies paid to the other contracting party. If, however, the illegal agreement is no longer found to be necessary or is withdrawn from or is not relied on (*Tribe v Tribe* [1996] Ch 107), or is frustrated (*Patel v Mirza* [2015] Ch 271), a claim can succeed.

The law here is not entirely consistent or satisfactory. For example in the case of *Tinsley v Milligan* [1994] 1 AC 340, property was purchased in the name of Tinsley (although both parties contributed to the business which paid the mortgage and outgoings, ie made a financial contribution to acquisition) so that Milligan could continue to claim benefits. When the couple split up, Milligan sought to claim a beneficial interest in the property under a purchase money resulting trust. The issue of fraud regarding social security benefits – notably housing benefits – was raised, but in this case held not to defeat the claim to a beneficial interest because this arose on the basis of financial contribution to acquisition rather than the benefit fraud itself. The decision in *Tinsley* was not unanimous, and it is clear that across different areas of law (trusts, contract and tort) there is uncertainty regarding the proper approach to a defence based on illegality. Indeed the House of Lords in *Tinsley* called for action in this area of law and, rather belatedly in 2010, the Law Commission published its report on 'The Illegality Defence' (Law Com No 320). This included a proposed draft bill, the Trusts (Concealment of Interests) Bill, which seems not to have progressed at all. Nevertheless *Tinsley* remains good law at least insofar as it must be shown that the illegality was relied on – see *Sharma v Top Brands Ltd* [2016] PNLR 12; *Hniazdzilau v Vajgel* [2016] EWHC 15 (Ch).

4.2.5 Resulting trust of the shared home

A version of the presumed purchase money resulting trust has also been used in cases where a couple are living together and where, typically, one person is the legal owner of property and the other has contributed to its purchase but is not on the legal title. Usually the problems arise when the couple's relationship gets into difficulty and they separate. As Diplock LJ said in the case of *Ulrich v Ulrich and Felton* [1968] 1 WLR 180, at 188–9:

> When these young people pool their savings to buy and equip a home or to acquire any other family asset, they do not think of this as an 'ante-nuptial' or 'post-nuptial' settlement, or give their minds to legalistic technicalities of 'advancement' and 'resulting trusts'. Nor do they normally agree explicitly what their equitable interests in the family asset shall be if death, divorce or separation parts them. Where there is no explicit agreement, the court's first

> task is to infer from their conduct in relation to the property what their common intention would have been had they put it into words before matrimonial differences arose between them. In the common case today, of which the present is a typical example, neither party to the marriage has inherited capital, both are earning their living before marriage, and the wife intends to continue to do so until they start having children. They pool their savings to buy a house on mortgage in the husband's name or in joint names and to furnish and equip it as the family home. They meet the expenses of its upkeep and improvement and the payments of instalments on the mortgage out of the family income, to which the wife contributes so long as she is earning. In such a case, the prima facie inference from their conduct is that their common intention is that the house, furniture and equipment should be family assets ...

If they are not married, the wide powers of property allocation conferred on the courts under divorce legislation – the Matrimonial Causes Act 1973 – are not available to them. They are unlikely to have arranged their interest under contract, and so it falls to equity to try to resolve the matter. The situation may also arise in other pooled resource/occupation cases. For example in *Bull v Bull* [1955] 1 QB 234, CA, the dispute was between a mother and son. Both had contributed to the purchase of a property, but the son had contributed more and the property was registered in his name. When he married a few years later, it was agreed that his mother could reside in the now matrimonial home of the son. Perhaps not unsurprisingly, this domestic arrangement soon got into difficulties. The son wanted the mother to move out and she wished to remain, arguing that despite his name being on the legal title, she was a beneficial owner under a resulting trust. The court found that she had not intended a gift to her son, but rather to retain a beneficial interest in the property which would give her a roof over her head (the upshot of course would be that the property would have to be sold to get the mother out of it and the equity divided between the son and the mother).

In many respects these cases are not dissimilar from the presumed purchase money resulting trust. The problem that can arise in cohabitation cases is the shared living over an extended period of time during which there have been various contributions to the home by both parties, most of which may not be formally recorded and recollections of which may be confused. The court is then called on to consider whether these contributions are sufficient to give rise to a beneficial interest in the property. For example in the case of *Springette v Defoe* [1992] 2 FLR 388, CA, the couple started off by cohabiting in Mrs Springette's council flat. They then moved into a council house as joint tenants. Shortly thereafter the council offered to sell them the house they were occupying at a price which was vastly discounted as a consequence of Mrs Springette having been a council tenant for over 11 years. The mortgage was in joint names with both agreeing to contribute to the mortgage repayments, and Mrs Springette also contributed some savings to the balance of the purchase price. When they split up,

Mr Defoe claimed a 50% share in the house (both were on the legal title but there had been no agreement at the time of purchase regarding beneficial shares). The court, however, awarded Mrs Springette a 75% share on the basis of the value of the council tenant discount and the deposit from her savings. It is clear from this case that the contribution must be in money or money's worth (the value of the discount here) and attributable to the acquisition of the property, although this may be the ongoing acquisition via mortgage repayments.

Payments which are not directed at acquisition do not give rise to a beneficial interest under a resulting trust. This is clear from the case of *Pettitt v Pettitt* [1970] AC 777. This was a claim by the husband that he had a beneficial interest in the proceeds of sale of the matrimonial home that had been bought with proceeds of the sale of a property his wife had inherited. For the purposes of a resulting trust, the issue was whether the husband had acquired a beneficial interest as a result of work he had undertaken on the property, which he claimed had increased its value. Lord Reid clearly stated the law:

> As regards contributions, the traditional view is that, in the absence of evidence to the contrary effect, a contributor to the purchase-price will acquire a beneficial interest in the property: but as regards improvements made by a person who is not the legal owner, after the property has been acquired, that person will not, in the absence of agreement, acquire any interest in the property or have any claim against the owner. (at 794)

He went on to suggest that where the improvements were substantial then it would be inequitable to distinguish between the party who paid for improvements and the party who paid the mortgage, similarly where one party through good housekeeping or by paying all the other outgoings enabled the other to maintain mortgage payments. This he suggested was not one of those cases, and so Mr Pettitt was not entitled to a beneficial share of the proceeds of sale. Lord Upjohn did suggest, obiter, that if the facts fitted, it might be possible for a husband (or presumably a wife) to raise an estoppel if he or she had been encouraged to believe that he or she had or would have a beneficial interest in the property and incurred a detriment in reliance on that (see below).

4.2.6 Calculating an interest under the resulting trust

If a beneficial interest is found under a resulting trust then the determination of entitlement is calculated according to the contribution to acquisition and any pro rata increase in the value of the property. This is very much a mathematical calculation and may fail to take into account circumstances or conduct which cannot be easily reduced to pounds and pence. It is more suitable for dealings at 'arm's length' rather than intimate cohabiting situations. On the other hand, a mathematical formula gives the court a clear and consistent tool to use in calculating beneficial shares, so that where, for example, the resulting trust is being used where a trust has failed, the court can clearly establish what goes back to whom.

4.3 Constructive trusts

4.3.1 Traditional uses of the constructive trust

The constructive trust can be used by the court to safeguard property which has been identified as being in the hands of someone who is not beneficially entitled to it. A recent example arose in the case of *National Crime Agency v Robb* [2014] EWHC 4384 (Ch), where eight defrauded investors brought a successful proprietary claim under the Proceeds of Crime Act 2002 to those proceeds which could be successfully traced (for tracing see **Chapter 6**). The advantage of using the constructive trust in this way means that property is safeguarded from other creditors or claimants, and the person who has control of the property is denied any beneficial interest in it and must manage the property as a trustee.

Where property is acquired by a trustee in breach of trust (see **Chapter 6**), it may be declared to be held on constructive trust by the trustee, or indeed in certain situations by a third party who was not the original trustee but received property knowing it to be trust property. Similarly, a constructive trust may be used where a fiduciary other than a trustee (see **Chapter 5**) breaches his or her fiduciary duty and makes a material gain as a consequence of doing so. See for example *AG for Hong Kong v Reid* [1994] 1 AC 324, where bribes received by a Crown civil servant were used to purchase property in New Zealand. The court held that the bribes and the property were held on constructive trust for the person to whom the fiduciary duty was owned – here the Crown (see also the application of *Reid* in *Tesco Stores Ltd v Pook* [2003] EWHC 823 (Ch) and *Kent CC v Knowles* [2014] EWHC 1900 (QB), both bribes cases).

Reid, however, was challenged as an inappropriate precedent in *Sinclair Investments (UK) Ltd v Versailles Trade Finance Ltd (in administration)* [2012] Ch 453, in respect of the imposition of a proprietary claim under a constructive trust rather than a personal remedy for equitable accounting of the trust funds, the latter being preferred following the much older case of *Lister & Co v Stubbs* (1890) LR 45 Ch D 1. In *FHR European Ventures LLP v Cedar Capital Partners LLC* [2014] Ch 1, a case involving secret profits made by a fiduciary gaining a large commission on the sale of property, the court tried to bring some order to the current law, suggesting that there were three situations arising where a fiduciary obtained a benefit in breach of fiduciary duty:

(1) where the benefit was an asset belonging beneficially to the principal (the person who had appointed the agent and to whom the agent owed a fiduciary duty – see **Chapter 6**) – this would give rise to a constructive trust;

(2) where the benefit had been obtained by the fiduciary taking advantage of an opportunity which was properly that of the principal (a *Boardman v Phipps*-type situation ([1967] 2 AC 46)) – this would give rise to a constructive trust;

(3) all other cases – where a personal rather than proprietary remedy would apply.

It should perhaps be pointed out that Lewison LJ made the following observation on the current state of the law:

> If the law is to be made simpler and more coherent ... then that suggests a need to revisit the very many longstanding decisions in Category 2 cases and to provide an overhaul of this entire area of the law of constructive trusts in order to provide a coherent and logical legal framework. If that can be done at all by the courts, rather than Parliament, it can only be accomplished by the Supreme Court. That indicates a need for informed debate and ultimately determination by the Supreme Court: (1) whether the *Sinclair* case was right to decide that the *Lister* case is to be preferred to the *Reid* case; (2) in terms of constructive trusts and proprietary relief for breach of fiduciary duty, what are the principles to distinguish opportunity cases within Category 2 and those within Category 3; (3) what is the true jurisprudential nature of the constructive trust in this (and by necessity other) areas of the law, including whether it is – or should be – an institutional trust at all or something else. In considering those matters, there are important issues of policy, and the relative importance of different policies, to assess, including deterring fraud and corruption; the ability to strip the fiduciary of all benefits, including increases in the value of benefits, acquired by breach of duty, and vehicles or third parties through which those benefits have been channelled; the importance attached to the protection of those to whom fiduciary duties are owed; and the position of other creditors on the fiduciary's insolvency who may be prejudiced by a constructive trust or proprietary relief in favour of the fiduciary's principal but who, in the absence of such a trust and relief, would benefit from increases in value of assets acquired by the fiduciary's fraud, corruption or wrongdoing. (para 116)

While it has been argued that English law does not recognise the 'remedial constructive trust', in fact the constructive trust is used when a remedy or solution is sought. For example, the constructive trust has been used to locate the beneficial interest in the hands of a husband seeking to avoid the payment of tax and to deny his wife any property interest on the breakdown of the marriage (*M v M* [2013] EWHC 2534 (Fam)).

4.3.2 The constructive trust and the shared home

This 'new' form of constructive trust emerged in the 1970s as equity's answer to the claims of cohabitees who, while not on the legal title of the shared home, nevertheless believed they had an interest in the property. These cases primarily involved couples who, while not married, were living together, and in some cases had been doing so for some time, and then split up, with the legal owner of the property denying the other party any proprietary interest. In developing this particular use of the constructive trust, the courts were reacting to a social and economic situation. By the 1970s, divorce had become much easier with less social opprobrium attaching to it. Cohabitation became more common in the socially liberal era of the 1960s and 1970s, and in the 1980s the release of public housing onto the private market through the 'right to buy' given to council tenants to buy the homes they lived in, together with a marked policy shift towards owner-occupants and a freeing up of the mortgage market, meant that many more people were investing in real estate. The consequences of this are with us today. Many people cohabit, either in intimate partner relationships or as a pragmatic solution to the lack of affordable housing, and many people pool their resources with others to 'get on the housing ladder'. '"Common Law Marriage" and Cohabitation' (House of Commons Briefing Paper No 03372, 13 June 2018) provides an excellent summary of the current situation and discusses the difficulties around property rights for cohabitees, amongst other things. The Paper sets out the following statistics:

Opposite sex cohabiting couples	Same sex cohabiting couples
▪ 1996 – 1.5 million	▪ 1996 – 16,000
▪ 2017 – 3.2 million	▪ 2017 – 101,000
▪ More than doubled	▪ Increase of 530%

Figure 4.4 Recent changes in society

However, this form of constructive trust is not limited to domestic relationships. Its use has been considered by the Court of Appeal in relation to the purchase of a property by friends in *Gallarotti v Sebastianelli* [2012] EWCA Civ 865, and it may extend to business relationships, for example a bed and breakfast business in *Agarwala v Agarwala* [2013] EWCA Civ 1763, where the claimant's sister-in-law was the legal owner of the property and had taken out the mortgage owing to his poor credit rating. He, however, built up the business, ran it and repaid the mortgage. The court held that the sister-in-law held the property on constructive trust. In a similar vein, the Privy Council in *Marr v Collie* [2017] UKPC 17 deemed the use of the constructive trust appropriate to resolve a dispute over the ownership of various assets jointly owned by a couple in a close personal relationship.

The problems of disputed beneficial ownership can easily be overcome by clear agreements relating to beneficial ownership in property, regardless of legal title, and there is provision in conveyancing processes for this to be done (which lie outside the scope of this book). Unfortunately this is not always done, and so the situation arises in which, as indicated, the non-legal owner is claiming a share in the property on the grounds that the legal owner holds the property on trust for both of them. This situation is not dissimilar to that found in *Paul v Constance*, discussed in **Chapter 2**. The distinction is that, there, the property was money and no formalities were required to be complied with to create an express trust. In these constructive trust cases, the property is land and the claimant is assisted by the provisions of s 53 of the Law of Property Act 1925, as mentioned above.

4.3.2.1 When will this type of constructive trust arise?

There are two situations:

(a) where both parties are on the legal title – and so hold as joint tenants in law – but have not agreed on their beneficial interests;
(b) when the legal title is held by A, but B claims a beneficial interest.

In the first case, the claimant will not have to establish that he or she has a beneficial interest, only the quantum of that interest. In the second case, the claimant will first have to establish that he or she has a beneficial interest and then the quantum of that interest. Clearly, therefore, in the second example the claimant has a more difficult task.

In order to determine if a claimant has a beneficial interest, the courts, notably in the case of *Lloyds Bank v Rosset* [1991] 1 AC 107, drawing on the earlier case of *Gissing v Gissing* [1971] AC 886, have developed a number of guiding principles.

Flowing from *Rosset* we have two situations:

(1) express intention regarding the beneficial interests in the property stemming from conversations or discussions at the time of acquisition;
(2) in the absence of express intention, implied intention inferred from the conduct of the party claiming a beneficial interest.

This type of trust is therefore based on the common intention of the parties evidenced in different ways. Lord Bridge in *Rosset* suggested that both *Pettit v Pettit* (above) and *Gissing v Gissing* (above) were examples of this approach. Further to but not distinct from, in both cases the claimant must demonstrate that he or she incurred a detriment as a consequence of his or her understanding that he or she was to have an interest in the property. A common intention without some kind of detriment is insufficient (*Layton v Martin* [1986] 2 FLR 227). If there is no evidence of express intention or intention which can be inferred from the conduct of the parties in respect of beneficial interests in the property, then the non-legal owner will not succeed in claiming a beneficial interest behind a constructive trust (*Windelar v Whitehall* (1990) 154 JP 29).

A (legal owner) B claims a beneficial interest

arising from

Express agreement between A and B

+

Detriment on B's part

or

Detrimental reliance by B which gives rise to implied agreement between A and B

Figure 4.5 Constructive trust and the shared home

4.3.2.2 Express agreement

When people move in with each other, they may not always discuss the proprietary interests in the shared home, especially if, as will be the case in these constructive trust claims, they have not had a discussion as to the percentage of beneficial interests or completed a declaration of trust. What the court is looking for as evidence of express agreement is some recollection of a discussion of some kind regarding the property, however imperfectly remembered. As Lord Bridge put it in *Rosset* (at 132), there must be a finding of an actual 'agreement, arrangement, or understanding' between the parties which must 'be based on evidence of express discussions between the partners, however imperfectly remembered and however imprecise their terms may have been'. There will of course be evidential difficulties and probable challenges by the other party, especially if the cohabitation has continued for a number of years and if there have been a number of property transactions during that time when homes have been bought and sold, new mortgages taken out and so on. *Oxley v Hiscock* [2005] Fam 211 is an example of a case where there were discussions regarding ownership of the property. The judge at first instance had found evidence of such a discussion, and in the Court of Appeal Chadwick LJ held:

> The true relevance is that her [the judge in the court below] finding that there was a discussion between the parties as to whose name should appear on the registered title … is only explicable on the basis that they both intended—and expressed that intention to the other—that each should have a beneficial share in the property. It is that feature which, to my mind, provides the foundation for Mrs Oxley's claim in constructive trust or proprietary estoppel; and which distinguishes that claim from one founded on resulting trust alone. (at 218)

4.3.2.3 Excuse cases

Although this form of constructive trust is referred to as a common intention trust, in fact some cases seem to point in the opposite direction. While one party has one intention, or understanding about the property, the other has a very different intention. These are referred to as excuse cases and can be illustrated by cases such as *Eves v Eves* [1975] 1 WLR 1338, where the man who was the legal owner of the property admitted that not putting his cohabiting partner's name on the legal title on the grounds that she was not 21 had been an excuse; and *Grant v Edwards* [1986] Ch 638, where the man told his female cohabitee that she should not be put on the title deeds as this could prejudice her pending matrimonial proceedings. Lord Bridge in *Rosset* suggested that both *Eves* and *Grant* were examples of express intention constructive trusts, ie *Rosset* category 1 types. These cases can be explained on the basis that the actions of the men in both cases suggest either that a conversation took place about ownership or, at the very least, demonstrate some acknowledgement of the potential interest of the women.

These types of cases are relatively rare, although the issue arose again in the Court of Appeal case of *Capehorn v Harris* [2015] EWCA Civ 955, where an excuse was made that it would too expensive to put the claimant's name on the title deeds. However, there was no evidence of an agreement to share and no detrimental reliance so the beneficial interest was not established. This leads us on to the second essential element – detriment.

4.3.2.4 Detriment

Where there is evidence of an express agreement regarding the intention of the parties in respect of the beneficial interest in the property (*Rosset* category 1), this detriment can be anything which the claimant did which they would not have done unless they understood that they had an interest in the property. This can include non-financial detriment, such as undertaking extensive renovations (*Eves v Eves* (above)) or giving up a well-paid job and supporting the other party in their business ventures (*Hammond v Mitchell* [1991] 1 WLR 1127). The detriment must be referable to the common intention to have a beneficial interest in the property.

Where a claim under *Rosset* category 2 is made (ie implied agreement arising from detriment), it appears from *Rosset* that this detriment has to be financial and directed at the acquisition of the property – it may be contribution to the initial deposit or subsequent contribution to the mortgage repayments. So, for example, in *Midland Bank Plc v Cooke* [1995] 4 All ER 562, the financial contribution was a gift given to the couple jointly. The courts have held that where there is financial assistance to a newly married or engaged couple, the usual inference is that it is a gift to both of them (*Abbott v Abbott* [2007] UKPC 53). Contributions not referable to acquisition have been rejected (see for example *Burns v Burns* [1984] Ch 317).

In *Rosset* itself, Mrs Rosset was claiming that she had a beneficial interest in the property which supported a claim to an overriding interest against the bank's claim for possession (a person in actual occupation of property referable to a proprietary interest has an interest that overrides the claim of a third party under the Land Registration Act 1925, s 70). Mrs Rosset based her claim on her contributions to supervising renovation projects and undertaking decorating work. On the facts, the court held that Mrs Rosset did not have a beneficial interest, and so the court did not need to go on to determine her beneficial share (compare the outcome of a *Rosset* category 2 (inferred intention) constructive trust in *Re Purseglove* [2006] EWHC 1762 and *Webster v Webster* [2008] EWHC 31 (Ch)).

Rosset has not been affirmatively followed in all subsequent cases. In *Stack v Dowden* [2007] 2 AC 432 at 448, Lord Walker suggested that

> The law should … (take) a wide view of what is capable of counting as a contribution towards the acquisition of a residence, while remaining sceptical of the value of alleged improvements that are really insignificant, or elaborate arguments (suggestive of creative accounting) as to how the family finances were arranged.

Stack was followed in *Abbott v Abbott* [2007] UKPC 53, where it was suggested that in order to determine the parties' intentions, the law should be less prescriptive and more holistic, looking at the whole course of conduct between them, including in this case that the parties had arranged their finances entirely jointly and undertaken joint liability for the repayment of the mortgage. According to Baroness Hale in *Abbott*:

> The law has indeed moved on … The parties' *whole course of conduct* in relation to the property must be taken into account *in determining their shared intentions* as to its ownership.

This more holistic approach may blur the lines between deciding if the claimant has a beneficial interest and the quantum of that interest (see for example *Happenish v Allnatt* [2010] EWHC 392 (Ch)). In *Curran v Collins* [2015] EWCA Civ 404, the Court demonstrated a willingness to look beyond financial contributions, although here the claiming cohabitee was unsuccessful (had she been able successfully to argue that this was an 'excuse' case, non-financial contributions could have been considered anyway – see *Grant v Edwards* (above)). In *Aspden v Elvy* [2012] EWHC 1387 (Ch) substantial financial and physical contributions to a barn conversion were taken into account to confer a 25% share on a male claimant – whether just the physical labour would have been sufficient is doubtful.

If either *Rosset* category 1 or *Rosset* category 2 is satisfied, this establishes that the claimant has a beneficial interest in the property, thereby making the legal owner a constructive trustee. However, the court then has to determine the quantum or size of this beneficial interest

4.3.2.5 Quantifying the beneficial interest

As indicated above (at **4.2.6**), under a resulting trust the quantum is determined by a mathematical calculation governed by the amount of money which has been contributed by the claimant to the acquisition of the property.

This formula may be inappropriate in cohabitation situations, insofar as it fails to take into account the consequences of shared lives and the give and take of family life, especially over an extended period of time. For these reasons the constructive trust is preferred to the resulting trust in shared home situations, although it is evident from some of the cases that the mathematical calculation is not entirely absent in determining quantum in constructive trust cases.

In quantifying the beneficial interest, an initial distinction has to be made between the situation where A and B are registered as legal owners but have not declared what their beneficial interests are to be, and the situation where only A is on the legal title.

A and B as joint tenants in law

As joint tenants in law holding the property as co-owners, A and B have undivided shares in the whole but are notionally equal owners. It follows then that their beneficial interests unless established otherwise are equal.

Co-owners can only hold as joint tenants in law. They thus hold an undivided share in the property. Following the maxim '**equity follows the law**', the courts have held that where the cohabitees are joint tenants in law, there is a presumption that they are joint tenants in equity. This is a rebuttable presumption, but the person seeking to rebut it and claim a different percentage division bears the onus of doing so. In *Jones v Kernott* [2012] 1 AC 776, at 784, the equitable maxim was rejected and it was held:

> The presumption of a beneficial joint tenancy is not based on a mantra as to 'equity following the law' … There are two much more substantial reasons (which overlap) why a challenge to the presumption of beneficial joint tenancy is not to be lightly embarked on. The first is implicit in the nature of the enterprise. If a couple in an intimate relationship (whether married or unmarried) decide to buy a house or flat in which to live together, almost always with the help of a mortgage for which they are jointly and severally liable, that is on the face of things a strong indication of emotional and economic commitment to a joint enterprise. That is so even if the parties, for whatever reason, fail to make that clear by any overt declaration or agreement.

This issue arose in the case of *Stack v Dowden* [2007] 2 AC 432, where both parties were on the legal title but had not declared their beneficial interests. Despite cohabiting for 18 years and having four children together, the couple had kept their finances distinctly separate, indicating that they did not intend to share equally. A division of 65:35 was upheld in the House of Lords. As a starting point the court held that there is no presumption as to beneficial joint tenancy. The starting point is to presume a tenancy in common (in which there can be identified shares). The court then has to look to the intention as to shares. If this is not expressed then it has to be inferred by the court. A starting point may be contribution (as in a resulting trust) but may also be referable to expectation based on the relationship between the parties and the way in which the expectation arose.

In *Jones v Kernott* [2012] 1 AC 776, another co-ownership case where beneficial interest had not been indicated, the court explained that the presumption as to equal shares could be rebutted by showing that there was a different common intention at the date of acquisition. Their common intention was to be deduced objectively from their words and conduct. If it was not possible for the court to ascertain what this common intention was, either by direct evidence or by inference, then the court would consider shares which were fair having regard to the whole course of dealing between them. In *Jones* the court also envisaged the possibility of the intention as to shares changing subsequent to acquisition (see below).

In contrast, the Court of Appeal in *Wodzicki v Wodzicki* [2017] EWCA Civ 95 held that the appellant (the daughter of one of the joint legal owners) could not rely on *Jones* and was therefore not entitled to an interest in the house. The Court was clear that there would be no imputation of a common intention to provide her with a share on the basis of fairness and there was no reason to interfere with the equal shares held by her late father and his wife, the respondent.

Where A is on the legal title but B has established a beneficial interest

Here the court looks first to see if there is any evidence of what shares were intended by the parties. In the absence of this, Chadwick LJ in *Oxley v Hiscock* [2005] Fam 211 explained as follows:

> In a case where there is no evidence of any discussion between them as to the amount of the share which each was to have – and even in a case where the evidence is that there was no discussion on that point – the question still requires an answer. It must now be accepted that (at least in this court and below) the answer is that each is entitled to that share which the court considers fair having regard to the whole course of dealing between them in relation to the property. And, in that context, 'the whole course of dealing between them in relation to the property' includes the arrangements which they make from time to time in order to meet the outgoings (for example, mortgage contributions, council tax and utilities, repairs, insurance and housekeeping) which have to be met if they are to live in the property as their home.

It has been suggested that what the court is looking for is evidence of 'a joint enterprise' in respect of the shared home. Indicators of this joint enterprise might be whether the couple had children, the length of the relationship, whether they had a joint bank account and shared in the outgoings on the property, whether they pooled their resources and labour in their daily lives and generally behaved in such a way that it would be unconscionable to deny the non-legal owner a share. In *Oxley*, while the court adopted a broad approach based on what the court considered fair taking into account the whole course of dealing, nevertheless there is evidence of a resulting trust calculation at play, insofar as on appeal to the House of Lords, the 50:50 division was overruled and replaced with a 60:40 division, taking into account the disproportionate financial contribution each party had brought to the series of house purchases. What was 'fair', therefore, was influenced by the financial contribution.

In the case of *Graham-York v York* [2015] EWCA Civ 72, the Court of Appeal upheld a decision to give the non-legal owner 25%. In doing so the court found that the couple had not owned the home jointly, and although a beneficial interest behind a constructive trust was found on the basis of financial contribution and subsequent conduct, evidence indicated that the couple had not had 'a relationship in which love and affection were at the forefront' from which an intention to share equally in the property could be inferred.

4.3.2.6 Changing the beneficial share

The courts have recognised that changing circumstances may result in changes to the intended shares of the parties. While the court is hesitant to impute an intention to the parties, it has been suggested that the court can adopt the approach of inferring beneficial shares on the basis that if the parties had addressed their minds to that matter, they would have arrived at a different division of the beneficial interest. This was considered in the case of *Jones v Kernott* (above).

Where there has been a change of circumstance, however, it appears that a court may impute an intention to vary the beneficial share. In the case of *Barnes v Phillips* [2015] EWCA Civ 1056, the power of a judge to impute an intention as to changed shares was challenged, but it was held that

> The judge's use of 'impute' was intentional and appropriate. He was seeking to determine the shares in which the parties were to own the property following a change in the basis on which their beneficial interests were held. The imputation of intention was entirely permissible in that context where it was not possible to infer the parties' intention. Imputation was not permissible at the stage of determining whether there had been a common change of intention, only at the second stage of determining the respective shares where inference was not possible,

4.3.3 The overlap with proprietary estoppel

As seen in **Chapter 2**, proprietary estoppel may be raised to claim a property interest where formalities are not complied with and there is an incomplete gift or incompletely constituted trust. The requirements for raising an estoppel have similarities with the constructive trust, in particular to the first category from *Rosset*: assurance leading to reliance and the incurring of a detriment which would not have been incurred had the person who has suffered that detriment not believed or been encouraged to believe that he or she was acquiring a property interest. A recent example of the interplay between the two claims is provided in the High Court case of *Culliford v Thorpe* [2018] EWHC 426 (Ch). Undoubtedly, they are bound together by the underlying concept of unconscionability which lies at the heart of equitable intervention in both instances.

Lord Walker in *Stack v Dowden* (above) at 448–9 suggested the following distinction:

> Proprietary estoppel typically consists of asserting an equitable claim against the conscience of the 'true' owner. The claim is a 'mere equity'. It is to be satisfied by the minimum award necessary to do justice (*Crabb v Arun District Council* [1976] Ch 179, 198), which may sometimes lead to no more than a monetary award. A 'common intention' constructive trust, by contrast, is identifying the true beneficial owner or owners, and the size of their beneficial interests.

If a claim under a constructive trust fails or there is insufficient evidence to support such a claim, proprietary estoppel may still be raised. See for example *Arif v Anwar* [2015] EWHC 124 (Fam), in which it was held that while there was insufficient evidence to support a constructive trust for a son's contribution of money for the refurbishment of a property, there was sufficient evidence that he had allowed the money to be used in the belief that he would acquire some interest in the property, and he was awarded 25% to offset any possible detriment. A constructive trust and proprietary estoppel may also be raised in the alternative – see *Aspden v Elvy* (above) and, more recently, *Dobson v Griffey* [2018] EWHC 1117 (Ch).

The distinction lies in the outcome. If a proprietary estoppel is successfully raised, the court then goes on to order a remedy in order to do the minimum equity demanded by the circumstances, for example the payment of compensation, the conveyance of the fee simple, etc.

4.4 Is the constructive/resulting trustee the same as an express trust trustee?

The constructive or resulting trustee is placed in this position against his or her will. It is a trust imposed by law. As such the trustee in a constructive or resulting trust is not in the same position as the trustee under an express trust. First, the position is usually only a temporary measure. Secondly, because of the circumstances in which the trust arises, it is unlikely that the trustee is permitted to exercise any of the powers that an ordinary express trustee has. The constructive or resulting trust trustee may, however, be under broadly similar duties as an express trustee insofar as he or she is expected to act honestly, to safeguard the integrity of the trust property, to observe the obligations and expectations of a fiduciary and to account for the property.

In some respects the imposition of a trust leads to curious anomalies. For example, a breaching trustee or a third party who has received trust property knowing it to be transferred in breach of trust has the legal title vested in them by virtue of being or becoming a trustee. In other words, their ownership of the property is legitimised through the imposition of the trust. Of course the distinction is that they are not beneficially entitled and must now manage the property for the benefit of those who are entitled in equity to benefit.

4.5 The continuing role of unconscionability

Although not always overtly expressed, we find in the use of the resulting trust and the constructive trust echoes of the origins of the trust. These trusts are imposed in order to achieve fairness or in situations where it would be unconscionable to deny the applicant a beneficial interest. Often the trust is being imposed to address a wrong such as a breach of trust, a fraud or dishonesty – both criminal and moral. Thus the resulting and/or constructive trust, while managing to observe the maxim 'equity follows the law', manages to mitigate or soften the operation of that law.

4.6 Reforming the law

A reading of the cases shows that the law in this area is far from satisfactory, and indeed it may be quite a challenge for a lawyer to advise his or her client about possible outcomes because not only are the decisions of the courts very fact dependent, but the approaches of the judges to finding an equitable solution diverge, sometimes quite considerably.

Practitioners need a statutory solution to the question of property division on the dissolution of a cohabitation relationship. Even if the correct approach to acquisition of an interest can be proved, it is hard to quantify, particularly since the decision in *Jones v Kernott* where at first instance the beneficial interests were said to be divided 90:10 in favour of Ms Jones, the Court of Appeal said 50:50 and the Supreme Court decided 90:10 was 'fair'.

The problem of cohabitation and property rights was considered by the Law Commission in its consultation paper No 179, 'Cohabitation: The financial consequences of relationship breakdown' (2006), which was a sequel to a discussion paper 'Sharing Homes' (Law Com No 278) presented to Parliament in

2002. In 2007 the Law Commission presented its report, 'Cohabitation: the Financial Consequences of Relationship Breakdown' (Law Com No 307) to Parliament.

The report recommended a statutory scheme of financial relief on separation which would be available to eligible couples: those who had a child/children together and/or those who had cohabited for a minimum period of time. Outcomes would be determined by the contributions made by each party to the relationship, and couples would be able to opt out of the statutory regime by written agreement. In 2008 the Government announced that it would not be implementing the recommendations, pending research into a similar scheme operational in Scotland under the Family Law (Scotland) Act 2006. In 2011 it was announced, following consideration of this research and the Law Commission report, that no changes in the law relating to cohabitation would be forthcoming in that Parliament.

As set out above at **4.3.2**, numbers of cohabiting couples are rapidly increasing, and calls for reform from both within and outside Parliament continue to be made, including in several Private Members' Bills. However, the Bills have not progressed and the Government remains undecided on how to proceed with the proposed reforms (see '"Common law marriage" and cohabitation' (above)).

Consequently, while cohabitation continues to be popular, the law remains unchanged, ie the property rights of cohabitees who are not married or in a civil partnership are not governed by legislation. If those who acquire property together do not indicate at the time of conveyance or at some point thereafter their intended beneficial interest, it falls to equity to try and resolve these issues. As Waite LJ explained in the case of *Midland Bank Plc v Cooke* [1995] 4 All ER 562, 575:

> Equity has traditionally been a system which matches established principle to the demands of social change. The mass diffusion of home ownership has been one of the most striking social changes of our own time. The present case is typical of hundreds, perhaps even thousands, of others. When people, especially young people, agree to share their lives in joint homes they do so on a basis of mutual trust and in the expectation that their relationship will endure. Despite the efforts that have been made by many responsible bodies to counsel prospective cohabitants as to the risks of taking shared interests in property without legal advice, it is unrealistic to expect that advice to be followed on a universal scale. For a couple embarking on a serious relationship, discussion of the terms to apply at parting is almost a contradiction of the shared hopes that have brought them together. There will inevitably be numerous couples, married or unmarried, who have no discussion about ownership and who, perhaps advisedly, make no agreement about it. It would be anomalous, against that background, to create a range of home-buyers who were beyond the pale of equity's assistance in formulating a

> fair presumed basis for the sharing of beneficial title, simply because they had been honest enough to admit that they never gave ownership a thought or reached any agreement about it.

The transfer forms used in conveyancing do now require joint purchasers to declare whether they wish to hold the property as joint tenants or tenants in common. If the latter, then there is a box headed 'Declaration of Trust' where the parties declare whether they hold the property on trust for themselves in equal shares or some other arrangement which has to be set out in the box.

It does not provide for any detailed arrangements and conditions which may have been agreed between the parties. To properly deal with any such agreements then, a separate declaration of trust deed is best, but in practice, for the reason given above by Lord Waite, it is often hard to persuade the parties to pay for this at the start of what is hoped to be a long relationship.

4.7 Further reading

Georgina Andrews, 'The presumption of advancement: equity, equality and human rights' (2007) *Conveyancer and Property Lawyer* 340–51.

Paul S Davies, 'The Illegality Defence – two steps forward, one step back?' [2009] 73 *Conveyancer and Property Lawyer* 182–208.

Terence Etherton, 'Constructive trusts and proprietary estoppel: the search for clarity and principle' (2009) 2 *Conveyancer and Property Lawyer* 104–26.

Simon Gardner, 'Case Comment: Heresy – or not? – in family property: Bhura v Bhura (No.2) [2014] EWHC 727 (Fam); [2015] 1 FLR 153' (2015) *Conveyancer and Property Lawyer* 332–40.

Sarah Greer and Mark Pawlowski, 'Imputation, fairness and the family home' (2015) 6 *Conveyancer and Property Lawyer* 512–21.

Timon Hughes-Davies, 'Redefining the Quistclose trust' (2015) 1 *Conveyancer and Property Lawyer* 26–46.

Matthew Mills, 'Single name family home constructive trusts: is Lloyds Bank v Rosset still good law?' (2018) 4 *Conveyancer and Property Lawyer* 350–66.

Sukhninder Panesar, 'Unconscionability, Constructive Trusts and Proprietary Estoppel: Culliford v Thorpe' (2018) *Wills, Trusts & Estates Law eJournal*; (2018) 1(1) *Wolverhampton Law Journal* (free online).

Lionel Smith, 'Constructive Trusts and the no-profit rule' (2013) 72(2) *Cambridge Law Journal* 260–3.

William Swadling, 'Explaining resulting trusts' (2008) 124 *Law Quarterly Review* 72–102.

Stephen Wildblood QC, *Cohabitation and Trusts of Land*, 3rd edn (Thomson Sweet & Maxwell, 2016).

Helen Wood & Others, *Cohabitation – Law, Practice & Precedents*, 7th edn (Jordans, 2017).

This chapter has focussed on trusts which arise when the court considers there are circumstances which justify the finding of a beneficial interest outside the express private trust. In doing so, the court may be giving effect to the actual or presumed intention of the parties, or because it would be unconscionable to deny the claimant a beneficial interest, or due to a combination of factors which persuade the court to exercise its inherent equitable jurisdiction. In some cases these trusts are used to 'do justice', for example in cases where the constructive trust is used to bring property back into a trust, or where it is appropriate to impose a fiduciary duty on a person in order to deny that person absolute beneficial entitlement – for example a breaching trustee who has made a profit. These circumstantial trusts are also used to address property issues which arise because of a lack of legal alternatives, for example where unmarried cohabitees are in dispute about entitlement to the formerly shared home, or where one party has contributed to the purchase price but is not on the legal title, or where one party believes that he or she is acquiring a property interest and is then denied this. The continuing demand for equitable intervention in the absence of legislative action highlights the continuing contemporary relevance of these types of trusts.

test your knowledge

1. What is the distinction between a presumed resulting trust and an automatic resulting trust?
2. The case of *Lloyds Bank v Rosset* suggests that a constructive trust will arise in two situations. What are these, and what sort of evidence would a court be looking for to find that the claimant has a beneficial interest?
3. What guidelines inform the court in determining quantum once an implied trust is found, and how is the calculation of quantum made in the case of (a) resulting trusts; (b) constructive trusts where there is only one legal owner; and (c) constructive trusts where both parties are on the legal title but their beneficial shares are not declared?
4. To what extent is there still a role for proprietary estoppel?
5. What is the role of (a) intention, and (b) unconscionability in resulting and constructive trusts?

chapter 5

Trustees' Powers and Duties

After reading this chapter, you will be able to understand:

- the fiduciary relationship and fiduciary duties
- who may be a trustee
- how trustees are appointed and removed
- the duties and powers of trustees
- the express or statutory powers of trustees and how these must be exercised
- the relationship between trustees and beneficiaries, including the exercise of the duty of care and the powers of maintenance and advancement
- how trustees incur and avoid liability.

5.1 Introduction

The position of trustee is onerous and involves a range of obligations or duties, as well as various powers enabling them to carry out the functions of the role. You will discover that these powers and duties are inextricably linked, and for every power there are corresponding duties, sometimes specific to the power but always governed, at least, by the general overriding duties.

A trustee is regarded as a person who stands in a fiduciary position in respect of others and the property that he or she manages, so first of all we need to consider what the characteristics of this fiduciary role are.

5.2 Fiduciaries

Broadly speaking, a fiduciary relationship arises where one individual places trust and confidence in another to manage and protect property or money. The person in whom that trust is placed is referred to as a fiduciary. Examples of recognised fiduciary relationships are:

- trustee/beneficiary (*Keech v Sandford* (1726) 2 Eq Cas Abr 741);
- solicitor/client (*Re Hallett's Estate* (1880) 13 Ch D 696, CA);
- corporate director/company (*Regal (Hastings) Ltd v Gulliver* [1967] 2 AC 134);
- partners in commercial partnerships (*Featherstonhaugh v Fenwick* (1810) 34 ER 115);
- executor/heir (*Re Diplock* [1948] Ch 465);

- agent/principal (*O'Sullivan v Management Agency and Music Ltd* [1985] QB 428); and
- parties to a joint venture (*Murad v Al-Saraj* [2005] EWCA Civ 959, *Glenn & KEA Investments Ltd v Watson* [2018] EWHC 2016 (Ch)).

These relationships are ones where a service is carried out by the fiduciary on behalf of the person who has entrusted the fiduciary. Consequently, where there is a fiduciary relationship between one party and another, there are duties of loyalty and fidelity. The fiduciary is expected to act honestly and in good faith. Fiduciaries may of course be appointed under contracts to carry out services, and where the transaction is a commercial one at arm's length, the court may find that it is not a fiduciary one (for example the relationship between a broker and a finance house was held not to be fiduciary in *Indata Equipment Supplies Ltd (t/a Autofleet) v ACL Ltd* [1998] 1 BCLC 412). However, it has been stated by Slade J in *English v Dedham Vale Properties* [1978] 1 WLR 93 that

> the categories of fiduciary relationships … should (not) be regarded as falling into a limited number of straight-jackets or as being necessarily closed. They are, after all, no more than formulae for equitable relief.

Millett LJ gives us a working definition in the case of *Bristol and West Building Society v Mothew* [1998] 1 Ch:

> A fiduciary is someone who has undertaken to act for or on behalf of another in a particular matter in circumstances which give rise to a relationship of trust and confidence. The distinguishing obligation of a fiduciary is the obligation of loyalty … This core liability has several facets. A fiduciary must act in good faith; he must not make a profit out of his trust; he must not place himself in a position where his duty and his interest may conflict; he may not act for his own benefit or the benefit of a third person without the informed consent of his principal. This is not intended to be an exhaustive list, but it is sufficient to indicate the nature of fiduciary obligations. They are the defining characteristics of the fiduciary.

These principles have been more recently confirmed by Neuberger LJ in *Sinclair Investments (UK) Ltd v Versailles Trade Finance Ltd (in administration)* [2012] Ch 453 at 470, where he stated:

> The distinguishing obligation of a fiduciary is the obligation of loyalty which has several features: (i) a fiduciary must act in good faith; (ii) he must not make an unauthorised profit out of his trust; (iii) he must not place himself in a position where his duty and his interest may conflict; (iv) he may not act for his own benefit or the benefit of a third person without the informed consent of his principal.

5.2.1 Duty not to profit

> It is an inflexible rule of a Court of Equity that a person in a fiduciary position ... is not, unless otherwise provided, entitled to make a profit; he is not allowed to put himself in a position where his interest and duty conflict. (*Bray v Ford* [1896] AC 44, per Lord Herschell; see also *Keech v Sandford* (1726) 2 Eq Cas Abr 741)

As explained by Lord Russell in *Regal (Hastings) Ltd v Gulliver* [1967] 2 AC 134:

> The rule of equity which insists on those, who by use of a fiduciary position make a profit, being liable to account for that profit, in no way depends on fraud, or absence of bona fides ... The liability arises from the mere fact of a profit having, in the stated circumstances, been made.

Because fiduciaries are entrusted to act on behalf of others, equity adopts a strict approach to this rule. For example, in the case of trusts, it used to be the case that a trustee could not be remunerated for his or her services. Today, trustees may be compensated for expenses, and professional trustees may make reasonable charges (see for example the Trustee Act 2000, ss 29 and s 31, and below at **5.8**). Indeed, as in other situations where one party performs a service for another, there may be express arrangements in place for remuneration - for example in a trust deed or contract of agency. The strict approach of equity can be seen, however, in the case of *Guinness v Saunders* [1990] 2 AC 663. Here there was a procedure whereby the director could be remunerated, but that procedure had not in the circumstances been followed. The House of Lords held that the payment awarded to the director was made in breach of this rule.

A similarly strict approach can be seen in the case of *Boardman v Phipps* [1967] 2 AC 46, where the solicitor to the trust, with the collaboration of one of the beneficiaries, invested trust monies and some of his own money in shares, knowledge of which had come to his notice as a result of his position vis-à-vis the trust. The shares did well, and both the solicitor and the trust benefitted. However, the House of Lords held that the solicitor held his own shares on trust for the beneficiaries because he could not be allowed to profit from his position. Exceptionally in this case, the court made an award of 'quantum meruit' in recognition of the good services that he had undertaken on behalf of the trust. The question is always whether 'the trustee acquire[d] the position in which he drew the remuneration by virtue of his position as trustee' (per Cohen J in *Re Macadam* [1946] Ch 730). In *Macadam*, a trustee was elected as a company director - and consequently entitled to receive remuneration - as a result of trustees using their voting powers. The court held that the trustee held any benefit on a constructive trust for the beneficiaries.

Guinness (above) and other cases illustrate a breach of fiduciary duty in non-trustee cases, and any profits made as a result are to be held on trust for those beneficially entitled. These include situations where a duty of loyalty was owed and was breached by the taking of a bribe/secret commission. See for example *AG for Hong Kong v Reid* [1994] 1 AC 324, *Reading v AG* [1951] AC 507 and *FHR European Ventures LLP v Cedar Capital Partners LLC* [2014] Ch 1 (above at **4.3.1**).

5.2.2 Conflict of interests

An illustration of this rule can be found in the case of *Guinness v Saunders* (above). Here one of the directors (Ward) was paid £5.2m for assisting in the takeover of Distillers by Guinness. The decision regarding this remuneration was made by Saunders but not by a committee of the board of Guinness as established under its own rules. Ward's fee was dependent on the value of the takeover bid. The court held that there was a clear conflict of interests here because Ward had a self-interest in getting as high a price as possible for the takeover, whereas Guinness had an interest in negotiating a low price for the takeover of Distillers.

5.2.2.1 Self-dealing

This rule is that the fiduciary cannot purchase the property entrusted to him or her in a fiduciary role. This is known as the self-dealing rule, and, put at its simplest, the fiduciary cannot be purchaser and seller of the same property because the interests of the purchaser and seller are different. This stems from *Ex parte Lacey* (1802) 31 ER 1228, followed in *Holder v Holder* [1968] 3 WLR 229. However, on appeal in *Holder v Holder* [1968] Ch 353, the Court held that the transaction could not be challenged by a beneficiary (it was unimpeachable) if: (a) the accused fiduciary (here an executor) had barely acted in that role; and (b) the beneficiary had acquiesced in the transaction. The true interpretation of the rule was that the purchase was voidable by the beneficiary within a reasonable time. The court may also retrospectively endorse such a transaction – see *Mills v Mills* [2015] EWHC 1522 (Ch).

5.2.2.2 Fair dealing

In contrast to the above, where the fiduciary either obtains the informed consent of the beneficiaries or those for whom he or she acts (see below) or is no longer in a position where there is a conflict of interests, then the self-dealing rule may give way to the fair-dealing rule. In the case of *Tito* v *Waddell* [1977] Ch 106, Megarry VC (obiter) differentiated these two rules:

> The self-dealing rule is ... that if a trustee sells the trust property to himself, the sale is voidable by any beneficiary ex debito justitiae, however fair the transaction. The fair-dealing rule is ... that if a trustee purchases the beneficial interest of any of his beneficiaries, the transaction is not voidable ex debito justitiae, but can be set aside by the beneficiary unless the trustee can show that he has taken no advantage of his position and has made full disclosure to the beneficiary, and that the transaction is fair and honest.

5.2.3 Acting with informed consent

As we shall see later, and as is implied above, a trustee may avoid liability by showing that the beneficiaries have consented to the breach of trust, provided that this consent is given freely, is fully informed, and all the beneficiaries have full capacity to give consent. Where a fiduciary acts for his or her own benefit, the courts have adopted varying degrees of latitude where informed consent has been provided.

These duties apply to all fiduciaries but should be kept in mind in particular when we consider trustees.

5.3 Who may be a trustee?

Anyone may be a trustee provided they have sufficient capacity. A child may in principle be a trustee, but a child cannot by law be the legal owner of land (Law of Property Act 1925, s 20). Therefore if the trust property is land, the appointment of a child as trustee would be inappropriate. Similarly, although a child may enter into contracts and therefore as a trustee manage trust property (other than land), these contracts may be voidable on reaching majority. Usually, therefore, minors (those under 18) are not appointed as trustees.

Any competent adult may be appointed as a trustee provided that he or she is habitually resident in the jurisdiction of the UK. Absentee trustees may be removed. Provided he or she is competent, the trustee need not be a professional trustee, and indeed in family trusts it is not unusual to find relatives appointed as trustees. The settlor him- or herself may be a trustee, as may one or more of the beneficiaries. The trustee may, however, be a professional trustee, such as a solicitor, or may be a corporate body having a separate legal personality, and indeed large trusts, such as pension funds or investment trusts, are managed by corporate trustees.

Where the trust property is land, there need to be two trustees in order to give a valid receipt for any sale of the land (Law of Property Act 1925, s 27(2) and Trustee Act 1925, s 14(2)), and there cannot be more than four trustees registered as legal owners of land (Trustee Act 1925, s 34(2)). With other forms of property, only one trustee is needed in principle, although it makes sense to have more than one for continuity (they are unlikely to die at the same time so the surviving trustee can appoint a replacement). Where the trustee is a trust corporation with its own legal personality then there is less likely to be a problem of trustees' dying or retiring.

The trustees to be appointed are named in the trust instrument. Where this is by a will, it is not unusual to find that the executors of the will are also named as trustees, although this does not have to be the case. A nominated trustee is not compelled to accept the post. A trustee may refuse the appointment – it can be quite an onerous task, as we shall see – and the best course of action is to do this by deed, but there have been cases where the courts have inferred a disclaimer from the circumstances (*Re Clout and Frewer's Contract* [1924] 2 Ch 230). Once the trusteeship has been accepted, it is not possible to disclaim, and a trustee wishing to retire must consider the other options set out below.

There is a maxim that **'a trust will not fail for want of a trustee'**. If necessary, therefore, the court will appoint a trustee under s 41 of the Trustee Act 1925, or the Public Trustee will intervene.

> **41 Power of court to appoint new trustees**
>
> (1) The court may, whenever it is expedient to appoint a new trustee or new trustees, and it is found inexpedient difficult or impracticable so to do without the assistance of the court, make an order appointing a new trustee or new trustees either in substitution for or in addition to any existing trustees or trustees, or although there is no existing trustee.
>
> In particular and without prejudice to the generality of the foregoing provision, the court may make an order appointing a new trustee in substitution for a trustee who lacks capacity to exercise his functions as a trustee, or is a bankrupt, or is a corporation which is in liquidation or has been dissolved.

The use of s 41 is not to be undertaken lightly as applications to court are expensive and potentially can result in unexpected outcomes. The applicable principles were laid down in *Ledderstedt v Broers* (1884) 9 App Cas 371 and as explained by Lewison J in *Thomas & Agnes Carvel Foundation v Carvel* [2007] EWHC 1314: 'the overriding consideration is ... whether the trusts are being properly executed; or as [Lord Blackburn] put it ... the main guide must be "the welfare of the beneficiaries".'

Additional trustees may be appointed by existing trustees if this is thought necessary (s 36(6)). Such appointments must be in writing and are permitted in the following circumstances:

- where the trustees wish to appoint additional trustees – this is restricted so that the total number of trustees must not exceed four;
- where a trustee wishes to retire – a replacement may be appointed; or
- where a trustee dies and a replacement is needed.

Section 36(6) of the Trustee Act 1925 states:

> Where, in the case of any trust, there are not more than three trustees—
>
> (a) the person or persons nominated for the purpose of appointing new trustees by the instrument, if any, creating the trust; or
>
> (b) if there is no such person, or no such person able and willing to act, then the trustee or trustees for the time being;
>
> may, by writing, appoint another person or other persons to be an additional trustee or additional trustees, but it shall not be obligatory to appoint any additional trustee, unless the instrument, if any, creating the trust, or any

statutory enactment provides to the contrary, nor shall the number of trustees be increased beyond four by virtue of any such appointment.

5.4 The removal and retirement of trustees

There are a number of circumstances where it might be desirable or necessary to end the appointment of a trustee, for example because a solicitor trustee retires from practice or a trustee is planning on living abroad or being out of the UK for an extended period of time. Alternatively, the beneficiaries or other trustees may be dissatisfied with the conduct of one of the trustees and wish to have him or her removed and replaced.

The settlor may have made express provision in the trust instrument regarding the appointment of further trustees.

A trustee wishing to retire under an express power in the trust instrument authorising his or her retirement may do so. It is, however, usually more sensible to use the statutory powers as they enable the vesting of the trust property in the continuing or new trustees.

However, a sole trustee or group of trustees all wishing to retire at the same time will not effectively divest themselves of their fiduciary responsibilities without the requisite number of replacement trustees being appointed at the same time and the trust property being properly vested in the replacements.

Therefore, the sensible course of action is for the trustee or trustees who wish to retire to ensure that proper arrangements are in place for the succession to the trusteeship when they retire, normally by way of the exercise of the statutory power of appointment of new trustees.

Under s 39 of the Trustee Act 1925, a trustee can retire voluntarily (if two people remain after his or her retirement) but must do so by deed which is signed by all the relevant persons – ie the person who has power to appoint trustees and the continuing trustees, as well as the retiring trustee.

Failing this, there is statutory provision under the Trustee Act 1925 for replacing trustees. This covers a number of situations:

- death of a last remaining trustee: the deceased trustee's personal representative(s) (either an executor if there is a will or administrator if there is no will) may take on the role (s 18(2)) or appoint a new trustee (s 36(1));
- death of a trustee leaving a diminished number of surviving trustees: the surviving trustees may appoint a new trustee (s 36(1));
- retirement of a trustee: this may be achieved by way of a deed requesting to be discharged from the duties of a trustee (s 39) to which the remaining trustees must consent, *or* requesting to be discharged and the appointment of a new trustee by the remaining trustees under s 36(1). In the absence of

disagreement, the usual method on retirement would be a deed of retirement and appointment of new trustee, which all the relevant parties sign and in which the title to the trust assets is transferred from the old to the new trustees.

- removal of a trustee: this may arise in cases of continuous absence from the UK of over a year or due to lack of capacity, or as a result of the trustee having been found unfit to be a trustee due to bankruptcy or a criminal conviction for dishonesty (s 36(1));
- removal by the court under s 41: this is usually in circumstances where the trustee is unwilling to vacate the office and the court is required to intervene because it would be 'difficult or impracticable to [remove the trustee] without the assistance of the court'. Similarly, the court might be approached where there was a request to remove a nominated trustee due to an actual or potential conflict of interests – *Re Weetman (Deceased)* [2015] EWHC 1166 (Ch). Usually the court will appoint a replacement at the same time.

One of the areas of contention when a trustee seeks to retire is the question of whether he or she should be discharged from his or her duties under the trust and indemnified against any breaches of trust. A trustee has a right of indemnity out of the trust fund for administrative expenses and other liabilities properly incurred. When a trustee therefore retires or is removed, the question is whether or not the lien is enough protection for the departing trustee or whether express indemnities need to be included in the deed of retirement.

Section 19 of the Trusts of Land and Appointment of Trustees Act 1996 further provides that the beneficiaries may direct a trustee to retire provided that at least two trustees or one trust corporation remain, and either a new trustee is appointed at the same time or the other trustees consent to the removal. Note the requirements of the legislation below:

> **19 Appointment and retirement of trustee at instance of beneficiaries**
>
> (1) This section applies in the case of a trust where—
>
> (a) there is no person nominated for the purpose of appointing new trustees by the instrument, if any, creating the trust, and
>
> (b) the beneficiaries under the trust are of full age and capacity and (taken together) are absolutely entitled to the property subject to the trust.
>
> (2) The beneficiaries may give a direction or directions of either or both of the following descriptions—
>
> (a) a written direction to a trustee or trustees to retire from the trust, and
>
> (b) a written direction to the trustees or trustee for the time being (or, if there are none, to the personal representative of the last person who was a trustee) to appoint by writing to be a trustee or trustees the person or persons specified in the direction.

(3) Where—
   (a) a trustee has been given a direction under subsection (2)(a),
   (b) reasonable arrangements have been made for the protection of any rights of his in connection with the trust,
   (c) after he has retired there will be either a trust corporation or at least two persons to act as trustees to perform the trust, and
   (d) either another person is to be appointed to be a new trustee on his retirement (whether in compliance with a direction under subsection (2)(b) or otherwise) or the continuing trustees by deed consent to his retirement,

   he shall make a deed declaring his retirement and shall be deemed to have retired and be discharged from the trust.

(4) Where a trustee retires under subsection (3) he and the continuing trustees (together with any new trustee) shall (subject to any arrangements for the protection of his rights) do anything necessary to vest the trust property in the continuing trustees (or the continuing and new trustees).

(5) This section has effect subject to the restrictions imposed by the Trustee Act 1925 on the number of trustees.

5.5 What must trustees do?

A trustee has both powers and duties. The former are discretionary in nature; the latter are mandatory. The exercise of the former may, however, be subject to mandatory rules, so that if the trustee decides to exercise a power, he or she must do so in a particular way or subject to certain guidelines.

There are certain general expectations of trustees (which also overlap with the general expectations of others in fiduciary roles), for example:

- to act even-handedly across the beneficiaries (ie not to show bias or favouritism). This can most easily be seen in relation to a successive interest trust, where it is essential for the trustees to maintain a balance between providing an income to the life tenant whilst protecting the capital for the remainderman (*Re Whiteley* (1886) 33 Ch D 347);
- to act in the best interests of the beneficiaries (*Buttle v Saunders* [1950] 2 All ER 193);
- to keep records and produce accounts; and
- to keep the beneficiaries informed (see *Lewis v Tamplin* [2018] EWHC 777 (Ch) for a recent consideration of this long-rumbling issue).

One of the first duties of the trustees is to locate or ascertain the trust property and determine who the beneficiaries are. Both these tasks are essential if the trustees are to carry out their fundamental duty, which is to administer the trust property in the best interests of the beneficiaries and to distribute it according to the settlor's wishes.

Sometimes this is quite straightforward, for example in a small private express family trust where the family home is left 'to my wife for life and in remainder to be divided equally between my surviving children', but where a trust provides for successive interests or involves a range of assets, it might be more complex. Consequently, while the duties of trustees will be similar in all trusts – including charitable trusts – the powers may vary quite considerably.

The trustees have the power to realise certain assets of the trust and to reinvest the value of these assets unless the trust deed stipulates otherwise. So, for example, trustees might decide to sell real estate belonging to the trust and reinvest the proceeds in a portfolio of shares. Where the trust includes personal property or reality (land and/or buildings), the trustees have a duty to insure the property and secure it, or more generally to safeguard the trust assets. Trustees very rarely, however, have to consult with the beneficiaries or obtain their consent. However, when taking decisions, the trustees must act unanimously (*Luke v South Kensington Hotel Co* (1879) LR 11 ChD 121) unless authorised by the court or trust instrument.

The powers and duties of trustees are governed by case law and by statute (the Trustee Acts 1925 and 2000, the Inheritance and Trustees' Powers Act 2014 and the Trusts of Land and Appointment of Trustees Act 1996). However, it is also important to note that the starting point should always be the trust deed, if there is one, because express provisions can override the statutory provisions.

The drafting of a trust deed, therefore, is critical not only to the creation of the trust but also to its ongoing administration. The settlor may vary the scope of the trustees' powers and also, to a certain extent, limit or exclude the trustees' liability for breach of duty. When we talk about the statutory or case law-based provisions, we are referring to the default provisions that would apply if there were no trust deed or if the deed were silent or unclear on a particular matter.

As indicated above, duties are mandatory and must be followed. If in breach of a duty, a trustee may be sued personally by the beneficiaries and may have to pay compensation or be ordered to, for example, restore property to the trust from his or her own funds. *Buttle v Saunders* [1950] 2 All ER 193 is a case relating to trust investments where the trustees were held liable to the beneficiaries for breach of their duty to safeguard the assets of the trust, which is a fundamental common law duty.

In this chapter we will consider the following duties:

- the common law duty of care and the duty of care under the Trustee Act 2000 (see **5.6**);
- duties specific to the powers of investment and delegation (see **5.7.1** and **5.7.2**).

5.6 The duty of care

Section 1 of the Trustee Act 2000 states:

> (1) Whenever the duty under this subsection applies to a trustee, he must exercise such care and skill as is reasonable in the circumstances, having regard in particular—
>
> (a) to any special knowledge or experience that he has or holds himself out as having, and
>
> (b) if he acts as trustee in the course of a business or profession, to any special knowledge or experience that it is reasonable to expect of a person acting in the course of that kind of business or profession.
>
> (2) In this Act the duty under subsection (1) is called 'the duty of care'.

This is not a radical departure from the position under the common law. In *Speight v Gaunt* (1883) 9 App Cas 1, we find the prudent man of business standard, and in the later case of *Bartlett v Barclays Bank Trust Co Ltd (No 2)* [1980] Ch 515, we find a higher standard of care being expected where the trustee is a trust corporation or holds itself out to have particular expertise or specialised knowledge. There is, therefore, a different standard of care required of a lay trustee, compared with a professional trustee. The court would take into account the individual's own knowledge and experience, and if the trustee is a professional then a higher standard will be imposed (see also the explanatory notes to the Act, para 13).

This is an overarching duty that applies to all of the powers considered below that may be conferred on a trustee, and it applies regardless of the source of the power, ie from the statute or via express provision.

The duty exists to provide a check against the wide powers of trustees under the Act, to protect the beneficiaries and to try to ensure that the trustees act prudently and carefully. It sets out clearly the duty of care for trustees and as such is the standard that must be met in order to avoid a negligence claim. Failure to comply with s 1 may result in liability to pay damages. You should note, however, that this section must be read in conjunction with 5.9 below on exclusion of liability.

5.7 Trustees' powers

Powers are discretionary in nature, which means that the trustees are not necessarily obliged to carry out the power, although they may be required to consider whether to exercise their discretion. The powers determine what the trustees are allowed to do, the extent of their authority, and they have developed over time in such a way that the source of the powers is a mixture of statutory and case law. Generally speaking, the court will not interfere with the exercise of trustees' discretions, although a beneficiary may have cause to complain to the court if the trustees are failing to consider their powers at all, exercise such powers ultra vires (ie beyond the mandate they are given) or are mala fides (ie act in bad faith) in their considerations. When exercising a power, the trustee must act within its terms, and so a trustee may be liable if he or she acts in excess of these powers. An example can be found in the case of *Turner v Turner* [1984] Ch 100, in which the court held that trustees appointed under a discretionary trust

> when exercising their discretionary powers were under a fiduciary duty to consider all the issues pertinent to each proposed appointment prior to its execution, and, since they were unaware that they had any discretion and did not read or understand the effect of the documents they were signing, it followed that they never had applied their minds to the exercise of their discretion and were in breach of that duty; and that, accordingly, the power to appoint had not been validly exercised ...

While the settlor may make express provision for the trustees to have various powers, the most common are:

- investment of the trust fund;
- delegation of powers by trustees;
- payment of income for the maintenance of beneficiaries and payment of capital for the advancement of beneficiaries.

In practice, solicitors drafting wills and/or trust deeds are likely to refer to standard provisions as set out in the Standard Provisions of the Society of Trust and Estate Practitioners (STEP). This has the advantage of keeping costs down for clients and ensuring that provisions are not inadvertently omitted. However, the use of these can also result in wills and trust deeds that are not always intelligible to the lay person, including testators, settlors and executors/trustees.

5.7.1 The power of investment

Investment is unique in that the trustees are under a duty to invest but also have a power to invest. The duty to invest comes from the common law (*Re Wragg* [1919] 2 Ch 58) but clearly ties in with other fundamental duties that the trustees owe, such as safeguarding the trust assets and acting in the best interests of the beneficiaries. In the Privy Council case of *Dominica Social Security Board v Nature Island Investment Co Ltd* [2008] UKPC 19, it was held that

> The word 'investment' did not have a precise legal meaning, but its natural meaning in a financial context was the acquisition of an asset to be held as a source of income.

5.7.1.1 Historical developments

The current law regarding the power to invest is found in the Trustee Act 2000, but it is useful and interesting to look at the position prior to 2000. The Trustee Act 2000 replaced the Trustee Investments Act 1961 where, unless there were express provisions in the trust deed, the choice of investments was limited to those mentioned in the schedules to the Act. These permitted investments were financial investments and were divided into two categories: narrow- and wide-range. Wide-range investments were the riskier investments, such as shares in limited companies, and narrow-range investments included the safer options of bonds or savings accounts. If trustees wanted to invest in the wide-range category, they had to separate the fund into two and comply with certain restrictions as to the amount that could be invested in the wide-range category. This severely curtailed the power of trustees to 'play the market'.

In the Law Commission Report (No 260), 'Trustees' Powers and Duties', that led to the passing of the Trustee Act 2000, these fund-splitting requirements were referred to as 'crude and administratively burdensome'. Indeed the provisions of the 1961 Act were viewed with such disdain that Lord Goodhart commented during the second reading of the Trustee Bill in 2000:

> The 1961 Act created an extremely complex and restrictive structure ... which made reliance on the statutory powers very unattractive. Indeed, my view – and I am not entirely joking – was that any lawyer drafting a trust deed who failed to include a much wider power of investment overriding the powers under the 1961 Act would have been guilty of professional negligence.

This quote also indicates to us the importance of the trust deed and the ability of the settlor to shape the powers of the trustees via an express provision, even where statute sets out a very clear system or regime.

Fortunately, the Trustee Act 2000 contains a wide power of investment under s 3, which we shall now turn to.

5.7.1.2 The general power of investment

Section 3(1) of the Trustee Act 2000 states that 'a trustee may make any kind of investment that he could make as if he were absolutely entitled to the assets of the trust'. This confirms a gradual development in the common law prior to the passing of the Act which conferred greater autonomy on trustees to make investments. *Speight v Gaunt* (1883) 9 App Cas 1 was one of the early leading cases on trustees' duties as regards investment (and also the appointment of agents), and here it was held that the trustee would not be liable for losses to the trust if he acted as the prudent man following the usual and regular course of business (cf *Re Whiteley* (1886) 33 Ch D 347, where it was found that this standard had not been met). Much more recently, the case of *Nestle v National Westminster Bank Plc* [1993] 1 WLR 1260 has endorsed this approach. Leggatt LJ, considering the duty of the bank, expressed it thus:

> It was ... a duty 'to take such care as an ordinary prudent man would take if he were minded to make an investment for the benefit of other people for whom he felt morally bound to provide' [referring to *Re Whiteley* (above) at 355]. The trustee must have regard 'not only to the interests of those who are entitled to the income, but to the interests of those who will take in future'

> (ibid) … 'A trustee must not choose investments other than those which the terms of his trust permit' [referring to *Speight v Gaunt* (above) at 19]. [Further] the trustee must also 'avoid all investments of that class that are attended with hazard' [referring to *Learoyd v Whiteley* (1887) 12 App Cas 727, 733]. The power of investment 'must be exercised so as to yield the best return for the beneficiaries, judged in relation to the risks of the investments in question; and the prospects of the yield of income and capital appreciation both have to be considered in judging the return from the investment' [referring to *Cowan v Scargill* [1985] Ch 270, 287A].

In this case the bank was not held liable.

The power under the Trustee Act 2000 enables the trustees to do virtually anything with the trust fund, although there are limits of course and we will consider the duties later in this section.

There is no mention in s 3 of the types of investments that may or may not be selected and no definition of investment is given in the Act. Again it is interesting to consider the historical position in this regard. Traditionally, investment could only be for the purposes of income production (*Re Wragg* (above)) so, for example, the trustees could buy a house to rent out or place money in a savings account in order to generate interest on it. The idea of investing for capital growth, ie that the asset itself, such as the house, would increase in value, was not considered as a viable objective for investment by trustees. There were practical reasons for this, going back to the 19th century, not least because successive interest trusts (referred to as strict settlements) were common then, so it was essential for trustees to ensure that income was being produced to support the person who had the immediate beneficial interest for his or her lifetime (the life tenant – often a surviving spouse), rather than worrying too much about increasing the capital value of the fund for the remainder beneficiaries (eg the children).

However, by the 1980s, attitudes to investment were changing. In particular the privatisation of utilities and other services meant that cheap shares were released on to the market for the ordinary public to buy, and the purchase and sale of shares became much more diverse and widespread. Even before the Trustee Act 2000, the approach of the courts had changed. Certainly by the 1990s, cases such as *Harries v Church Commissioners for England* [1992] 1 WLR 1241 demonstrated the modern approach to investment that we now enjoy. In *Harries*, the court held that where property is held as an investment, the purposes of the trust will be best served by the trustees seeking to obtain the maximum return, whether this is by way of income received or growth in the value of the capital asset itself. Clearly it will depend on the type, structure and value of the trust fund in question, so it is not without its limitations.

This approach was supported by the Law Commission in its Report (No 260) – 'Trustees might legitimately invest in antique or silver paintings in the expectation that they will increase in value' – and by Parliament in para 22 of the explanatory notes to the 2000 Act.

Section 6 of the Trustee Act 2000 explicitly provides that the settlor may amend the statutory power via an express provision extending, restricting or indeed excluding s 3.

5.7.1.3 Investment in land

Section 8 of the Trustee Act 2000 authorises investments in freehold or leasehold land in the UK and also permits the land to be held either as an investment, for occupation by a beneficiary or for any other reason.

This also marks an expansion of the law. The previous default position did not permit trustees to invest in land without an express provision in the trust deed. It is also significant for the fact that it mentions the possibility of a beneficiary living in the property, which addressed the historical case law. According to *Re Power's Will Trusts* [1947] Ch 572, for example, even where there was an express power to invest in land, a beneficiary was not permitted to occupy the property. The underlying rationale behind this was of course to ensure that rental income was produced by renting to a third party.

This rather perverse reasoning of the court did not preclude a settlor making provision for a life tenant to occupy trust property, and indeed this was common if that life tenant was the surviving spouse and the family home was left on trust. The distinction lies in making new investments in property rather than placing on trust existing property.

Section 9 allows for the extension, exclusion and restriction of s 8 in the trust instrument.

5.7.1.4 Duties relating to investment

The Trustee Act 2000, s 1 duty of care (considered above) applies to investment, so the trustees must take reasonable care when selecting and managing investments.

Section 4 of the Trustee Act 2000 sets out the standard investment criteria. The trustees are required to have regard to the suitability of investments and the need for diversification of investments, although exactly how this applies to the trust will depend upon what is appropriate in the circumstances. Relevant factors include the structure of trust, the age and type of beneficiaries and the value of the fund. So, for example, it would be important to achieve a balance between income and capital growth in a successive interest trust. This approach also ensures that the trustees act in accordance with their duty to act impartially between the beneficiaries. It is also essential that the trustees review the investments regularly.

During the second reading of the Trustee Bill, Lord Goodhart stated:

> It may be perfectly reasonable for a £1million trust to gamble £20,000 on a speculative dot com business whereas it would plainly not be reasonable for the trustees of a £100,000 fund to put half of it into dot coms.

The requirement to consider the suitability and diversification of investments reflects the modern portfolio theory, which focuses on the risk level of the portfolio as a whole rather than the risk level of each individual investment. In *Nestle v National Westminster Bank Plc* (above), the court made specific reference to this theory.

More recently, in *Daniel v Tee* [2016] EWHC 1538 (Ch), the High Court considered the suitability of investments made by trustees of a family trust when they chose to invest a large portion of the fund in shares, including shares in risky technology sector companies. The court concluded that this strategy was one that no reasonable trustee could have made.

5.7.1.5 Ethical investments

A question that has been referred to the courts on a number of occasions is whether the trustees may take into account the personal view or requests of the settlor, the beneficiaries or indeed their own beliefs when investing. The Trustee Act 2000 did not address this point specifically, although para 23 of the Explanatory Notes makes reference to the possible inclusion of ethical considerations. During the second reading of the Bill, however, Lord Wilberforce took the view that it was not yet settled whether ethical considerations fell within the scope of the standard investment criteria.

In order to give the matter full consideration, it is necessary to look at the prior case law. The starting point is that trustees have a common law duty to act in the best interests of the beneficiaries, and this has been held, on numerous occasions, to mean the best financial interests of the beneficiaries.

In *Buttle v Saunders* (above), the trustees were selling a piece a land belonging to the trust and had orally agreed to sell the land. Subsequently, and before they had signed any paperwork, the trustees received a higher offer. However, the trustees felt morally obliged to complete the sale with the first buyer and did so. The court held that although the trustees may have followed what they considered to be the honourable course of action, their overriding duty was to the beneficiaries and this was to obtain the best price possible for the property. The trustees were therefore in breach of duty.

Following this approach, in *Cowan v Scargill* [1985] Ch 270, the court held that the trustees could not take their own views into account or the views they believed the beneficiaries may have in relation to a particular investment. This was in the context of the mineworkers' pension scheme and money from the fund being invested in overseas energy companies.

In the *Harries* case (above), however, the court sought to rationalise this strict rule somewhat. It was suggested here that trustees could pursue an ethical investment policy if the selected investments were financially sound. In other words, where the ethical investments could be shown to be as good as or better than the non-ethical investments, the principle of acting in the best financial interests of the beneficiaries would not be breached. It was acknowledged that there are many companies around to invest in and plenty of potential to make a good return.

Despite the relatively relaxed view in *Harries*, the guidance on this is by no means clear and trustees are still in a risky position if they choose to restrict investments. The best solution to the problem is where an express provision is included in the trust deed by the settlor stating that the trustees must avoid a particular type of investment.

A settlor having a particular wish to retain certain investments in the trust portfolio or desiring the trustees to choose a particular type of investment would in practice be encouraged by the draftsman to include these wishes in the trust deed or a separate letter of wishes. It would be unlikely that professional trustees would choose to invest in ethical investments in priority to other investments if they were not appropriate for the trust to invest in, nor without the authority of the trust deed or with the backing of a letter of wishes from the settlor.

5.7.1.6 Duty to take advice

Prior to exercising the power of investment, trustees must obtain and consider proper advice, having regard to the standard investment criteria (Trustee Act 2000, s 5; *Daniel v Tee* (above)). The trustees should obtain advice unless they reasonably conclude that in all the circumstances it is unnecessary or inappropriate (s 5(3)). Examples of situations where it might be unnecessary or inappropriate can be found in the Explanatory Notes to the Act (para 28) and include: where the trustees have sufficient knowledge or expertise themselves; or where the investment is so small that the cost of obtaining advice would be disproportionate.

'Proper advice' is defined in s 5(4) as 'the advice of a person who is reasonably believed by the trustees to be qualified to give it by virtue of his ability in and practical experience of financial matters related to the proposed investment'. It does not state that the adviser has to be acting in the course of a business or have relevant professional qualifications. In practice this provision is taken to mean that you seek appropriate advice from the right adviser, eg land advice from a land agent, heritage assets advice from, say, Sotheby's etc, and of course advice about stocks and shares from a suitable broker.

However, this should be read in light of s 19 of the Financial Services and Markets Act 2000 which states that anyone carrying on investment business should be authorised or exempt by the appropriate regulating body, which will include having the relevant qualifications. This provision does not bind the trustees as such but rather the provider of the advice, although given that such regulation exists it would seem reasonable for a trustee to consult a properly authorised individual.

Moreover, the trustees are bound by the duty to act in the best interests of the beneficiaries at all times and by the duty of care (see **5.6**). In *Daniel v Tee* (above) the court reiterated the importance of having an appropriate investment strategy before obtaining advice and of undertaking regular reviews (in accordance with s 4 above).

5.7.2 The power to delegate

There are two types of delegation – individual and collective – and they are quite different from each other.

5.7.2.1 Individual delegation

A trustee may delegate all of his or her functions to a third party under s 25 of the Trustee Act 1925 (as amended by the Trustee Delegation Act 1999 but not the Trustee Act 2000). This is done by power of attorney and can operate for a maximum of 12 months. A trustee may do this, for example, if the trustee knows that he or she will not be available to carry out his or her role as trustee for a short period of time.

However, there is a significant disadvantage to individual delegation as the trustee is strictly liable for the acts and defaults of the appointed agent. For this reason it is only used where absolutely necessary.

A trustee power of attorney might be used when a trustee is going into hospital or away on holiday at a time when the trust is actively engaged in transactions for which all the trustees may have to sign. If the trustee is going abroad for work or with a view to settling abroad, a power of attorney would be discouraged and the trustee would be asked to retire.

5.7.2.2 Collective delegation

The power to delegate allows the trustees to appoint an agent to carry out some of their functions for them. This is particularly attractive in relation to functions that require particular expertise or skills that the trustees do not possess, the best example being the investment of trust funds.

Again we must look at the default position under statute but would also look at the trust deed to see whether any express provisions exist.

Prior to the Trustee Act 2000, trustees could delegate administrative tasks only under s 23 of the Trustee Act 1925. They were not able to delegate any decision-making powers or discretions, including importantly the power to invest (*Rowland v Witherden* (1851) 3 Mac & G 568). This was a significant hindrance to trustees, and so it was common to find powers of delegation in trust deeds in order to avoid the restrictions of s 23.

The Law Commission Report (No 260) described the default rule under s 23 as

> … a serious impediment to the administration of trusts. Trusteeship is an increasingly specialised task that often requires professional skills that trustees may not have. Far from promoting the more conscientious discharge of the obligations of trusteeship, the prohibition on delegation of fiduciary discretions may force trustees to commit breaches of trust in order to achieve the most effective administration of the trust.

The report led to the provision trustees may now rely upon in s 11 of the Trustee Act 2000.

Section 11(2) allows trustees of non-charitable trusts to delegate their functions, except those listed in sub-paragraphs (a) to (d) which include, for example, decisions about distributing to beneficiaries and the power to appoint another trustee. Importantly, trustees may now, under the default provision, delegate their investment functions to an expert.

We must then look to s 12 in order to clarify who may be appointed as an agent. Section 12 states that the trustees may appoint one or more of their own number, so if one of the trustees has the necessary skills, he or she may act as the agent for all. It also states that the agent may not be one of the beneficiaries. There is no indication in the statute that the agent must be professionally qualified or acting in the course of a business, although any appointment would be subject to the general duty of care (see **5.6**).

It is therefore necessary to look at the duties of the trustees when appointing an agent to see whether these place any limits on the selection process.

Interestingly, the law prior to the Trustee Act 2000 was more specific about the type of agent. This would have been applicable where the trust deed contained an express power to appoint an agent, and the duty when selecting came from the case of *Re Vickery* [1931] 1 Ch 572. It was based upon the general duty of good faith of trustees and was described as being an ordinary subjective approach to act in good faith but with two further conditions. Trustees should:

- use their discretion when selecting; and
- only employ an agent to act in the usual course of his or her business.

Under *Vickery*, the trustee appointing an agent would only be liable for the acts of that agent if he or she were in wilful default of the above criteria.

This has been replaced by the Trustee Act 2000 provisions, but it does seem at odds with the taking of reasonable care to allow trustees to appoint another lay person to undertake investment powers on their behalf.

The Trustee Act 2000 sets out a number of relevant duties for trustees who are delegating. First is the s 1 duty of care, set out at **5.6**, so trustees must take reasonable care when selecting and monitoring the agent.

There are also further specific duties in relation to delegation. Section 15 sets out the requirements that trustees must follow if they are to delegate their asset management functions, including investment, acquisition, disposal and management of property. The trustees must prepare a written policy statement providing guidance to the agent. It should set out the objectives for the trust, including such matters as the desired balance between income and capital growth. The statement should also inform the agent of any restrictions in the trust deed, for example certain categories of investments to be avoided. The duty of care in s 1 applies to the preparation of the statement by the trustees.

Section 22(2) requires the trustees to review the policy statement and to revise and replace it as necessary. The trustees must also ensure that the statement is being complied with so they cannot sit back and let the agent act without any supervision.

Clearly there is a range of duties that trustees must comply with when delegating, and these are generally common sense matters of good practice. Trustees may wonder, therefore, whether they are liable for any mistakes made by the agent, as this will clearly affect the decisions made by trustees when appointing and monitoring their agents. Section 23 of the Trustee Act 2000 states that, unlike individual delegation under s 25 of the Trustee Act 1925, the trustees are not strictly or automatically liable for the acts or defaults of the agent. However, the trustees may be liable if they have failed to comply with the duty of care when selecting the agent, preparing the policy statement or reviewing matters during the agency period.

Policy agreements are necessary for any delegation by trustees of administrative work, so if the trust is large and employs an estate manager, even though he or she should be given a contract of employment, there is also a need to provide a policy statement as to what tasks are to be delegated, performance of which must be reviewed regularly.

Investment policy agreements do need care and in practice will be overlooked by less organised trustees. The Society of Trust and Estate Practitioners (STEP) has developed a suitable draft document to consider and provides members with regular updating of a suitable benchmark to use in such a policy document against which to judge whether the agent is providing the required level of service.

5.7.2.3 Nominees and custodians

Section 16 of the Trustee Act 2000 provides for the appointment of nominees. This was a new power in 2000 and allows trustees to appoint a third party, typically their agent, to hold the legal title to assets as nominee for the trustees. The rationale for using nominees is that it allows the agent to deal with an asset quickly, ie selling and buying shares without having to revert to the trustee on each occasion. Most brokers offer nominee accounts to hold stock electronically for investors for this very reason.

Under s 17 trustees may appoint custodians, and again this was a new statutory power. Custodians are simply people who undertake the safe custody of assets or title documents. Solicitors commonly offer this service and keep smaller items such as jewellery or documents such as share certificates for clients in their strong room. Where the trust property includes works of art or family heirlooms, the use of a custodian with appropriate facilities is very useful.

It is interesting to note that s 19 restricts the category of potential nominees and custodians to persons carrying on a business which consists of or includes acting as nominee or custodian. This is clearly in stark contrast to the wide group of potential agents under s 12.

5.7.3 Maintenance and advancement

5.7.3.1 Maintenance

The power of maintenance gives trustees the discretion to maintain an infant beneficiary.

According to the statutory provision under s 31 of the Trustee Act 1925, as amended by the Inheritance and Trustees' Powers Act 2014, the power applies in the following circumstances:

- Trustees may use the **income** arising from the fund (examples of income are interest, rent and dividends).
- It can be applied for the **maintenance, education or benefit** of the beneficiary. The definition of this is interpreted very widely by the courts. While the beneficiary is an infant, payment is discretionary.
- Payments are usually made to a parent or guardian of the child, or sometimes directly to a third party such as a school. Trustees should obtain a receipt for their records.
- The power can be used to maintain a beneficiary under the age of 18, unless this age limit has been amended in the trust deed.
- Once a child reaches 18, he or she then becomes entitled to receive the income on his or her share and the payment is no longer discretionary.

The requirement of reasonableness

Section 31 of the Trustee Act 1925 states that the trustees may pay out such sum from the income as is reasonable. This means that a payment could be challenged at a later date, and so it became common practice for trust deeds to amend s 31 and remove the requirement of reasonableness from the power of maintenance in order to protect trustees. For example, it was often left to the discretion of the trustees as to whether the power was exercised and, if so, how.

As a result of this widespread practice, the Inheritance and Trustees' Powers Act 2014 amends s 31 so that the default rule now is that trustees have an unfettered discretion when deciding whether and how to use the power of maintenance. However, it only applies to trusts created or interests arising on or after 1 October 2014. So, older trusts and interests will still be bound by the original wording of s 31, subject to any express provision in the deed.

Note that if income is not distributed via the power of maintenance, it must be accumulated in the trust and distributed to the beneficiary when he or she becomes entitled to his or her share of the capital.

5.7.3.2 Advancement

The power of advancement provides trustees with the discretion to give a beneficiary some of the capital at an earlier date than that stated in the trust deed. For example, the settlor may have specified that the beneficiaries receive their share at the age of 25, but one of them may require a lump sum at the age of 20 to help start up a new business venture.

Section 32 of the Trustee Act 1925 sets out the power of advancement and states that it applies in the following way:

- The trustees may pay out money from the **capital** of the trust fund.
- It may be used for the **advancement or benefit** or the beneficiary. Again this is interpreted widely (*Re Pilkington's Will Trusts* [1964] AC 612) to mean any use of the money which will improve the material situation of the beneficiary, or indeed it may be used to discharge a moral obligation (*Re Clore's Settlement Trusts* [1966] 1 WLR 955 – in which the court upheld payments to charities set up by the settlor). See, however, *X v A* [2005] EWCC 2706, in which the court refused to allow trustees to make an advancement to a beneficiary so that she could pay this to a charity.
- The beneficiary is required to bring any advancement received into account upon final distribution, ie it is deducted from his or her final share.
- Consent must be obtained from anyone with a prior interest in possession.

Limits on the amount that may be distributed

Section 32 of the Trustee Act 1925 states that the trustees may only advance up to one half of the vested or presumptive share of a beneficiary. Again, it was common practice to include an express provision in the trust deed amending or removing this restriction. The Inheritance and Trustees' Powers Act 2014 has now amended s 32 and removed the limit of one half. The new rule applies to trusts created or interests arising on or after 1 October 2014, and prior to that date the one half limit remains in place.

The 2014 Act has also clarified that trustees may advance assets to beneficiaries as well as cash.

In practice, sometimes trusts become uneconomic to run and everyone would like to bring them to an end early. The new law is welcome as it enables the power of advancement to be used to bring a trust to an end before the vesting date; whereas the old version meant that, without an express amendment to the statutory provision, it was not possible to bring a trust to an end early unless all the beneficiaries agreed, were of age and capacity and together absolutely entitled to the beneficial interests.

5.7.3.3 The duty of care for maintenance and advancement

The relevant duty for these powers is the old common law duty from *Speight v Gaunt* (above), rather than s 1 of the Trustee Act 2000. The standard of care that must be borne in mind by trustees when deciding whether to use the powers of maintenance and advancement, and then how much to distribute, is to act as a prudent man of business managing his own affairs.

In the context of advancement, this means the trustees must be satisfied that the advancement would be for the benefit of the beneficiary. They do not need to obtain evidence that the money has been applied in a particular way, but should at least enquire as to its application (*Re Pauling's Settlement Trusts (No 1)* [1964] Ch 303).

Note that powers of maintenance and advancement are discretionary. The infant beneficiaries are not entitled to be maintained or to demand some of the capital early, and the courts are usually reluctant to interfere with decisions of the trustees in these matters unless they relate to an issue such as the reasonableness of a payment under s 31, where there is a specific ground for challenge.

It would have to be a highly valuable trust to challenge the refusal of maintenance through the courts – the costs of taking this action would be high and there would be no guaranteed chance of success. However, it might be part of a bigger dispute which might be evidence of the need to remove a trustee who was not acting in the best interests of the beneficiaries.

5.8 Remuneration

It is very common for trust deeds to include a charging clause, and realistically a professional trustee would not agree to act if there were no agreement for him or her to be paid.

Payment for trustees can be authorised via the deed, but it is also possible for the beneficiaries to collectively agree a payment, provided that they all have the necessary capacity, which includes being at least 18. The court can also, exceptionally, authorise payment and has done so in cases such as *Boardman v Phipps* [1967] 2 AC 46.

However, until the Trustee Act 2000 there was no statutory authorisation for remuneration. The Law Commission took the view that modern trusteeship is a complex task requiring professional skills and therefore payment for services rendered was appropriate (if not essential due to market conditions, as mentioned above).

Accordingly, s 29 of the Trustee Act 2000 provides that a trustee who acts in a professional capacity is entitled to reasonable remuneration from the trust funds, so long as the other trustees agree in writing to the payment. Section 28(5) defines 'professional capacity' as acting in the course of a profession or business providing services in connection with the management or administration of trusts, and states that the services provided must fall within that type of work.

The payment is restricted to 'reasonable remuneration', which means reasonable in the circumstances for the provision of the particular services (s 29(3)). The explanatory notes at para 105 set out further guidance, including that regard must be had to the nature of the trust and the attributes of the trustee. Interestingly, s 29(4) states that payment can be made for services that could have been provided by a lay person, for example photocopying or simple record-keeping. The charges made by a professional acting for a trust were raised in *Pullan v Wilson* [2014] EWHC 126 (Ch):

> In my judgment, a professional trustee is not necessarily entitled to charge by reference to his normal or standard charging rates ... To hold otherwise would be to deprive a court of equity of any effective control over a trustee's remuneration.
>
> ... one must have regard to the nature and the value of the services which are performed, and to the propriety, reasonableness and proportionality of using the services of the level of fee earner who is providing them.

From this case it is clear that where there is a remuneration clause in the trust, s 29 will not apply.

In addition, s 31 allows trustees to claim back expenses properly incurred whilst acting on behalf of the trust, for example travel costs.

Members of the Law Society and STEP must draw to the attention of a testator the likely costs of acting as executor and trustee, should the testator wish to appoint them to either of these roles. It would therefore be usual in professionally drafted wills and trusts for the charging clause to be wide, to cover the costs of using agents and of undertaking work which a lay person could have undertaken. Some may even provide for honaria for certain trustees for undertaking particular tasks. It is important that those considering setting up trusts in which professional trustees are used balance likely costs against the value of the trust fund and the intended distribution to beneficiaries.

5.9 Exclusion from liability

Another common clause found in trust deeds is the exclusion clause (*Barnsley v Noble* [2016] EWCA Civ 799). This means a provision excusing the trustees from liability for wrongdoing. However, it is important to note that while such clauses may protect the trustees from liability for negligence, they cannot exclude liability for fraud or dishonesty. The leading case is *Armitage v Nurse* [1998] Ch 241. Here it was held that if trustees deliberately committed a breach in good faith, honestly believing they were acting in the best interests of the beneficiary, this did not amount to fraud, and an exclusion from liability clause could exempt the trustee even if he or she had been 'idle, imprudent, careless or wilful in discharging his [or her] functions.' This case is, moreover, authority for the proposition that a trustee will only be found liable for fraud if there is a fraudulent intention and proof of dishonesty.

This means that the protection afforded by the common law duty of care and s 1 of the Trustee Act 2000 as outlined in this chapter may be removed if the deed contains an exclusion from liability clause.

Unsurprisingly, the existence of such clauses is the cause of a great deal of debate amongst academics and the legal profession. The Law Commission has considered the issue on a number of occasions, both before and after the Trustee Act 2000, but did not make any recommendations to restrain the use of exclusion from liability clauses. Consequently the Act is silent on the matter.

Further discussion around this issue can be found in **Chapter 6** on breach of trust.

Professional practice seems to be that no professional trustee would act as trustee without a suitable clause for exclusion from liability. This is not because professional trustees would expect to act carelessly, but because trust administration is much more litigious than it used to be, and justifying actions as reasonable will always come down to a question of judgment, with which it is hard to be sure a court will agree.

5.10 Further reading

Gino Dal Pont, 'Wilful default revisited – liability for a co-trustee's defaults' (2001) *Conveyancer and Property Lawyer* 376–86.

LM Clements, 'Bringing trusts into the twenty-first century' (2004) *Web Journal of Current Legal Issues* 2.

Matthew Conaglen, 'A re-appraisal of the fiduciary self-dealing and fair-dealing rules' (2006) 65(2) *Cambridge Law Journal* 366–96.

David Harris, 'Investments by professional trustees in private companies and partnerships' (2005) *Private Client Business* 167–75.

William Moffett, 'Case Comment: Considering entitlement' (2018) 202 (Dec) *Trusts and Estates Law & Tax Journal* 4–8.

Shelly Saluja, 'The law relating to trustee exoneration clauses' (2014) *Trust Law International* 27–37.

Rosy Thornton, 'Ethical investments: a case of disjointed thinking' (2008) 67(2) *Cambridge Law Journal* 396–422.

David Hayton et al, *Underhill & Hayton Law of Trusts & Trustees*, 19th edn (LexisNexis, 2016).

Lynton Tucker et al, *Lewin on Trusts*, 20th edn (Sweet & Maxwell, 2018).

Trustees are pivotal in the administration of trusts and in giving effect to the settlor's intentions. For this reason the trust instrument is always the starting point for determining what they can do. The powers given to trustees may therefore be extensive or constrained. In the absence of specific provision and where not expressly excluded, the powers and duties of trustees are governed by the common law and by statute, notably the Trustee Act 1925, the Trustee Act 2000, the Trusts of Land and Appointment of Trustees Act 1996 and the Inheritance and Trustees' Powers Act 2014.

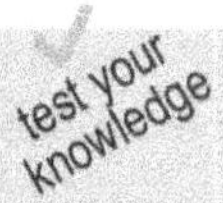

1 To what extent have trustees' powers of investment been liberated by the Trustee Act 2000?
2 What limitations on the trustees' power of advancement were addressed by provisions in the Inheritance and Trustees' Powers Act 2014?
3 Why is the ruling in the case of *Armitage v Nurse* considered by some to be controversial?
4 To what extent are trustees absolved from liability for the acts of their agents under the Trustee Act 2000?
5 Do you think that the standard of care in the Trustee Act 2000 is sufficient to safeguard beneficiaries?

chapter

6 Breach of Trust, Tracing and Remedies

After reading this chapter, you will be able to understand:

- the type of conduct that gives rise to a breach of trust
- the range of remedies available to the beneficiary
- the limits to the liability incurred by trustees and others
- the process of tracing trust property in common law and equity into the hands of the errant trustee and others in certain circumstances
- the interaction of common law and equity in the area of remedies.

6.1 Introduction

During the course of your study of equity and trusts, you will have considered situations where a breach of trust may arise, such as where a trustee fails to comply with one of his or her fiduciary duties. You will be aware by now that integral to the beneficiary principle is the need for a court to be able to order performance in favour of the beneficiary, and for there to be a beneficiary who has *locus standi* to bring an action (in other words, the right to bring an action in court). You may also have met the maxim that '**equity will not act in vain**', meaning that a court will be reluctant to exercise its equitable jurisdiction if an order cannot be enforced. Similarly you will have encountered the equitable maxims, '**He who seeks equity must do equity**' and '**He who comes to equity must come with clean hands**'. Affording a remedy to a claimant is fundamental to the origins of equity, as those who sought the intervention of the early Lord Chancellors did so because they could not find justice in the King's courts – the courts of common law – often because their particular claim fell outside the forms of action or procedural claims recognised by the King's courts. The availability of equitable remedies is not limited to cases of breach of trust; indeed one of the important consequences of the merger of the courts of equity and of common law in the late 19th century was that all courts could use equitable remedies. It should be remembered, however, that these are discretionary and predominantly personal remedies – operating *in personam* – although, as we shall see in the case of the trust, it appears that equity may provide remedies which recognise the proprietary claims of an aggrieved party and therefore operate *in rem* in certain circumstances.

In this chapter we will explore the issues that must be addressed when considering a breach of trust, including identifying when a breach has occurred, what harm has been caused by whom and to whom, who can be held liable for that breach and why, and if there are limits or defences to that liability. Once liability for breach is established, there is the question of what remedies are appropriate or possible in the circumstances, and whether these are only equitable or may also be common law remedies. Although we are focussing on breach of trust here, it is important to remember that one of the great contributions of equity was to enlarge the range of remedies available to claimants, for example by developing various forms of injunction, the order for specific performance and the idea of equitable compensation. Unsurprisingly therefore, we find in this chapter reference to remedies that may be encountered in other areas of the law – such as contract and tort.

It should also be noted that the civil aspect of a breach may not always be considered in isolation in practice. For example, if a trustee has stolen money from a trust fund, or has been engaged in some form of fraudulent conduct, then there would of course be criminal consequences as well. Here, however, we shall concentrate on civil liability.

One of the equitable maxims (see **Chapter 1**) is that '**equity acts in personam**', that is equity acts against an identified person. This goes back to the historical development of equity, where equity acted on a person's conscience. In consequence, it is often held that the remedies available in equity are personal, not proprietary. This is generally true, but sometimes it is necessary to bring a person within the 'net' of equity to hold them liable. Where trust property is misappropriated, equity offers a number of processes whereby that property can be brought back to the trust or the loss made good. One of these is the process of tracing trust property, which enables a claimant to find out what has happened to his or her property and literally to trace where it has gone. Once the property is traced then an order can be made against the person who has the property – or its equivalent. In this chapter we shall also be considering this process and the consequences that flow from it for the beneficiary.

6.2 Breach of trust

Breach of trust is not an isolated topic and clearly flows on from other areas already covered in this book, for example fiduciaries' and trustees' powers and duties. If a breach of trust results in loss to the trust fund or an unauthorised gain for the trustee then the trustee may be liable to compensate for the loss or to account for the profit made.

6.2.1 Identifying the breach

The first task is to identify the breach that has occurred. This may happen where the trustee:

(a) *does any act he ought not to do*, for example where the trustee acts in excess of the powers conferred on him or her, either under the trust deed or under statute. This might be, for example, purchasing an investment property outside the UK in breach of the power to buy land under s 8 of the Trustee Act 2000. Or it could involve a situation where the trustee has acted outside of the powers set out in the trust deed, such as investing in oil companies where there is a clear prohibition on doing so in the deed. The breach may be entirely innocent, as in the case of *Re Diplock* [1941] Ch 253 where executors paid out around £250,000, which was the residue of the deceased's estate, to some 130 charitable institutions thinking the bequest was valid. In fact it was found that the bequest – that the executors apply the residue for 'such charitable institution or institutions or other charitable or benevolent object or objects in England' – was invalid as the purposes were not wholly charitable (see **Chapter 3**). This was affirmed on appeal to the House of Lords (*Chichester Diocesan Fund and Board of Finance (Incorporated) v Simpson* [1944] AC 341);

(b) *fails to do something he or she ought to do*, most commonly failing to comply with one of the numerous duties imposed on trustees. Examples would be failing to distribute the trust property, or failing to maintain a balanced portfolio of investments.

Note that where the beneficiaries – provided they have capacity – have condoned a breach in advance then there will be no liability on the part of the trustee unless there is some form of inequitable conduct, such as undue influence, misrepresentation or fraud.

6.2.2 Causation

Once the breach has been identified, we must consider whether the breach is causally linked with any loss to the trust fund or to any profit made by the trustee, and the usual rule is that without such a link, there will be no liability.

The relevant test for causation here is the 'but for' test, and you may be familiar with this from your studies in other areas, such as tort law.

The relevant approach was clarified in *Target Holdings Ltd v Redferns* [1996] AC 421, a House of Lords case. The claimant company agreed to loan £1.5m for the purchase of two properties. The properties were being sold for £2m but unbeknown to the lender were in fact only worth £775,000, and so there was insufficient security given to the lender. The defendants were the solicitors acting for both the claimant company (lender) and the purchasers of the properties. The claimant had sent the money to the defendants some days before completion, but the defendants released the money to the purchasers before completion, which was in breach of trust. The purchase went ahead and subsequently the purchasers defaulted on the mortgage held by the lender. The claimant called in its security and discovered the disparity in valuation. There was insufficient money raised from the sale of the properties to repay the claimant, and so it sought to sue the solicitors in relation to the breach of trust that occurred with a view to making up the shortfall.

It was held that the solicitors were not liable because the evidence showed that even if the solicitors had released the money at the correct time, on completion, and had therefore not been in breach, this would not have changed the outcome because completion would have gone ahead in the same way and there would still have been insufficient security. In other words the loss would still have occurred even without the breach of trust. The court confirmed the use of the 'but for' test in the context of a breach of trust, ie looking at whether, but for the breach, the loss would still have occurred. Here the loss would still have arisen and therefore did not cause the loss.

Target Holdings has been followed in a number of cases, most recently in the case of *AIB Group (UK) Plc v Mark Redler and Co Solicitors* [2015] AC 1503. According to Lord Toulson:

> Absent fraud, it would not ... be right to impose or maintain a rule that gives redress to a beneficiary for loss which would have been suffered if the trustee had properly performed its duties.
>
> It would be a backward step ... to depart from [or 're-interpret'] Lord Browne-Wilkinson's analysis in *Target Holdings Ltd v Redferns* [1996] AC 421 [of the equitable principles of compensation for breach of trust].

6.2.3 Remoteness of damage

A closely linked issue is that of remoteness of damage, for example whether the claimant must establish that the trustee's breach is the only cause of the loss or whether it is sufficient to show that it is one of the causes. There may have been a third party involved in the breach who was also dishonest or negligent. The case law is not entirely clear but, according to the *Target Holdings* case, the common law principles relating to remoteness do not apply, and all that is required is satisfaction of the 'but for' test in order to hold the defendant trustee liable. This may be quite hard to prove. For example, in the case of *Nestle v National Westminster Bank Plc* [1993] 1 WLR 1260, the claimant complained that the trust had lost value due to the investment policy of the trustees. While it was conceded by the court that the trustees had misunderstood their powers of investment, the court held that the onus was on the claimant to establish that she had suffered loss as a result of the trustees' breach of duty, and she had failed to do so – largely because of the difficulty of establishing what other shares would have been worth had the trustees invested in them.

6.2.4 The nature of liability

A trustee will be liable for his or her own breaches, but to what extent will he or she be liable for the acts of a co-trustee or an agent, for example?

6.2.4.1 Liability for acts of a co-trustee

The general rule is that trustees are not vicariously liable for the acts of a co-trustee; they are only liable for their own breaches. However, a non-active or passive trustee may be liable for neglecting to take the necessary steps to prevent a breach occurring, which ties in with the duty to act unanimously when taking decisions (*Luke v South Kensington Hotel Co* (1879) LR 11 ChD 121, as noted in **Chapter 5**).

Bahin v Hughes (1886) 31 Ch D 390 provides an old authority on this point. Here the active trustee made an improper investment – she informed the passive trustee and he did nothing to prevent her. The passive trustee was held liable for the breach alongside the active trustee on the basis that he had been in a position to supervise his co-trustee and prevent the improper investment that eventually led to a loss to the trust fund. This demonstrates that equity will not recognise or assist a 'sleeping' trustee.

Where more than one trustee is held to be in breach, their liability will be joint and several. In other words, any of them can be held to be liable for the full loss and the beneficiary can choose to pursue one or more of the trustees. This can be very harsh on the passive trustee who may have to pay an equal share of the compensation or indeed the whole sum. The position has been mitigated to some extent by the Civil Liability (Contribution) Act 1978, which allows the court to apportion liability between trustees according to what is just and equitable in the circumstances and having regard to the extent of each party's responsibility for the damage (s 2(1)).

Alternatively, a trustee may be entitled to an indemnity from a co-trustee. The situations where this may arise include:

- where one of the trustees has acted in a fraudulent manner – the fraudulent trustee may be required to indemnify the other trustee(s) (*Re Smith* [1896] 2 Ch 590);
- where a co-trustee has specialist knowledge. This does not mean that every 'professional' trustee would always be required to indemnify – each case will turn on its own facts. An example is *Head v Gould* [1898] 2 Ch 250;
- if one of the trustees is also a beneficiary of the trust – he or she may be required to indemnify the other trustee(s) to the extent of his or her beneficial interest.

When a trustee retires, the general rule is that liability for future breaches ceases, provided that the retirement has been effective. The outgoing trustee may be liable for breaches that occurred during his or her trusteeship unless an indemnity is obtained upon leaving (as discussed in **Chapter 5**). Following retirement, a trustee will only continue to be liable if he or she retired in order to facilitate a breach (*Wright v Morgan* [1926] AC 788, PC) or left knowing that the future of the trust was in jeopardy (*Head v Gould* [1898] 2 Ch 250).

6.2.4.2 Liability for acts of agents

You will recall from **Chapter 5** on trustees' powers and duties that trustees may delegate their responsibilities in accordance with the relevant statutory authority, subject to the terms of the trust deed.

Individual delegation by way of power of attorney under s 25 of the Trustee Act 1925 is a little used power and for good reason. Section 25(7) imposes strict liability on the appointing trustee.

On retirement, a trustee may seek indemnity from the continuing trustees in respect of any prior or subsequent breach of trust, and so place the burden of compensating the beneficiaries onto others. The question of whether an indemnity should be given, particularly in relation to past breaches of trust, and if so to what extent, can be a fraught matter to resolve.

Collective delegation on the other hand, under s 11 of the Trustee Act 2000, does not lead to strict liability. Section 23 of the 2000 Act provides that the trustee will only be liable for the acts or default of the agent if he or she has failed to comply with the relevant duties when selecting and dealing with the agent. Accordingly, provided that the trustee has taken reasonable care (s 1) when choosing the agent, has provided a policy statement (s 15) and keeps the agent's activities under review (s 22) then he or she should not incur liability if the agent makes a mistake. The trustee might, moreover, be covered by an exclusion of liability clause (see below) which will exclude liability for his or her own defaults and those of the agent indirectly.

6.2.5 Assessing the extent of liability

There are two main measures of liability – any loss caused to the trust and any unauthorised gain received by the trustee.

If the actions or omissions of the trustee have resulted in a loss to the trust fund, the court may order that the trustee pay compensation so that the trust is restored to the position it would have been in had the breach not taken place (*Bartlett v Barclays Bank Trust Co Ltd (No 2)* [1980] Ch 515).

In this context, the liability of the trustee is compensatory, but this cannot quite be equated to common law damages because the focus of the compensation is slightly different. In equity, the court prefers to risk overcompensating the beneficiary rather than allowing a defaulting trustee to profit from the wrong that he or she has committed. So there is some focus on the wrongdoer, whereas in tort, for example, the focus is squarely on the claimant and his or her loss.

The loss to the fund is assessed at the date of judgment rather than the date of breach, with the full benefit of hindsight, again putting the claimant's position first (see *Target Holdings v Redferns* (above) and *Hulbert v Avens* [2003] EWHC 76 (Ch)). For example, a trustee who improperly retained an unauthorised investment would be liable for the difference between the value of the investments when the case comes to court and the value of the investments at the time they should have been sold (*Fry v Fry* (1859) 54 ER 56).

If, on the other hand, the trustee has made an unauthorised gain as a result of his or her breach, then the gain may be used as a measure of liability. The amount of liability is generally calculated by reference to the highest value of the profit made between the date of breach and the date of judgment (*Nant-y-glo and Blaina Ironworks Co v Grave* (1878) 12 Ch D 738), although this case does not appear to have been widely followed.

If a case involves both a loss to the trust fund and a profit made by the trustee then the claimant must elect which to claim; he cannot recover both. In the Privy Council case of *Tang Man Sit (deceased) v Capacious Investments* [1996] AC 514, which of course is only persuasive and not binding, Tang was involved in building houses on a piece of land. He agreed to assign some of the properties to the claimant once they were built but, instead of doing so, he rented the houses out without the claimant's knowledge. This action caused both a loss to the claimant, as well as a gain to Tang, in terms of the rents he received. The claimant asked for both the loss and profit, but the court held that these were alternative remedies and he must choose between them; he could not have both. This was followed in the case of *Ramzan v Brookwide Ltd* [2011] 2 P & CR 32, in which it was affirmed that 'the claim for damages for breach of trust and the claim for loss of profit were not cumulative remedies but alternative and inconsistent remedies'. However, it is open to the claimant to choose the one that is most favourable to him or her, or the court could treat the claimant as having elected to receive the larger award (*Ramzan*).

Interest is generally payable by the defaulting trustee on any sums due to the trust. This will generally be simple interest unless the trustee has been fraudulent or received an unauthorised gain, in which case it is likely to be compound.

One final issue that sometimes arises in relation to measure of liability is whether a trustee who has caused a loss to the fund is permitted to set off gains made in other transactions for the trust. The general rule is no, and in *Dimes v Scott* (1828) 38 ER 778 a trustee who had made a gain for the trust in one investment was not permitted to set this off against the loss he had incurred in another investment in order to reduce his liability.

However, more recently in *Bartlett v Barclays Bank* (above), the court decided that if the gain and loss are part of the same transaction or part of the same wrongful course of conduct then it may be possible to set gains off against losses sustained. This approach has been criticised due to the uncertainty over what is meant by 'part of the same transaction'.

6.2.6 Relief from liability

There are number of ways in which a trustee's liability may be limited or indeed avoided altogether.

6.2.6.1 Limitation

Section 21(3) of the Limitation Act 1980 governs time limits which apply to actions by a beneficiary to recover property or to bring a claim for breach of trust. Such actions must generally be brought within six years of the date on which the right of action accrued.

However, s 28 of the Act provides the following variations to the limitation period:

- Where a person is under a disability, which includes being under the age of 18 or of unsound mind, time will not start to run until the disability ceases.
- Section 32(1) provides that where a trustee deliberately conceals a fact relevant to the right of action, time will not start to run until the beneficiary becomes aware of the concealment.
- Finally, there is no time limit for actions against a trustee who has acted fraudulently or to recover trust property in the possession of a trustee. These are said to be outside the scope of the Act (s 21(1); *Wassell v Leggatt* [1896] 1 Ch 554). For a recent consideration of these rules, see *First Subsea v Balltec* [2017] EWCA Civ 186 on s 21(1)(a) – fraudulent transactions; and *Burnden Holdings v Fielding* [2018] UKSC 14 on s 21(1)(b) – actions to recover trust property.

Alongside the statutory limitation rules, there also exists the equitable doctrine of laches (see **Chapter 1** and the equitable maxims). 'Laches' is an old French word denoting delay in asserting a right, coupled with remissness or negligence on the part of the claimant. The rule may be used where there has been an unreasonable delay on the part of the claimant in pursuing the claim, such that it would be unconscionable for him or her to be allowed to proceed (*Re Sharpe* [1892] 1 Ch 154). The defendant must show substantial delay plus the existence of circumstances that would make it unfair for the claimant to be awarded a remedy. This might involve, for example, considering any hardship caused to the defendant, the nature of the remedy sought or the conduct of either party. In more recent cases, such as *Patel v Shah* [2005] EWCA Civ 157, a broad approach based on unconscionability was used when assessing whether the defence of laches was successful in defeating a claim. The doctrine of laches will not apply where a statutory limitation applies (see *Re Pauling's Settlement Trusts (No 1)* [1964] Ch 303 and *Green v Gaul* [2005] 1 WLR 1890).

6.2.6.2 Consent of the beneficiaries

As indicated above, it is possible for the beneficiaries to consent to a breach of trust, whether at the time or by granting a release after the event (*Re Pauling's Settlement Trusts (No 1)* above). There are no particular formalities required, such as the consent being in writing, and the court will consider each case on its own facts. However, the beneficiaries must have full legal capacity in terms of age and being sound of mind (*Overton v Banister* (1844) 67 ER 479), and the beneficiaries must have acted freely, with full knowledge of the facts and without any undue influence placed upon them (*Boardman v Phipps* [1967] 2 AC 46).

6.2.6.3 Relief granted by the court

According to s 61 of the Trustee Act 1925, the court may relieve the liability of a trustee in whole or in part where the court is satisfied that the trustee has acted honestly, reasonably and ought fairly to be excused. *Re Evans (deceased), Evans v Westcombe* [1999] 2 All ER 777 serves as a useful example of the operation of s 61. A woman became the executor of her father's estate, and according to his will the estate was to be divided equally between herself and her brother. However, her brother had been missing for over 30 years and was thought to be dead. She took legal advice, purchased an insurance policy worth half the value of the estate to insure against the event of her brother turning up, and proceeded to distribute the whole estate to herself.

Inevitably, the brother turned up some years later and demanded his share. The policy did not cover the total sums due to him and so he brought a claim before the court. It was held that although the sister had wrongly received trust property, she was partially relieved of liability as she had acted honestly and reasonably in taking advice and making provision for the brother via the insurance policy. She was ordered to pay some interest to him only.

In *Daniel v Tee* [2016] EWHC 1538 (Ch) the court agreed that s 61 could apply to a situation involving poor investment decisions where trustees have acted to the best of their abilities and relied on advice from someone they reasonably believed to be a competent professional (eg under s 5 of the Trustee Act 2000).

6.2.6.4 Exclusion clauses

It is common practice for trust deeds to contain an exclusion clause protecting trustees from liability, and clearly this is something that a solicitor-trustee will be keen to include when drafting the trust instrument for the settlor. The case of *Armitage v Nurse* [1998] Ch 241 clarified that such a clause may only exclude liability for breach of a trustee's duty of care which is negligent, not fraudulent. This could potentially include gross negligence but not breach of a trustee's core fiduciary duties or for fraud or dishonesty – a limitation confirmed in the case of *Taylor v Midland Bank Trust Co Ltd (No 2)* [2002] WTLR 95. In *Armitage* the claims against the defendant related to failure to supervise management of trust investments adequately and so was a claim in negligence rather than fraud. Consequently the exemption clause operated to absolve the trustees from liability.

There have been examples where trustees, including professional trustees, caused catastrophic losses and yet were protected from personal liability. *Bogg and Others v Raper and Others* (1998) *The Times*, 22 April, CA, is one such case where mismanagement of the trust assets resulted in a loss of nearly £8m over a period of only two years. In *Bogg*, the court considered what the duty of the solicitor was when drafting the deed and including an exemption clause. It was held that there was a duty to advise the client about the terms of the deed, upon which the trustees would be acting, including informing the settlor of the effect of each clause, but there was no need for the client to obtain independent legal advice as there was no conflict of interest. Indeed, it is open to a trustee to insist upon an exemption clause and to refuse to act without one.

Unsurprisingly, this is a controversial issue, particularly in the context of professional trustees, and there have been calls for a tougher stance. However, the Trustee Act 2000 did not include any provision limiting the use of exclusion clauses, and in fact at Sch 1, para 7 it states that the s 1 duty of care is inapplicable where it is clear from the trust instrument that it is not meant to apply.

In the case of *Walker v Stones* [2001] QB 902, a little progress was made towards providing some justice to claimants. The court gave dishonesty a broad meaning and it was construed objectively, on the basis of what a reasonable trustee might have done in the same situation:

> Although the test of honesty might vary depending, inter alia, on the role and calling of the trustee, it was not sufficient in the case of solicitor-trustee to ask whether he had genuinely believed that he was acting honestly. Rather, in such a case it was also necessary to consider whether his so-called 'honest belief', though actually held, was so unreasonable that, by any objective standard, no reasonable solicitor-trustee could have thought that what he did or agreed to do was for the benefit of the beneficiary.

The outcome in the case was that the solicitor-trustee was prevented from relying on the exclusion clause.

In 2016, the Court of Appeal dealt with a dispute over the interpretation of a standard form exemption clause contained in a will trust in *Barnsley v Noble* [2016] EWCA Civ 799. Despite arguments to the contrary by the claimant, the court demonstrated leniency towards the non-professional trustees and refused to deprive them of the protection afforded by the exemption clause. This is an uncontroversial decision: most would agree that a lay trustee acting honestly and conscientiously ought to be shielded from liability.

The Law Commission has considered the issue of exemption clauses and professional trustees on a number of occasions, including in the report that led to the Trustee Act 2000. Subsequently, in 2003, it carried out a consultation which included a proposal that professional trustees should not be able to rely on exclusion clauses. However, when the report was published in 2006 (No 301, para 6.65), the final recommendation was far less stringent and merely suggested that any paid trustee who includes an exclusion clause in the trust deed must, before creation of the trust, take such reasonable steps to ensure that the settlor is aware of the meaning and effect of the clause.

In the event, the Commission entered into agreements with various regulatory bodies rather than enforce their view by new legislation. The result is that, in the guidance accompanying the Solicitors' Code of Conduct, the solicitor is recommended to: 'take reasonable steps before the trust is created to ensure that your client is aware of the meaning and effect of the clause. Extra care will be needed if you are, or anyone in or associated with your firm is, or is likely later to become, a paid trustee of the trust.' And: 'where you or another person in, or associated with, your firm is considered acting as a paid trustee you should not cause to be included a clause in a trust instrument which has the effect of excluding or limiting liability for negligence without taking reasonable steps before the trust is created to ensure that the settlor is aware of the meaning and effect of the clause.'

There was a real concern that if the Law Commission recommended that exclusion clauses should be abolished, no professional would want to act as a trustee. Given the increasingly onerous requirements on trustees and the complexity of dealing with investments, it was felt that to have no professional trustees would be a step too far. A prudent trustee will look for a suitable indemnity clause, act with caution in the management of the trust assets and retire at an appropriate time without overstaying his or her usefulness.

6.3 Tracing

In the event of a breach of trust or breach of fiduciary duty resulting in a loss to the claimant or an unauthorised profit for the fiduciary, the claimant will be seeking to obtain a remedy. This remedy may involve a return of misappropriated assets or profits and/or the payment of compensation by the defendant. If the objective is the former then the claimant will be relying on proprietary rights which attach to the assets taken. If necessary, the claimant can also demand that the defendant pay monetary compensation where, for example, the return of the assets does not fully satisfy the claim. In this section we look at the rules of tracing which help a claimant to track what has happened to the assets taken by the defendant, but, before doing so, it is important to understand the difference between the proprietary and personal remedies and thereby understand the potential value of being able to trace assets and rely on the proprietary rights that attach to them.

The table below sets out the key advantages and disadvantages of proprietary and personal claims. There are pros and cons with each, but where the asset can be traced and proprietary rights attach to it, there are clear benefits to be gained.

Table 6.1 Proprietary and personal claims

Proprietary remedy	**Personal remedy**
Strengths	*Strengths*
Claimant can potentially take the asset itself, including any increase in value	Does not depend on the continued existence of the asset
Claimant will have priority over other creditors of the defendant (eg on insolvency)	Not affected by any fall in value of the asset
Weaknesses	*Weaknesses*
No benefit where the right to trace has been lost (eg where the asset has been dissipated)	Dependent on the personal wealth of the defendant/ability to pay
If the value of the asset has fallen, there will be a loss (then consider the personal claim)	No priority over other creditors of the defendant

There are two types of tracing – common law and equitable – and although there are some similarities between the two, there are also significant differences. For the beneficiary claimant, equitable tracing will be the appropriate course to pursue, and so this will be the main focus of the section on tracing.

It is not only possible to trace into the hands of the trustee or fiduciary who initially held the claimant's property, but also to pursue a third party who acquires such property. The position of a third party varies depending upon their state of knowledge and whether they provided consideration for the property or not. The process of tracing only locates the property and so, finally, it will be necessary to look at the remedies that might be available.

Tracing allows a claimant to find out what has happened to his or her property, to follow where it has gone and to identify it in the hands of another. Tracing might be used as part of a claim by either an equitable or legal owner of property where the property has been misappropriated and the claimant is seeking a remedy such as rescission or perhaps compensation.

In the leading case of *Foskett v McKeown* [2001] 1 AC 102, Lord Millett stated:

> Tracing is thus neither a claim nor a remedy. It is merely the process by which a claimant demonstrates what has happened to his property, identifies its proceeds and the persons who have handled or received them, and justifies his claim that the proceeds can properly be regarded as representing his property.

So, the process of tracing is concerned with the claimant's property and the transmission of that property away from the claimant. It might involve, for example, a trust asset being misappropriated by a trustee or simply where money has been stolen from the legal owner's bank account. In these situations the legal or equitable owner has a proprietary interest in the asset and so is able to use tracing to find out where it is.

The tracing rules differ depending on whether the claimant originally had the legal or equitable title to the property in question. For legal owners, common law tracing may be available although, as we shall see, its scope is rather narrow so equitable tracing may be more useful. Equitable owners – such as beneficiaries of a trust – can only use equitable tracing.

It should be noted that the existence of the two separate tracing processes has been criticised, in particular by Lord Millett in *Foskett*. You may also like to look at the case of *Trustee of the Property of FC Jones (A Firm) v Jones* [1997] Ch 159 which has been criticised as blurring the boundaries between the two types of tracing.

6.3.1 Common law tracing

Where a legal owner has been deprived of his or her property, he or she may be able to use tracing to identify the property, or property substituted for it, in the hands of the defendant. There is also a process called 'following' at common law, which is another means of locating property and simply refers to the process of following the asset as it moves from hand to hand.

At common law, the claimant may continue to trace where the asset has been converted into another form, for example from cash into shares or from jewellery into cash. In the old case of *Taylor v Plummer* (1815) 3 M&S 562, Plummer handed over money to a broker asking him to use it to purchase bonds on his behalf. The stockbroker instead used the money to buy gold and some American investments and then prepared to leave for North America. Plummer caught up with the broker and took the gold and certificates from him. The broker was then made bankrupt and the court had to decide whether Plummer was entitled to the assets or whether they should be distributed amongst the broker's creditors. It was held that Plummer could retain the assets as they were an ascertainable product of his money and so they belonged to him.

In the more recent case of *Lipkin Gorman v Karpnale* [1991] 2 AC 548, the court confirmed that common law tracing could be applied to intangible assets, in that case a chose in action or debt owed to the claimant. *Lipkin* was followed in *London Clubs Management Ltd v Revenue and Customs Commissioners* [2014] UKFTT 1060 (TC) in which HMRC was trying to trace tax liability when stakes were converted into various other forms of gambling chips and prizes.

However, common law tracing has some significant limitations which means it is rarely used, and it cannot be used at all for equitable owners, such as beneficiaries of a trust, because the claimant must be the legal owner of the property (*MCC Proceeds Inc v Lehman Brothers International (Europe)* [1998] 4 All ER 675).

An even bigger problem is that common law tracing is only available if the court is able to identify the property as a direct traceable product of the original asset. This difficulty has mostly manifested itself in the context of the claimant's money being mixed in a bank account with money from another source. In *Re Diplock, Diplock v Wintle* [1948] Ch 465, Lord Greene stated:

> If two sums are mixed … their identity is lost to the eye of the common law, which is unable to detect their continued existence.

In *Agip (Africa) v Jackson* [1991] Ch 547, the claimant was trying to trace money paid to the defendants as a result of fraud. The money was transferred electronically and passed through an interbank clearing account. The Court of Appeal decided that the claim should fail as it was not possible to trace the claimant's money once it had been mixed with other funds. It had ceased to be identifiable as the claimant's property once it had passed through the clearing account where it had been mixed with other funds. As Fox LJ said:

> Money can be followed at common law into and out of a bank account … provided that it does not cease to be identifiable by being mixed with other money in the bank account derived from some other source.

We must therefore turn our attention to equitable tracing which, as you would imagine, is much more flexible and caters specifically for the beneficial owner.

6.3.2 Equitable tracing

Let us take a simple trust example to illustrate the mechanics of tracing:

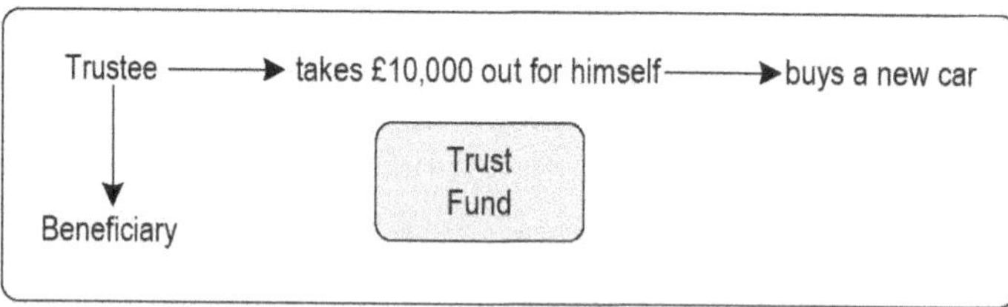

Figure 6.1 Equitable tracing

Here we can see that the trustee has committed a breach of trust by taking money out of the fund and spending it on a new car for his own use. When this comes to light, the beneficiary will wish to recoup the loss caused to the trust. This can be done by tracing the money that came from the fund and now resides in the car, and ultimately asking the court to, for example, order the trustee to sell the car and return the money to the trust. The beneficiary is not the legal owner of the trust fund and therefore cannot use common law tracing, so we must look to equitable tracing instead.

In order to trace in equity, the claimant must first satisfy two requirements:

- a fiduciary relationship between the claimant and the person who initially held the legal title; and
- an equitable proprietary interest in the property.

In *Re Diplock* (above), the executors of Caleb Diplock's will had wrongly distributed £250,000 of his residuary estate amongst various charities. They did so on the authority of a clause in a will that later turned out to be invalid. The money should really have passed to his next of kin, and so those representing the next of kin brought an action to recover the money. Tracing was used to find out what had happened to the money, and the court confirmed the prerequisites:

- The need for an initial fiduciary relationship was easily satisfied as executors of a deceased's estate are a type of fiduciary. It was not necessary to show that the charities were in a fiduciary relationship with the claimants; it was the people who had initially held the funds who had to be in a fiduciary position, namely the executors. Of course, there are many different types of fiduciaries, including solicitors and directors, for example.
- The equitable proprietary interest will usually follow quite easily once the fiduciary relationship has been established and, in *Diplock*, the next of kin were in a position to say that, as true beneficiaries of the estate, they had an equitable interest in the funds. It should be noted that the interest can arise under an express, resulting or constructive trust.

In the same way, the prerequisites will easily be satisfied in our example above because the trustee is the initial fiduciary and the beneficiary has an equitable proprietary interest in the trust fund.

The need to satisfy these prerequisites has been criticised, again most notably by Lord Millett in *Foskett v McKeown* [2001] 1 AC 102, where he stated, obiter, that there was no logical justification for insisting on the fiduciary relationship as a requirement for tracing in equity. The courts are usually quite generous in accepting the existence of the fiduciary relationship in the context of tracing in any event.

It is now necessary to consider the rules around the process of tracing, and this differs slightly depending on whether the property has been mixed or not and whether the funds have been placed in a bank account.

6.3.3 Rules governing equitable tracing

6.3.3.1 Unmixed funds

This is the most straightforward situation, and the possible outcomes are as follows:

- The property is returned in its original state, for example a trustee takes a painting from the trust and hangs it in her house, and the court orders the return of the painting.
- The property has been passed on to a third party, for example the trustee gives the painting as a present to her sister. Here the beneficiaries would be entitled to trace the painting into the sister's hands and have it returned to the trust. This would be the case regardless of whether the sister knew that the painting was trust property. Further detail is given below regarding the status of third parties (see **6.4**).

- The trustee sold the painting for, say, £200. The beneficiaries could trace into the sale proceeds received by the trustee, which means they would be tracing their equitable interest from the painting into the money that has been substituted for it. It may be possible to trace into the hands of the purchaser but only if he or she had knowledge of the breach of trust.
- Trust money of, say, £500 is taken by a trustee and used to buy a piece of jewellery. In this case the beneficiaries could trace the money into the jewellery and their interest now resides in the jewellery. They would be entitled to take either the jewellery itself or have a charge over it to the amount of trust money used (*Re Hallett's Estate* (1880) 13 Ch D 696).

You should also note that if any of these courses of action results in a loss to the beneficiaries because, for example, the sale of the jewellery in the last example did not raise sufficient money to cover the £500 owed to the trust, then the beneficiaries would be entitled to sue the trustee personally to obtain compensation for the shortfall.

6.3.3.2 Mixing of trust funds and trustee's funds

This would include scenarios where a trustee misappropriates trust money and mixes it with her own, or buys an asset with the mixed fund.

The basic position here is that the beneficiary may trace his or her money into the mixed fund or the asset acquired with it and, again, the claimant would have the right to a charge over the fund or asset for the amount of trust money used (*Re Hallett* (above)). In an interesting development in *Brazil v Durant International Corporation* [2015] 3 WLR 599, the court suggested that backward tracing of bribes was possible. Recognising the complexity of banking transactions today and the ease with which money can be moved around so that the interconnectedness of transactions is effectively disguised, the court held that non-chronological transactions could constitute a valid chain of transactions if the court was satisfied that the various steps were part of a coordinated scheme. Importantly, for the rule in *Foskett* (see below), the court held that equitable tracing should not be defeated by criminals manipulating bank accounts so that a debit appeared before a credit. This was a Privy Council case from Jersey and so not binding, but it will be interesting to see if it is followed. Where the beneficiary acquires a charge in this way, he or she will become a secured creditor to the extent of the charge, which can be enforced by requiring the asset to be sold. This puts the beneficiary in a good position, not only in terms of being able to receive his or her money back, but also if the trustdee is made bankrupt as he or she will have priority over the other creditors of the trustee.

Another option that might be considered as an alternative is that the beneficiary could take the asset purchased with his or her money or take a proportionate share of the asset (*Re Tilley's Will Trusts* [1967] Ch 1179, *Foskett* (above)). So, for example, if the asset is shares and they are a good investment, the beneficiary may prefer to take the shares in his or her name. This would be particularly attractive if the asset has increase in value.

In *Foskett*, Lord Millett confirmed:

> Where a trustee wrongfully uses trust property to provide part of the cost of acquiring an asset, the beneficiary is entitled at his option to claim a proportionate share of the asset or to enforce a lien upon it to secure his personal claim against the trustee for the amount of the misapplied money.

The trustee in *Foskett* took trust money and put it towards the purchase of a life insurance policy in favour of his children. He subsequently took his own life and the policy paid out around £1m. It was held that the claimants could trace into the proceeds from the policy in proportion to the amount of trust money that had been used.

6.3.3.3 Mixing of trust funds with funds of another innocent party

Here, for example, trust funds are taken and mixed by the trustee with money from another trust or an innocent third party.

The rule here, from cases such as *Diplock* and *Foskett* (above), is that innocent contributors are treated equally between themselves and so would share the fund or asset purchased *pari passu* or rateably. The innocent parties can agree to take the asset itself, as explained above, and would become tenants in common over the asset with shares proportionate to the amounts claimed (*Sinclair v Brougham* [1914] AC 398), including any increase in value. None of the innocent parties would have priority over the other but would share rateably; this means that if the asset has dropped in value they would each bear that loss proportionately too.

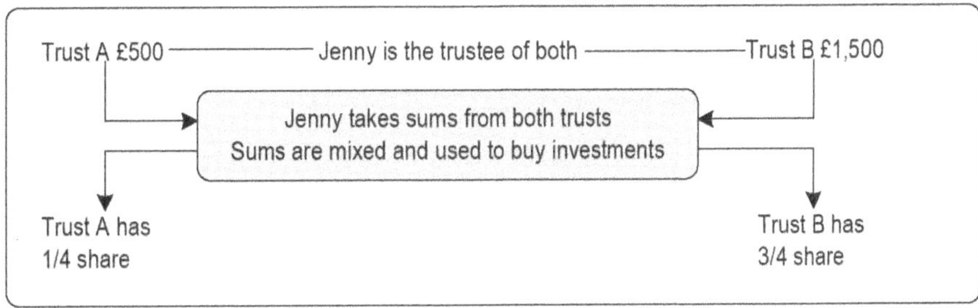

Figure 6.2 Mixing of trust funds

6.3.3.4 Funds mixed in a bank account

There are a number of rules that may come into play when funds are mixed in a bank account, some of which are the same as or similar to those already discussed, but there are also some important differences specific to the bank account context.

The rule in *Re Hallett*

If the trustee mixes his or her own money with trust money in a bank account and subsequently makes a withdrawal from the account, then a general rule that may be applied is that the trustee is presumed to have taken his or her own money out of the account first (*Re Hallett* (above) – based on the presumption of honesty). This will be particularly attractive to the claimant where the money withdrawn has been dissipated and so he or she cannot trace into it, and where there are funds left in the account after the withdrawal into which he or she can trace.

The rationale behind this rule is that the trustee is presumed to be acting honestly, giving him or her the benefit of the doubt, and that the remaining money in the account belongs to the beneficiary. In the words of Lord Jessell MR in *Re Hallett*, 'whenever an act can be done rightfully, [a man] is not allowed to say … that he has done it wrongfully'. This is something of a legal fiction, which while it appears to give the inadvertent wrongdoer – such as a lay trustee – the benefit of the doubt, it also confers greater merit on defaulting and often dishonest trustees than perhaps is deserved!

T's bank account	£ In	£ Out	£ Balance
T's money	100		100
B's money	100		200
T's living expenses		100	**100**

Figure 6.3 Re Hallett example

In this example, using *Re Hallett*, the trustee (T) would be assumed to have spent his own money first, and so the £100 remaining in the account belongs to the beneficiary (B).

The rule in *Re Oatway*

In circumstances where money has been withdrawn from a mixed fund in a bank account and used to purchase an asset, the beneficiaries will be entitled to trace into the asset and to take a charge over the asset to secure their claim. For mixed bank accounts, this rule comes from the case of *Re Oatway* [1903] 2 Ch 356, and Joyce J explained the rule as follows:

> When any of the money drawn out has been invested, and the investment remains in the name … of the trustee, the rest of the balance having been afterwards dissipated by him, he cannot maintain that the investment which remains represents his money alone, and that what has been spent and can no longer be traced and recovered was the money belonging to the trust.

In *Oatway*, the deceased, formerly a solicitor, had mixed his own money with trust money in a bank account, made a withdrawal and purchased shares with it. He then dissipated the rest of the money in the account. The court held that the beneficiaries were entitled to take a charge over the shares and that the shares or proceeds thereof belonged to the trust rather than the deceased's estate.

Although at first glance this rule may seem to conflict with the rule from *Re Hallett*, the underlying objective is the same, and that is that the trustee is obliged to satisfy the claims of the beneficiary before setting up his or her own personal claim to funds or other assets. *Oatway* will not apply if it would be inequitable or unconscionable to do so (*Turner v Jacob* [2006] EWHC 1317 (Ch)).

As explained above, following cases such as *Foskett*, it is possible for the claimant to take a proportionate share of the asset purchased, including any increase in value.

	£ In	£ Out	£ Balance
T's money	100		100
B's money	100		200
Shares		100	100
Living expenses		100	0

Figure 6.4 Re Oatway example

In this example, using *Re Oatway*, the money used by the trustee (T) to purchase the shares is presumed to be the beneficiary's £100, thus allowing the beneficiary (B) to trace into the shares.

The rule in *Roscoe v Winder*

Where the beneficiaries are seeking to trace into a balance remaining in an account, the rule in *James Roscoe (Bolton) Ltd v Winder* [1915] 1 Ch 62 provides that the beneficiaries are not permitted to claim an amount exceeding the lowest intermediate balance in the account since the date of mixing of the funds (see also *Bishopsgate Investment Management Ltd (in liquidation) v Homan* [1995] Ch 211).

In other words, withdrawals that reduce the balance in the account to a sum lower than the amount of trust money originally paid in must include withdrawals of the trust money (in whole or in part). The trust money remains reduced despite any subsequent payments in unless the defendant shows an intention to repay the trust money or the payments in represent the traceable proceeds of the original trust money.

This rule was applied in the case of *Bishopsgate v Homan* (above), which concerned the misappropriation of pension funds belonging to employees of Robert Maxwell. Following Maxwell's death, it was discovered that large sums of pension fund money had been paid into various bank accounts and then been spent. One of the accounts in question, with National Westminster Bank, had gone back into credit by the time of Maxwell's death and the court had to decide whether the claimants could trace into this account.

Applying *Roscoe*, the court held that the claimants could not trace into the account as there was no evidence that Maxwell intended the money paid in subsequently to replace the missing pension funds. As Dillon LJ commented:

> It is difficult to suppose, however, that in the circumstances of Robert Maxwell's last days ... Robert Maxwell intended to make good the misappropriation of the BIM pension monies by the cryptic expedient of arranging to put the account with the Nat West Bank back into credit.

	£ In	£ Out	£ Balance
T's money	100		100
B's money	100		200
Holiday		175	**25**
T's money	100	100	125

Figure 6.5 Roscoe v Winder example

In this example, applying the rule in *Roscoe v Winder*, the beneficiary (B) may only trace into a maximum of £25 in this bank account, unless the court is satisfied that the trustee (T) paid in the final £100 with the intention of replenishing the beneficiary's money.

6.3.3.5 Overdrawn accounts

The rule with overdrawn accounts is that it is not possible to trace through an overdrawn bank account, whether it was overdrawn at the time the money was paid in or became overdrawn subsequently (*Re Goldcorp Exchange Ltd (in receivership)* [1995] 1 AC 74, *Re Tilley* (above), *Bishopsgate v Homan* (above)).

Where the account is overdrawn at the time trust funds are paid in, any trust money used to clear the overdraft will be considered dissipated. An overdraft facility is akin to a loan or debt owed by the account holder to the bank, and if money is used to pay it off then the general rule is that money cannot be returned. In any event, the bank could claim to be a bona fide purchaser for value (see **6.4.1** below).

6.3.4 The equitable doctrine of subrogation

There is an exception to the general rule that the payment of debts using trust money will be classed as dissipation and thereby defeat a tracing claim, and this is by virtue of the equitable doctrine of subrogation.

The principle is that if a trustee uses trust funds to pay off a secured debt, such as a mortgage, the beneficiaries may be subrogated to the security of the charge. This means that when the trust money is used to pay off all or part of the money owing, the beneficiary will stand in place of the lender or chargee and become a secured creditor in relation to the property charged.

In *Burston Finance v Speirway Ltd* [1974] 1 WLR 1648, Walton J said:

> Where A's money is used to pay off the claim of B, who is a secured creditor, A is entitled to be regarded in equity as having had an assignment to him of B's rights as a secured creditor.

Boscawen v Bajwa [1995] Ch 211 also provides a useful case example. Here, a building society advanced money for the purchase of a property to be secured by a mortgage. The solicitors used the money to pay off an existing mortgage on the property before completion and then the purchase fell through at the last minute. It was held that the building society's money could be traced through the payment made by the solicitors to the previous lender, and this kept the mortgage alive for the benefit of the building society. The building society therefore had security by way of a charge over the property in place of the previous lender.

6.3.5 The rule in *Clayton's* case – mixing of the funds of two or more innocent parties in a bank account

We must also consider the position where the funds of two or more innocent parties are mixed in an account and the ways in which the court might approach the competing claims of these parties.

The rule in *Clayton's* case (*Devaynes v Noble* [1816] 1 Mer 572) is one possible method of determination, and, quite simply, in the words of Lord Grant MR (in *Clayton*), 'it is the sum first paid in that is the first drawn out'. This is often referred to as the 'first in first out' rule.

	£ In	£ Out	£ Balance
Trust A money	100		100
Trust B money	100		200
Rent/bills		100	100 **(B's)**

Figure 6.6 Clayton example

So if money from trust A is paid in first and then money from trust B second, when the trustee withdraws a sum to pay for her rent and monthly bills, for example, the money will be taken first from trust A's money and, once that is used up, from trust B's money. In the example above, therefore, the remaining £100 would belong to trust B.

Clearly, this could result in a harsh outcome for trust A, if its money is dissipated and trust B is able to trace into the remaining balance in the account or into an asset purchased later with money from the account. Consequently, the first in first out principle is considered to be a rule of convenience rather than an absolute principle.

In *Barlow Clowes International Ltd (in liquidation) v Vaughan* [1992] 4 All ER 22, several thousand people had invested in a collective investment portfolio and all this money had been mixed in various bank accounts. The money was misappropriated and the scheme collapsed, with the result that there was insufficient money left to satisfy the claims of all investors.

The court had to decide how the remaining funds could be divided amongst the contributors, and the court considered the rule from *Clayton's* case. It was held that if the application of *Clayton* would be impractical, would result in injustice between the competing parties or would be contrary to the intentions of the parties concerned, then it could be displaced if an alternative method of distribution was available.

The outcome in *Barlow Clowes* was that the court allocated the funds on a pro rata basis, in proportion to each investor's original contribution. It would have been inappropriate to use *Clayton* here as that would run contrary to the collective nature of the scheme. *Barlow Clowes* was followed in the case of *National Crime Agency v Robb* [2014] EWHC 4384 (Ch), where a number of investors had been defrauded by a property developer and were seeking to get back their money under the Proceeds of Crime Act 2002. The court applied a pro rata approach.

Similarly in *Russell-Cooke Trust Co v Prentis* [2003] EWHC 1206 (Ch), *Clayton* was disapplied on the grounds that it would have been complicated and expensive to undertake a first in first out analysis of the transactions. Compare, however, the case of *Commerzbank Aktiengesellschaft v IBM Morgan Plc* [2004] EWHC 2771 (Ch) in which *Clayton* was applied.

6.3.6 Loss of the right to trace

Broadly speaking there are three situations where the right to trace will cease. These are:

- where the property is no longer identifiable (also referred to as dissipation). The best example of this is when the trustee takes trust money and spends it in such a way that it is not possible to trace any further. In *Re Diplock* (above), Lord Greene stated:

  > The equitable remedies presuppose the continued existence of the money either as a separate fund or as part of a mixed fund or as latent in property acquired … if such existence is not established, equity is as helpless as the common law itself.

  Examples of such dissipation of trust funds would include the fiduciary purchasing a meal in a restaurant or paying for a holiday;
- where property has been sold to a bona fide purchaser for value (see **6.4.1** below);

- where it would be inequitable to trace into the hands of an innocent third party (see **6.4.2** below).

Again, note that if the right to trace is lost, the claimant may still sue the initial fiduciary for compensation. However, this type of personal claim (the right in personam) will not be helpful if the fiduciary has no personal wealth or has been declared bankrupt, and so the proprietary right (the right in rem) attaching to a fund or asset puts the claimant in a much better position.

6.4 Third parties to the trust

You will have realised that it is possible to trace not only into the hands of the initial fiduciary who held the property or who made a secret profit, but also into the hands of a third party who has subsequently received the property in question. We must therefore consider the position of these third parties and exactly what rights a claimant would have if attempting to trace into their hands.

6.4.1 Bona fide purchaser for value without notice

Definition

> A third party who has provided consideration and does not have knowledge of the breach.

For example, a trustee takes a painting from the trust and then sells it on to an art dealer with the intention of keeping the sale proceeds himself. The purchasing dealer is not aware that the trustee stole the painting from the trust.

Tracing rule

In such a situation, it is not possible to trace into the hands of the bona fide purchaser for value, but the claimant can trace into the money received by the fiduciary.

6.4.2 Innocent volunteer

Definition

> A third party who has not provided any consideration and does not have knowledge of the breach.

For example, the trustee takes the painting and gives it as a present to his fiancée but she is not aware that the painting came from the trust. Because she is a 'volunteer', ie has not provided any consideration for the painting, for example under a contract of sale, she is distinguishable from the dealer in the previous example. It is important that she has no actual, implied or constructive notice of the fact that the property has been acquired and transferred in breach of trust, otherwise she is not 'innocent'.

Tracing rule

The general rule is that it is possible to trace into the hands of an innocent volunteer but not if it would be inequitable to trace (see below). Where it is possible to trace against an innocent volunteer, this would generally be limited to recovery of the initial sum plus interest and not any profit that the third party might have made, for example.

Inequitable results

We must return to the case of *Re Diplock* (above) in order to understand the situations where tracing against an innocent volunteer may not be permitted. In *Diplock*, the next of kin pursued the charities to recover money wrongly distributed to them by the executors of the will. The charities were innocent volunteers as they received the money as a gift and did not know about the breach committed by the executors in wrongly distributing the estate. However, some of the money had been used to make alterations and improvements to buildings belonging to some of the charities, and it was this fact that led to the inequity in *Diplock*.

Lord Greene acknowledged that the improvements to the buildings may not have even added any value to them. If the court was to allow the beneficiaries to trace the money into the land and grant them a charge over it, the only way they could recover their money would be to force a sale of the land, and this would have produced a particularly harsh result for the charities given their innocence.

So, although the rules of equitable tracing recognise the property rights of the claimant and in general put the claimant's interests first, there is some flexibility in circumstances where tracing might cause real harm to the third party in receipt of trust property.

This does not mean, of course, that innocent volunteers will always be able to raise the *Diplock* defence; they must show why, on the facts of their case, tracing would produce an inequitable outcome (*Kleinwort Benson Ltd v Lincoln Council* [1999] 2 AC 349).

There is a separate, more modern defence known as 'change of position' which, it could be argued, has subsumed the rule from *Diplock*. As Lord Goff explained in *Lipkin Gorman v Karpnale* (above):

> I do not wish to state the principle any less broadly than this: that the defence is available to a person whose position is so changed that it would be inequitable in all the circumstances to require him to make restitution.

There is some support in *Boscawen v Bajwa* (above) to suggest that the change of position defence is a logical development of the inequitable results rule from *Diplock*. A change of position would occur where the innocent recipient of an asset can show that he or she has changed his or her position in some way following receipt of and in reliance upon acquisition of the asset.

Change of position – example

Alice innocently receives a gift of £5,000 from her partner Frank, who is the trustee of the King family trust. Frank had wrongfully taken the money from the trust as he wanted to impress Alice with a generous gift. She uses the £5,000 to buy a car. Alice then spends £2,000 that she had saved up for a car to pay for a holiday to Greece with Frank. Her decision to book the holiday was in reliance on the unexpected gift from Frank. In such a case, the court is likely to decide that any claim brought by the beneficiaries of the King family trust would be limited to £3,000, not the full £5,000.

6.4.3 Knowing recipient

Definition

> A third party who may or may not have provided consideration for the asset received but who does have knowledge of the breach.

So it is the issue of knowledge that transforms a third party from a bona fide purchaser for value or an innocent volunteer into a knowing recipient. The definition of knowledge is by no means clear or easy to pin down and is discussed below.

Tracing rule

It is possible to trace into the hands of a 'knowing' recipient and this third party becomes a constructive trustee over the asset received, which means that the claimant may also sue the knowing recipient for a personal remedy or compensation.

This dual right of action against a knowing recipient means that it would be extremely attractive to a claimant if he or she is able to demonstrate that a third party has the relevant knowledge.

According to *El Ajou v Dollar Land Holdings Plc* [1994] BCC 143, three criteria must be satisfied in order to demonstrate that a person is a knowing recipient, and these are:

- disposal of the claimant's assets in breach of fiduciary duty (see **6.2.1** above);
- **receipt** by the defendant of assets which are traceable as representing the claimant's assets; and
- **knowledge** on the part of the defendant that the assets received are traceable to the breach of duty.

Receipt

The claimant must be able to show that the defendant (the alleged knowing recipient) has received the asset. This would be satisfied by, for example, the receipt of a gift by the third party or where he or she has purchased an asset from the trustee or other fiduciary. Merely entering into a binding contract to acquire an asset will not amount to receipt: the asset must pass to the third party (*Criterion*

Properties Plc v Stratford UK Properties LLC [2004] 1 WLR 1846) and the receipt must be the 'direct consequence' of the breach (*El-Anjou* above and see *Courtwood Holdings v Woodley Properties Ltd* [2018] EWHC 2163 (Ch) for an example of a case where this was not made out).

Knowledge

The thorny question is what do we mean by 'knowledge'? Over time, the courts have attempted to define and explain the concept of knowledge, and although there have been developments at various points throughout its history, there are still no clear-cut criteria. To be clear, in order to possess knowledge, the defendant does not need to have been dishonest or fraudulent (cf dishonest assistance at **6.4.5**). As Vinelott J stated in *Eagle Trust Plc v SBC Securities Ltd* [1992] 4 All ER 488, 'it is not necessary ... to show that the defendant was in any sense a participator in a fraud', although, as you will see, some of the cases on knowing receipt do relate to schemes perpetrating elaborate frauds, and those involved often do behave in a clearly dishonest manner.

Broadly speaking, knowledge can be divided into three categories – (a) implied (where for example a person (the principal) appoints another (the agent) to carry out a task, and that agent has actual knowledge and this is attributed to the principal), (b) actual and (c) constructive. It is fairly clear that if someone is told directly about the breach that they will have actual knowledge, but what is not so clear is where the boundary between actual and constructive knowledge lies, what would amount to constructive knowledge and where constructive knowledge ends and becomes 'no knowledge'.

In *Baden v Société Générale pour Favoriser le Développement du Commerce et de l'Industrie en France SA* [1993] 1 WLR 509, the court set out a fivefold classification in an attempt to define and categorise knowledge:

- actual knowledge;
- wilfully shutting one's eyes to the obvious (amounts to actual knowledge); (*Manifest Shipping v Uni-Polaris Shipping* [2003] 1 AC 469)
- wilfully or recklessly failing to make enquiries (amounts to actual knowledge) (*Cantor Fitzgerald v Bird* [2002] IRLR 867);
- knowledge of the circumstances which would indicate the facts to an honest reasonable person (constructive knowledge);
- knowledge of the circumstances which would put an honest and reasonable person on enquiry (constructive knowledge).

The first three, amounting to actual knowledge, could be said to involve intention on the part of the knowing recipient, whereas the final two, equating to constructive knowledge, would be more akin to negligent behaviour on the part of the recipient.

This seems like it could be useful guide but, unfortunately, and perhaps inevitably given the nature of the nebulous task of both defining knowledge and applying it to a set of facts, the cases are difficult to interpret and reconcile with each other. Indeed, the courts have often warned against the dangers of interpreting the categories as being rigid or self-contained (eg Scott LJ in *Polly Peck International v Nadir* [1992] 2 Lloyd's Rep 238 at 243).

In cases such as *Karak Rubber Co v Burden* (No 2) [1972] 1 WLR 602, *Belmont Finance Corp v Williams Furniture Ltd (No 2)* [1980] 1 All ER 393 and *Agip (Africa) v Jackson* [1991] Ch 547, the court accepted that either actual or constructive knowledge would suffice when deciding whether someone was a knowing recipient. Whereas in, for example, *Re Montagu's Settlement Trust* [1987] Ch 264, *Eagle Trust v SBC Securities* [1993] 1 WLR 484 and *Cowan de Groot Properties v Eagle Trust* [1992] 4 All ER 700, the court insisted on the presence of actual knowledge. In the *Eagle Trust* cases, the court took the narrower view of knowledge on the basis that commercial transactions and dealings had to be based on trust rather than constant suspicion.

In *Montagu* (not a commercial case), Megarry VC commented on the five categories set out in *Baden* (above) and was of the opinion that the first three, equating to actual knowledge, would suffice. However, he doubted that the fourth and fifth categories of constructive knowledge were enough to move a recipient out of the categories of innocent or bona fide on the basis that carelessness would not justify the imposition of a constructive trust. Interestingly, he went as far as to say that he would not attempt to grapple with the precedents on this issue and acknowledged that difficulties arose from the fact that some of the judgments had been given without full consideration of all the relevant authorities in the area.

The facts of *Montagu* related to the receipt by the 10th Duke of Manchester of certain trust assets, in breach of the trust of which he was a beneficiary. Megarry VC carried out an assessment of the activities that had taken place and the state of knowledge of the Duke when he took possession of and dealt with the assets in question. During the course of this assessment, Megarry VC considered the doctrine of 'imputed knowledge' and whether the Duke might have been said to have known about the breach by virtue of the fact that his solicitor had the requisite knowledge. This line of construction was rejected on the facts.

Arguments were also put forward regarding the possibility that the Duke had previously been familiar with the extent of the trust assets but had subsequently genuinely forgotten which items belonged to the trust. Megarry VC took the view that even if the Duke had once known this information, the correct approach was to focus on his knowledge at the time of receipt.

Megarry VC went on to say that the crucial question is whether the conscience of the recipient has been sufficiently affected to justify the imposition of a constructive trust and held that on this basis the Duke was not a knowing recipient.

You will recall, from **Chapter 4** dealing with constructive trusts, that a key element for the imposition of such a trust is that the constructive trustee has behaved in an unconscionable manner, or where it would be unconscionable to deny the rights of the (potential) beneficiary of the constructive trust.

Here again, we see more recently the courts relying on the idea of unconscionability as an important factor to be taken into account when making decisions within the realm of equity. Subsequently, in 2000, in the case of *Bank of Credit and Commerce International (Overseas) Ltd v Akindele* [2001] Ch 437, Nourse LJ felt that there should be a move away from attempting to categorise knowledge, and rather a broader and possibly simpler approach should be used which emphasises that underlying rationale behind the constructive trust. He said a single test would suffice:

> The recipient's state of knowledge must be such as to make it unconscionable for him to retain the benefit of the receipt.

This, he said, would avert the difficulties of definition and allocation that previous categories led to, although he did acknowledge that there may be difficulties with application.

In *Akindele*, the defendant escaped liability even though he was aware of rumours regarding the bank's activities. The court took the view that unless he had reason to believe the allegations, his conscience would not have been affected sufficiently and therefore he was not a knowing recipient.

The *Akindele* case has been the subject of criticism, for example in the House of Lords case, *Criterion Properties Plc v Stratford UK Properties LLC* [2004] 1 WLR 1846, but it has not been overruled and is still considered to reflect the current state of the law. Cases such as *City Index Ltd v Gawler* [2008] Ch 313 and *Madoff Securities International Ltd (in liquidation) v Raven* [2013] EWHC 3147 (Comm) provide subsequent examples of the court confirming the *Akindele* approach, although both were relatively straightforward with *City Index* involving actual knowledge and *Madoff* at the other end of the scale where there was clearly no unconscionability.

The current position regarding the definition of knowledge remains unsatisfactory – the meaning of unconscionability is inherently vague and the courts still refer to the *Baden* categories alongside the *Akindele* test (*Armstrong GmbH v Winnington Networks Ltd* [2013] Ch 156; *Group Seven Ltd v Nasir* [2017] EWHC 2466 (Ch)). However, as suggested by Carnworth LJ in *Criterion Properties* (above), there may be some value in leaving the definition vague, especially given the wide variety of situations in which these issues can arise (breach of trust, breach of fiduciary duty, commercial and non-commercial scenarios).

6.4.4 Dishonest assistance

The dishonest assistant is in a distinct category because this involves someone who dishonestly assists in or procures the breach of trust. It is irrelevant whether the third party actually received trust property as part of the breach and also whether the fiduciary him- or herself was dishonest or fraudulent.

If someone is held to be a dishonest assistant, he or she will be liable to the claimant for the loss occasioned by the breach but, unlike the knowing recipient, he or she is not a constructive trustee. In other words, the remedy is personal, not proprietary. Lord Millett clearly explains the position in *Twinsectra Ltd v Yardley* [2002] 2 AC 164, as follows:

> It is fault-based not receipt-based. The defendant is not charged with having received trust monies for his own benefit, but having acted as an accessory to a breach of trust. The action is not restitutionary; the claimant seeks compensation for wrongdoing.

The meaning of dishonesty

The concept of dishonesty has been the subject of some debate over the years since it was explained in the leading case of *Royal Brunei Airlines v Tan* [1995] 2 AC 378. *Tan* was a Privy Council case and involved a travel agent company engaged to sell tickets for an airline. Payments received from customers were held on trust for the airline, and in breach of this the money was paid into the company's own account and used for its own business purposes. The company went into insolvency and so the airline brought an action against Tan, its managing director and principal shareholder. The claim alleged that Tan had dishonestly assisted in the misappropriation of the funds belonging to the airline, and he was held to be personally liable to compensate the airline. Lord Nicholls stated that the standard to be applied when assessing dishonesty involved an objective test but with a subjective element.

In *Twinsectra* (above), Lord Hutton framed it as a 'combined test' involving both objective and subjective elements. It required asking whether the defendant's conduct was 'dishonest by the ordinary standards of reasonable and honest people and that he himself realised that by those standards his conduct was dishonest'.

However, in 2005, the Privy Council again considered the meaning of dishonesty in the case of *Barlow Clowes International Ltd (in liquidation) v Eurotrust International Ltd* [2006] 1 WLR 509, and the Court confirmed the test as set out in *Tan* but attempted to provide further clarification. Lord Hoffmann stated that there was an element of ambiguity in working out what was meant by the requirement that the dishonest assistant must have appreciated that what he was doing was dishonest by the standards of honest and reasonable men. He explained that the test did not require the defendant to have reflected on what is meant by the 'standards of honest and reasonable people', but rather that his knowledge of the transaction in question should be such as to render his participation in it contrary to the normal acceptable standards of honest conduct.

As Lord Millett had opined in his strong dissenting judgment in *Twinsectra*, the subjective element of the test allows the court to take into account factors such as the defendant's experiences and intelligence, not that he had to realise that his behaviour was dishonest by comparison to a set of ordinary standards of honesty.

Following *Twinsectra* and *Barlow Clowes*, the court in *Starglade Properties Ltd v Nash* [2010] EWCA Civ 1314 explained that the standard to be applied is the ordinary standard of honest behaviour. This standard is applied by the court to the conduct of the specific individual, possessing the knowledge and qualities he or she actually enjoyed. The subjective understanding of the person concerned as to whether his or her conduct was dishonest is irrelevant. It is also irrelevant that there may be a body of opinion that regards the ordinary standard of behaviour as being set too high. More recently, the Supreme Court considered the meaning of dishonesty in the case of *Ivey v Genting Casinos (UK)* [2017] UKSC 67 and, referring to *Barlow Clowes* (above), clarified again that the test was an objective one and there is no need to show that the defendant appreciated that his or her behaviour was dishonest (see further *Group Seven Ltd & Ors v Notable Services LLP & Ors* [2019] EWCA Civ 614).

Finally, on the issue of dishonesty, it is quite common for both the trustee and the dishonest assistant to have been dishonest, but this is not necessary. It is possible to have a scenario where the trustee has behaved properly but a third party has acted dishonestly. As Lord Nicholls said in *Tan*, 'What matters is the state of mind of the third party sought to be made liable, not the state of mind of the trustee', and the court must be careful to carry out a full assessment of all the relevant evidence in this regard (see *Clydesdale Bank v Workman* [2016] EWCA Civ 73 where, after careful consideration of the evidence, two solicitors were found not to have been dishonest).

The meaning of assistance

Assistance requires active participation in the breach, either by procuring it or helping out in some way. There must be a causal link between the breach and the assistance, or, in other words, the defendant's 'assistance' must have occurred in relation to the breach in question (*Brown v Bennett* [1999] 1 BCLC 649).

A good case example is *Brinks Ltd v Abu-Saleh* (No 1) [1995] 1 WLR 1478, which concerned the laundering of stolen money from Brinks Mat during a robbery at Heathrow Airport in 1983. The claim for dishonest assistance was against Mrs Elscombe, who accompanied her husband on a number of trips to Switzerland couriering money from the robbery. They both knew there was something untoward about the arrangement but not where the money had come from.

The court held that she was not liable as she had not actually 'assisted' in the wrongdoing. The courier arrangement was with her husband and she was not a party to it. She simply went along on some of the trips for a free holiday, and the court said that this was not enough to make her a dishonest assistant.

Table 6.2 Remedies against third parties – summary

Type of third party	Proprietary remedy?	Personal remedy?
Bona fide purchaser for value	No	No
Innocent volunteer	Yes (subject to it being inequitable)	No
Knowing recipient	Yes	Yes
Dishonest assistant	No	Yes

6.5 Equitable remedies

There are a variety of equitable remedies and (as indicated previously) these are not confined to the context of equitable claims, such as a breach of trust, but may be awarded to provide a solution in other areas of law, from family cases to contract claims and intellectual property matters. However, whatever the context, the equitable remedy is only available at the discretion of the court, unlike, for example, damages for breach of contract, where the award is automatic once the claimant has proved his or her case. Having said that, the courts are bound by certain rules, including the maxims of equity, and so the decision to award an equitable remedy is not entirely arbitrary.

6.5.1 Rectification and variation of trusts

The general rule is that the terms of a properly constituted trust must be strictly adhered to. However, there may be circumstances where it is necessary to amend, correct or even remove certain clauses or to vary the terms of the trust more broadly.

6.5.1.1 Rectification

The equitable remedy of rectification is most commonly used in the context of contracts, trust deeds and wills to address the consequences of mistake (*RBC Trustees v Stubbs* [2017] EWHC 180 (Ch) and *Millar v Millar* [2018] EWHC 1926 (Ch)) or fraud (*Collins v Elstone* [1893] P 1). Rectification of a voluntary provision, such as a trust deed or will, can take place where the settlor's or testator's intentions have not been properly reflected in the document, for example where the solicitor made a drafting error (*Lawie v Lawie* [2012] EWHC 2940 (Ch)). The burden of proof rests with the person seeking rectification, most commonly a beneficiary (existing or potential) of the trust or will or the settlor herself, in the case of a lifetime settlement.

6.5.1.2 Variation of a trust

If the beneficiaries of a trust, who are all competent adults and absolutely entitled to the trust property, are in unanimous agreement, they may bring the trust to an end and each take their share. This is known as the rule in *Saunders v Vautier* ([1841] 4 Beav 115). This is clearly the most extreme example of variation – termination of the trust.

If there is a need to vary the beneficial interests under a trust, the procedure set out in the Variation of Trusts Act 1958 will be used. The Act is considered to be a statutory extension of the rule in *Saunders v Vautier* and permits variations of trusts involving all types of beneficiaries. The Act allows the court to vary or revoke all, or any part, of an express private trust and its application may not be expressly excluded. Cases brought under the Act are often pursued for tax reasons but the scope of the Act is not limited to such circumstances.

Section 1 of the 1958 Act states that the court may vary the terms of the trust 'if it thinks fit' and, in making its decision, the court:

- must balance the various competing interests of the beneficiaries (*Re Weston's Settlements* [1969] 1 Ch 223);
- may consider the moral and social benefits as well as the financial consequences of the variation (*Re Holt's Settlement* [1969] 1 Ch 100); and
- will usually consider the settlor's intentions as part of the process but does not have to follow them (*Goulding v James* [1997] 2 All ER 239).

A practical example of the use of variation under the 1958 Act would be altering a provision in a trust deed for the appointment of new trustees, as in *Bathurst v Bathurst* [2016] EWHC 3033 (Ch). However administrative variations are usually undertaken using s 57 of the Trustee Act 1925, and a recent example of this can be found in *Gelber v Sunderland Foundation and Others* [2018] EWHC 2344 (Ch), where the court authorised the appointment of a sole trustee and the payment of a substantial sum to charity.

6.5.2 Rescission

Rescission can sometimes be appropriate in a case involving a breach of trust, and allows a contract or other transaction to be reversed where it has been carried out in an unconscionable or morally reprehensible manner. For example, where assets have been transferred out of the trust in breach, rescission may be used to order that the asset be returned back to the trust, even where the asset is in the hands of a third party.

6.5.3 Declarations

Declarations offer a simple solution, particularly where, for example, trustees need guidance and clarification from the court. They are often used in the context of trustees' powers, and the court can make a declaration setting out how the trustees should deal with a particular matter relating to the trust.

Cowan v Scargill [1985] Ch 270 was a case pertaining to the relevance of ethical considerations when trustees carry out the investment of trust funds. The court made a declaration that half of the trustees of the miners' pension fund were in breach of trust by refusing to agree to the adoption of an investment strategy with which they did not agree, on ethical grounds.

Although declarations are viewed by some as a lesser form of remedy, they are an important method by which the trustees can be required to comply with their duties, and also so that clarification can be obtained from the court setting out what the law is and how it applies in a particular situation.

A recent example of trustees faced with a fundamentally difficult decision in the face of opposition from the key beneficiary was *Cotton v Earl of Cardigan* [2014] EWCA Civ 1312, where the trustees of an impoverished estate sought confirmation from the Court that their decision to sell the estate property was properly taken. The Earl of Cardigan had brought several actions against the trustees, so it was prudent for the trustees to seek confirmation and guidance over this final act in the administration of the trust to protect the trustees from further actions.

6.5.4 Monetary compensation

Equity provides two flexible options to a claimant in terms of obtaining some form of monetary compensation.

6.5.4.1 Equitable compensation

This is similar to damages, and the basis of the remedy is to put the beneficiaries back in the position they would have been in, had the breach not occurred. If property has been taken from the trust, the ideal outcome would be for the property to be returned to the trust via restitution (ie giving it back), but this is not always possible, particularly where the asset has ceased to exist or if it cannot be traced. In such a situation, the claimant will have to rely on equitable compensation to provide a remedy for the loss caused. *Target Holdings* (above) provides an interesting discussion of this remedy and a comparison with common law damages, and see also more recently *Main v Giambrone* [2017] EWCA Civ 1193 where both were awarded.

6.5.4.2 Account of profits

Alternatively, the claimant may seek an account of profits, particularly where the errant trustee has made an unauthorised or secret profit.

Accounting for profits made may result in a higher sum being repaid than the original unauthorised sum taken and used by the trustees, and so it enables a fair recovery for the beneficiaries who would otherwise lose out. For example, a trustee who uses trust money to purchase a property who subsequently, due to a rising property market, would profit from the increase in value of the property, would gain at the expense of the beneficiaries if only the original money taken was repayable.

6.5.5 Specific performance

The remedy of specific performance most commonly arises in claims for breach of contract and is an order by the court requiring the defendant to carry out his or her obligations under the contract. For example, where one party has contracted to transfer an asset to another in return for cash consideration, if the first party refuses to complete the transfer, the court may make an order for specific performance requiring him or her to do so. An order of specific performance will only usually be made if damages are insufficient – typically in contracts for the sale of land on the grounds that each parcel of land is unique – and will not be made if the order would be inequitable or unenforceable. Equity will not compel performance of certain contracts of employment for example.

In a trust situation, the court may use specific performance to compel a trustee to perform his or her obligations under the trust. In *Re Tillott* [1892] 1 Ch 86, the trustees were ordered to hand over certain documents to the beneficiaries. Trustees may also be required to distribute the trust fund if they have failed to do so, although there are limits to this, so, for example, the courts will not generally interfere with the exercise of the trustees' power to select a beneficiary in a discretionary trust (*Re Blake* (1885) 29 Ch D 913).

Breach of an order for specific performance carries a heavy penalty as it amounts to contempt of court, which is punishable by a fine or imprisonment.

6.5.6 Injunctions

The injunction is a well-known remedy, often arising in family law cases, and again breach results in contempt of court. However, injunctions may be awarded in many contexts and are usually used as a preventative measure to either:

- order a party to cease doing an act (prohibitory). An example of this can be seen in the case of *Buttle v Saunders* [1950] 2 All ER 193 where an injunction was granted by the court to prevent the trustees from selling land to the lower bidder. An example of the prohibitory interim injunction is the freezing injuction (formerly known as a *Mareva* injunction) which operates to prevent a party from moving assets out of the reach of the claimant, pending a final trial of the issues (*FM Capital Partners v Marino* [2018] EWHC 2889 (Comm)); or, more rarely
- order someone to carry out a positive act (mandatory). One type of interim mandatory injunction is the search order (formerly known as an *Anton Piller* order) or seizing injunction, which can, for example, require a party to make premises or documents available for inspection in order to facilitate trial of the action being brought.

Both types of injunction have a number of strict criteria which have to be complied with, but a detailed analysis of the requirements for the granting of these injunctions is beyond the scope of this book.

Broadly speaking, injunctions may be either interim or final. The interim injunction, as the name suggests, is a holding measure which operates pending a full hearing of the issues by the court. They can often relate to urgent matters that may be heard without the other party present ('ex parte'), particularly where the other party is committing a wrong that needs to be halted quickly. They are not, however, granted lightly, and a prima facie case needs to be made out that the applicant has a strong case to bring before the court and the injunction is necessary to facilitate the administration of justice. Sometimes sureties have to be provided by the applicant and will be forfeited if the case fails. *Douglas and Others v Hello! Ltd (No 1)* [2001] QB 967, where the claimants wanted to stop the publication of wedding photographs, provides a good example.

A final injunction would be granted by the court as a remedy forming part or all of the final solution to a claim, and *Buttle v Saunders* (above) provides an appropriate example.

6.6 Further reading

Andrew Bowen, 'Case Comment: Tracing and substitute property: Relfo Ltd (In Liquidation) v Varsani [2014] EWCA Civ 360' (2015) 136 *Business Law Bulletin* 1-3.

Paul Davies, 'Section 61 of the Trustee Act 1925: Deus Ex Machina?' (2015) *The Conveyancer and Property Lawyer* 379–94.

Michael Haley, 'Legislative Comment: Section 61 of the Trustee Act 1925: a judicious breach of trust?' (2017) 76(3) *Cambridge Law Journal* 537–65.

Trevor Mascarenhas, 'Constructive trusts in fraud cases' (2011) 22(10) *International Company and Commercial Law Review* 318–21.

Robert Pearce, 'Case Comment: When must a bank repay stolen funds? Credit Agricole Corp and Investment Bank v Papadimitriou [2015] UKPC 13' (2015) *Conveyancer and Property Lawyer* 521–29.

Shelly Saluja, 'The law relating to trustee exoneration clauses' (2014) 28(1) *Trusts Law International* 27–37.

David Hayton et al, *Underhill & Hayton Law of Trusts & Trustees*, 19th edn (LexisNexis, 2016).

Lynton Tucker et al, *Lewin on Trusts*, 20th edn (Sweet & Maxwell, 2018).

This chapter has focussed on what remedies are available – primarily to beneficiaries but also in some cases to co-trustees – when things go wrong. Inevitably an aggrieved party does not just want to know what their rights are, but what they are entitled to as a remedy. As this chapter demonstrates, action is usually taken against the defaulting trustee, but there may be circumstances in which third parties are brought within the net of liability. The equitable maxim **equity acts in personam** is relevant here, recalling the early development of equity explained in the first chapter of the book. But it is also evident here that equity may appear to confer proprietary remedies in some cases, and there is academic debate on whether and to what extent equity acts *in personam* (against the person) or *in rem* (attaching to property). This chapter has also demonstrated that there are circumstances in which a remedy will be frustrated or impossible, so not all breaches or wrongdoing will lead to a happy outcome. Nevertheless it is important to bear in mind that the whole armoury of equitable remedies is available as well as, in some cases, legal remedies – for example where there is a contract. It is also evident that in the field of remedies, equity continues to be creative, seeking to do justice when good conscience requires it.

test your knowledge

1. To what extent can the liability of trustees be excluded and/or excused?
2. What is the role of causation in pursuing a remedy for breach of trust?
3. What are the advantages of equitable tracing over tracing in common law?
4. When will equitable tracing fail?
5. There are two types of situation in which a third party who is not a formal trustee to the trust may be held liable for a breach of trust. What are these and what criteria have to be satisfied?
6. Does the law relating to remedies favour the errant trustee or the aggrieved beneficiary?

INDEX